EVERYONE IS RIGHT

Roland Peterson

EVERYONE IS RIGHT

A New Look at Comparative Religion

and Its Relation to Science

Roland Peterson

DeVorss & Company
P.O. Box 550, Marina del Rey, CA 90294

ISBN: 0-87516-565-6
Library of Congress Catalog
Card Number: 86-70146

Printed in the United States of America

Contents

Introduction

Religion is one of the most emotion-charged subjects in the world—a subject that evokes strong feelings in many; and therein lies a serious problem. The emotions surrounding religion are often so strong that logic and clear thinking are pushed to the background. Many people who are very objective in other areas take fixed dogmatic positions on the subject of religion, leading at times to unnecessary conflict.

Man's emotions can be controlled by his mind, and we find that as more knowledge is gained, old prejudices are put aside, old emotions are overcome, and we see more clearly. One of the purposes of this book is to provide information on different religions and related subjects in a format that can help lead to a greater depth of understanding especially with respect to interrelationships. Shelley wrote, "The eye sees what it brings to the seeing." I trust that what is given here will provide more enlightenment for the reader to bring to the seeing with respect to religion and thereby facilitate seeing more clearly.

We are in an era of rapid change in the field of religion, a time in which there is an opening up of understanding, a flow of new thinking, and a widening general interest in spiritual subjects. More and more information is becoming readily available about different religions. Magazines, newspapers, and television are displaying a greater depth of fundamental understanding in their coverage. One of the most widely publicized signs of change in the churches was the Ecumenical Council called by the late Pope John XXIII with a charge to clear the cobwebs out of the Roman Catholic church. The changes in practices and, more significantly, in attitude which that produced are truly dramatic. Although not as well covered in the media, there have been corresponding changes in many other churches that have led to increased understanding.

To give an example of changing attitudes from my own observations, I can recall about thirty-five years ago sitting in a Lutheran Protestant church listening to the minister, a good and sincere man, discussing from

ix

the pulpit the grave errors of Catholics. I was somewhat impressed by what he had to say but also uneasy about the whole situation; it did not feel right to me. I found out much later that the liturgy and basic beliefs of the Roman Catholic and Lutheran churches were approximately the same, although the Catholic Latin mass helped to disguise the fact at that time. A few years after that, I happened to be in a Catholic church and heard a sermon to the effect that since Catholics were the only ones who had the right message, they had to be careful to show a uniform and consistent face to Protestants and others who were not of "the true faith."

I contrast those incidents with another one, twenty years later, in a different state. A Lutheran minister declared from the pulpit that all Christians belong to the same fundamental church, the "Body of Christ," whether Catholic or Protestant. Today, after the Ecumenical Council, hymns by Martin Luther are found in the missalettes in Catholic churches and are sung along with other formerly "Protestant" hymns. There is also a serious official dialogue taking place among the Roman Catholics, Anglicans, Lutherans, Reformed Alliance, Methodists, Pentecostals, and a number of orthodox churches on the subject of Christian unity.

This book does not, however, concern itself with the various Christian denominations, but looks rather at the major world religions and other sources of spiritual ideas from both East and West with a view toward understanding how they compare. The relationship between religion and science is also explored in some depth, and information is provided which may help to resolve the apparent disparity that exists between these fields.

The title of this book suggests the picture that emerges from this study. It is found that those religions which some Christians formerly labeled as heathen are founded on the same principles as those taught by Jesus Christ. We will also see that science and religion need not be at odds when each is properly understood.

There is a story from India that has been repeatedly used to illustrate the differences between religious viewpoints.

> Four blind men went to see an elephant. One, who touched its leg, said, "The elephant is like a pillar." The second, who touched the trunk, said, "The elephant is like a thick club." The third touched the belly and thought it to be like a big jar. The fourth, who felt the ears, concluded that the elephant was like a winnowing fan. Then they began to dispute amongst themselves as to the figure of the animal they had touched . . . in exactly the same manner do men quarrel among themselves about religion, each having seen some different aspect of the Deity.[1]

Different religions have also been likened to men climbing a mountain from different sides. They are all heading for the same goal but are not familiar with each other's path. Perhaps this book will help to shed some light on these different paths and show what I believe to be an overall pattern or common thread underlying all the major religions, suggesting that they may all derive from the same fundamental source.

This idea of a common source is certainly not a new one; in fact, some of the scriptures of the great religions declare that there is such a source. In the Hindu Svetasvatara Upanishad we read:

Thou, Lord God, bestowest all blessing, . . .
Of all religions thou art the source. . . .
The source of all scriptures thou art,
And the source of all creeds.[2]

In the Koran we find:

We verily gave Moses the Scripture, that happily they might go aright.
And we made the son of Mary and his mother a portent, and we gave them
a refuge on a height. . . .
And lo! This your religion is one religion and I am your Lord, so keep your
duty unto me.
But they [mankind] have broken their religion among them into sects, each
sect rejoicing in its tenets.
So leave them in their error till a time.

(Koran XXIII: 49–54)[3]

Christ said, "Other sheep have I which are not of this fold" (John 10:16), and St. Paul points out, "Every scripture inspired of God is profitable for teaching, for reproof, for correction, for instruction which is in righteousness, that the man of God may be complete, furnished completely unto every good work" (II Tim. 3:16–17).

The Buddha was asked the question, "What some style 'truth' the rest call empty lies; strife reigns. Pray, why do anchorites not speak in unison?" To which he replied, "There's one sole truth . . . to know which bars men's strife. But such a motley crowd of 'truths' have they evolved that anchorites, perforce, speak not in full accord.[4]

To avoid the "motley crowd of 'truths'," this study will confine itself to the fundamental scriptures and basic teachings of the founders and inspired teachers of the great religions and will not be concerned with practices, customs, ceremonies, rituals, variations in sects, theological argument and speculation, or any of the outer forms that have evolved over the years.

We shall begin in the next chapter to show that when fundamental scriptures are consulted, a remarkable uniformity in teaching emerges, even though the various religions can be assumed to have been established for different peoples at different times and would therefore show some variations in emphasis.

Christ said, "The sabbath was made for man, and not man for the sabbath" (Mark 2:27). This idea, of course, applies to all outer practices in religion, which exist to serve the people. Thay have value, but they must not be confused in importance with the more profound truths that form the basis of all major religions. Practices may be different to serve the particular needs of various races or localities. They are all subject to updating and improvement in response to the legitimate changing needs of the people as progress is made. We know that such modifications have been made over periods of time.

Perhaps the saddest commentary on the manner in which man has interpreted the message of the great religious teachers is the severe division between peoples of different faiths—and even worse, the armed conflict that has sometimes occurred as a result of religious differences. I believe that the more the followers of any religion learn about the fundamental teachings of other religions, and the less they focus on the man-made interpretations or extensions of these teachings, the fewer religious conflicts there will be.

The teachings of the esoteric doctrines, which have paralleled and, for those familiar with them, augmented religious teachings throughout recorded history are also reviewed here, and their relationship to religion and science is explored. These teachings are found to help bridge the gap between science and religion.

Many quotations from scriptures and other sources are used in this book, thereby allowing readers to come to their own conclusions regarding the significance of relationships illustrated and also to provide an undistorted picture of the teachings that are compared. This extensive use of quotations causes portions of the book to take on the character of a compilation, which may give the work some value as a reference source.

Perhaps a more complete title for this work would be, "Everyone Is Right, But Only Partly." It is the writer's opinion that the study of the various teachings considered here provides a far more comprehensive and undistorted view of reality than any one of them taken alone. Each of the different religions adds depth and dimension to our understanding. Science and religion both contribute valid information to the total picture, but the perception of each is limited in a fashion similar to that portrayed in the story of the elephant.

Finally, recognizing the often powerful influence of fixed ideas that may have been introduced early in life, it is recommended that in studying this book readers observe their reactions to the material presented. Note that which may cause a strong negative response and attempt to determine its source. Ask, "Am I being objective or am I responding emotionally to past prejudices?" Attempt to stand back from your emotions and prior concepts and make clear observations and evaluations. This is the path to expanded understanding. Remember that our particular religious background is usually a matter of where, when, and to whom we were born, and not necessarily something we arrived at independently. The following quotation seems appropriate here:

> See your prejudices, your opinions, your images, your experiences, see how they are going to prevent you from listening.[5]

PART I

A COMPARISON OF RELIGIOUS THINKING

1. Hinduism, Christianity, Buddhism, and Taoism: A Comparison

We begin with a comparison of the scriptures of four religions, one practiced mainly in the West and three Eastern religions, whose message for the world is still vital, useful and practical today in spite of the long period of time that has lapsed since the words were first given.

The late Thomas Merton, Trappist monk and well-known author of *Seven Storey Mountain* and other books, gives one thoughtful Christian's view of the value of the Asian religions.

> I believe that by openness to Buddhism, to Hinduism, and to those great Asian traditions, we stand a wonderful chance of learning more about the potentiality of our own traditions, because they have gone from the natural point of view, so much deeper into this than we have. The combination of the natural techniques and the graces and the other things that have been manifested in Asia and the Christian liberty of the gospel should bring us all at last to that full and transcendent liberty which is beyond mere cultural differences and mere externals—and mere this or that.[1]

The comparison that follows provides a means for those not familiar with the scriptures of all these religions to rapidly gain an understanding of relationships between fundamental teachings. The topics covered begin with basic teachings about man's relationship to man and the importance of fulfilling one's duty. This is followed by teachings on the nature of God and of man, some of the means to be used in man's spiritual advancement, and results to be expected as progress is made.

By selecting Hinduism, Christianity, Buddhism, and Taoism for the initial comparison, we are able to examine the possibility of a link in religious teaching between East and West. We already know that Christianity is an outgrowth of Judaism, and the quotation in the Introduction shows that the Koran links Islam with these two. The relationships of Judaism and Islam to other religious teachings will be explored in a later chapter.

The quotations used here to convey the fundamental teachings of Hinduism are from the most important Hindu scriptures, The Bhagavad Gita and the principal Upanishads. The Bhagavad Gita ("The Lord's Song"), which is probably the best-loved Hindu scripture, contains the recorded teachings of Sri Krishna. The Upanishads, the portion of the Vedas that deals with spiritual knowledge, are of more ancient origin, and in addition to being most highly regarded by Hindus, they have been praised by such Western thinkers as Goethe, Schopenhauer, and Emerson.

Almost all of the quotations used to show Christian belief are from the New Testament of the Bible. A few Old Testament quotations have also been used.

The Dhammapada, the Buddhist Book of Proverbs, is the teaching of the Buddha that is most frequently quoted here, but a number of other scriptures are also referred to.

Taoist quotations are almost exclusively from the brief but profound *Tao Te Ching* by the great sage Lao-tzu. This scripture is the most important source of Taoist teaching.

The topical listing of short quotations that follows has the advantage for comparative purposes of conveying a great deal of information in a compact format. However, one necessarily misses the overall flow and impact of the various scriptures, and for those with a deeper interest, reading the entire scriptures will prove most rewarding.

Finally, in looking at the organization of this book, the question might arise as to the placement of the tabular comparisons in this chapter and the much less extensive tables in several other parts of the book. Material such as this, which is not in narrative form, is commonly relegated to an appendix. However, the message conveyed by these comparisons and the common topics addressed by all these religions are so central to the theme of the book that it was believed best to place them before the reader's attention early in the text.

TOPICS FOR COMPARISON OF THE SCRIPTURES
OF HINDUISM, CHRISTIANITY, BUDDHISM,
AND TAOISM (with page references)

Note: The reference key for the tabulation that follows is given in the References and Acknowledgments section at the end of the book under the heading "Reference Key for Tabulation in Chapter 1."

1. LOVE AND SERVICE TO HUMANITY

Hinduism

Christianity

LOVE

True religion is to love, as God has loved them, all things, whether great or small. (Hitopadesa: W p. 142)

Who sees Me everywhere and all in Me . . . Loves Me in all.[2]

Them that worship me with love, I love; they are in me and I in them. (BG-A IX)

A new commandment I give you, that you love one another. (John 13:34)

God is love; and he who dwells in love dwells in God. (I John 4:16)

There is no fear in love; but perfect love casts out fear. (I John 4:18)

1. LOVE AND SERVICE TO HUMANITY

Buddhism   Taoism

LOVE

The ninth perfection is: *Loving-kind-ness.* As water quenches the thirst of the good and the bad alike, and cleanses them of dust and impurity, so also shall you treat your friend and your foe alike with loving-kindness. (*Sutta-Pitaka; Buddha-Vasma*: W p. 12)

May creatures all abound in weal and peace . . . all creatures weak and strong, all creatures great and small; . . . Let all-embracing thoughts for all that lives be thine—an all-embracing love for all the universe in all its heights and depths and breadth, unstinted love, unmarred by hate within, not rousing enmity. (*Sutta-Nipata*; T p. 47)

The excellence of friendship is measured by love. (8-B)

In governing the world,
Let rule entrusted be
To him who treats his rank,
As if it were his soul;
World sovereignty can be
Committed to that man
Who loves all people
As he loves himself. (13-B)

Hinduism

Christianity

LOVE IN RETURN FOR HATRED

He who regards
With an eye that is equal
Friends and comrades,
The foe and the kinsman,
The vile, the wicked,
The men who judge him,
And those who belong
To neither faction:
He is the greatest. (BG-S p. 64)

A man should not hate any living
creature. Let him be friendly and
compassionate to all. (BG-S p. 99)

He who sees all beings in the Self,
and the Self in all beings, hates
none. (U-I)

Love your enemies, bless them who
curse you, do good to them who
hate you, and pray for them who
spitefully use you and persecute you.
   (Matt. 5:44)

Resist not evil; but whoever shall
smite you on your right cheek turn
to him the other also. (Matt. 5:39)

If you love those who love you,
what thanks do you deserve? And if
you do good to them who do good to
you, what thanks do you deserve?
For sinners do so also. (Luke
   6:32–34)

To no man render evil for evil, but
provide good things. (Rom. 12:17)

Buddhism | ## Taoism

LOVE IN RETURN FOR HATRED

Buddhism

"He abused me, he beat me, he defeated me, he robbed me"—in those who harbor such thoughts hatred will never cease.
"He abused me, he beat me, he defeated me, he robbed me"—in those who do not harbor such thoughts hatred will cease. (D-3,4)

For hatred does not cease by hatred at any time; hatred ceases by love—this is an old rule. (D-5)

Let a man overcome anger by love, let him overcome evil by good, let him overcome the greedy with liberality, the liar by truth. (D-223)

Taoism

Return good for evil. (63-S)

Surely the good man is the bad man's teacher; and the bad man is the good man's business. If the one does not respect his teacher, or the other doesn't love his business, his error is very great. This is indeed an important secret. (27-B)

Hinduism	Christianity

HARMLESSNESS

Therefore I tell you: Be humble, be harmless. (BG-S p. 101)	Be wise as serpents and harmless as doves. (Matt. 10:16)

FAULTFINDING

Faults, mustard-small, of others, ye see well; your own as large as bel-fruit, ye see not. (Mahabharata)	Why do you behold the speck in your brother's eye but do not consider the beam in your own eye? (Matt. 7:3) Judge not, that you be not judged. (Matt. 7:1) If your brother trespasses against you, go and tell him his fault between you and him alone. (Matt. 18:15)

Buddhism

Taoism

HARMLESSNESS

Him I call indeed a brahmana who without hurting any creatures, whether feeble or strong, does not kill nor cause slaughter. (D-405)

Him I call indeed a brahmana who is tolerant with the intolerant, mild with the violent, and free from greed among the greedy. (D-406)

Him I call indeed a brahmana from whom anger and hatred, pride and hypocrisy, have dropped like a mustard seed from the point of a needle. (D-407)

God's way is gain that works no harm. (81-B)

A skillful soldier is not violent;
An able fighter does not rage;
A mighty conqueror does not give battle;
A great commander is a humble man.
You may call this pacific virtue;
Or say that it is mastery of men;
Or that it is rising to the measure of God,
Or to the stature of the ancients. (68-B)

FAULTFINDING

The fault of others is easily perceived, but that of oneself is difficult to perceive; a man winnows his neighbour's faults like chaff, but his own fault he hides, as a cheat hides the bad die from the player. (D-252)

A truly wise man tries to understand rather than to judge. (2-S)

Hinduism   Christianity

GOODNESS, RIGHTEOUSNESS

Find full reward of doing right in   Blessed are they who hunger and
right! Let right deeds be thy motive,   thirst after righteousness for they
not the fruit which comes from   shall be filled. (Matt. 5:6)
them. (BG-A II)

THOUGHTFULNESS AND GENTLE-KINDNESS

Their every action   Add . . . to brotherly kindness, char-
Is wed to the welfare   ity. (II Pet. 1:7)
Of fellow-creatures:
Such are the seers
Who enter Brahman*
And know Nirvana.† (BG-S p. 61)

---

*God.
†A high state of heavenly consciousness.

Buddhism

Taoism

GOODNESS, RIGHTEOUSNESS

From the Eightfold Path: *Right Effort*—always to strive for that which is good and avoid that which is evil. (*Vinaya-Pitaka; Maha-Vagga*: W p. 10)

If a man does what is good, let him do it again; let him delight in it: the accumulation of good is delightful. (D-118)

The virtuous man delights in this world, and he delights in the next— he delights in both. He delights and rejoices when he sees the purity of his own work. (D-16)

The highest goodness, water-like, Does good to everything and goes Unmurmuring to places men despise; But so, is close in nature to the Way. (8-B)

THOUGHTFULNESS AND GENTLE-KINDNESS

The thoughtless man, even if he can recite a large portion [of the law], but is not a doer of it, has no share in the priesthood, but is like a cowherd counting the cows of others. (D-19)

Earnest among the thoughtless, awake among the sleepers, the wise man advances like a racer, leaving behind the hack. (D-29)

Three things prize above all: gentleness, frugality and humility. For the gentle can be bold, the frugal can be liberal and the humble can become leaders of men. (67-W)

Hinduism   Christianity

COMPASSION

Do not withhold your compassion from those who ask for it. (Hitopadesa W p. 140)

Be self controlled! Be charitable! Be compassionate! (U-B)

He who has the goods of this world and sees his brother in need and closes his heart to him, how does the love of God abide in him? My dear children, let us not love in word, neither with the tongue, but in deed and in truth. (I John 3:17–18)

Blessed are the merciful for they shall obtain mercy. (Matt. 5:7)

CHARITY

Acts of sacrifice, almsgiving and austerity should not be given up: their performance is necessary. (BG-S p. 120)

The gift lovingly given, when one shall say "Now must I gladly give!" when he who takes can render nothing back; made in due place, due time and to a meet recipient, is gift . . . fair and profitable. (BG-A XVII)

Give and your wealth shall grow; give and you shall the more safely keep the wealth you have. (Hitopadesa W p. 142)

It is more blessed to give than to receive. (Acts 20:35)

God loves a cheerful giver. (II Cor. 9:7)

When thou doest alms, let not thy left hand know what thy right hand doeth; that thine alms may be in secret; and thy Father which seeth in secret himself shall reward thee openly. (Matt. 6:3–4)

And above all things have fervent charity among yourselves; for charity shall cover the multitude of sins. (I Pet. 4:8)

Buddhism

Taoism

COMPASSION

The heart that boundless pity feels
for all things that have birth, in such
a heart nothing narrow or confined
can ever be. (*Jatakas* 169-W p. 37)

True compassion is known by its
good deeds. (38-W)

In battle, 'tis compassion wins the
day;
Defending, 'tis compassion that is
firm;
Compassion arms the people God
would save! (67-B)

CHARITY

The first perfection is: *Giving*. As a
full jar overthrown pours out the liquid and keeps back nothing, even so
shall your charity be without
reserve—as a jar overturned. (*Sutta-
Pitaka; Buddha-Vasma*: W p. 11)

If virtue perishes, charity perishes.
(38-W)

2. DUTY

Hinduism

Christianity

DUTY

If, knowing your duty and your task, you bid duty and task go by—that shall be sin. (BG-AII)

He who knows what is right and does it not, to him it is sin. (James 4:17)

Do your allotted task, work is more excellent than idleness.

Be doers of the word, and not hearers only. (James 1:22)

In performance of plain duty man mounts to his highest bliss. By works alone ancient saints reached blessedness. (BG-AIII)

By works a man is justified and not by faith alone. (James 2:24)

Do your duty always but without attachment. (BG-S p. 46)

Now you shall hear how a man may become perfect, if he devotes himself to the work which is natural to him. A man will reach perfection if he does his duty as an act of worship to the Lord. (BG-S p. 129)

2. DUTY

Buddhism   Taoism

DUTY

Let no one forget his own duty for the sake of another's, however great; let a man, after he has discerned his own duty, be always attentive to his duty. (D-166)

The wise man's duty is to teach those who have not yet learned the way of nature; the duty of the ignorant man is to listen to these teachings and try to learn from them. Neither man should neglect his duty. (27-S)

Hinduism   Christianity

UNPLEASANT OR DIFFICULT TASKS

The good is one thing; the pleasant is another. These two, differing in their ends, both prompt to action. Blessed are they that choose the good; they that choose the pleasant miss the goal.

The wise prefer the good to the pleasant; the foolish, driven by fleshly desires, prefer the pleasant to the good. (U-K)

When a man is endowed with spiritual discrimination and illumined by knowledge of the Atman*, all his doubts are dispelled. He does not shrink from doing what is disagreeable to him, nor does he long to do what is agreeable. (BG-S p. 120)

If a man wishes to come after me, he must deny his very self, take up his cross and follow in my steps. (Mark 8:34)

He who will not take up his cross and come after me is not worthy of me. He who seeks only himself brings himself to ruin, whereas he who brings himself to naught for me discovers who he is. (Matt. 10:38–39)

If any would not work, neither should he eat. (II Thess. 3:10)

SLOTH

Activity is better than inertia. Act, but with self control. If you are lazy, you cannot even sustain your own body. (BG-S p. 45)

. . . be not slothful. (Heb. 6:12)

---

*The spiritual essence in man.

Buddhism   ## Taoism

UNPLEASANT OR DIFFICULT TASKS

Make yourself an island, work hard, be wise! When your impurities are blown away, and you are free from guilt, you will enter into the heavenly world of the elect. (D-236)

Rouse yourself! Do not be idle! Follow the law of virtue! The virtuous rest in bliss in this world and in the next. (D)

Take hard jobs in hand
While they are easy;
And great affairs too
While they are small.
The troubles of the world
Cannot be solved except
Before they grow too hard.
The business of the world
Cannot be done except
While relatively small.
The Wise Man, then, throughout his life
Does nothing great and yet achieves
A greatness of his own.

Choosing hardship, then, the Wise Man
Never meets with hardship all his life. (63-B)

SLOTH

He who does not rouse himself when it is time to rise, who, though young and strong, is full of sloth, whose will and thought are weak, that lazy and idle man never finds the way to knowledge. (D-280)

A man's work is never finished until the day he dies. . . . Never feel you have accomplished enough. (45-S)

Hinduism   Christianity

PATIENCE AND ENDURANCE

What God's Will gives   And ye shall be hated of all men for
He takes, and is contented,   my name's sake: but he that en-
Pain follows pleasure,   dureth to the end shall be saved.
He is not troubled;   (Matt. 10:22)
Gain follows loss,
He is indifferent. (BG-S p. 52)

Buddhism   Taoism

PATIENCE AND ENDURANCE

The sixth perfection is: *Patience*. As
the earth bears all that is cast upon
it, both the pure and the impure,
and feels no resentment nor rejoicing, so also shall you receive favors
and rebuffs alike with indifference.
  (*Sutta-Pitaka; Buddha-Vasma*: W
  p. 12)

Him I call indeed a brahmana who,
though he has committed no offense,
endures reproach, stripes and bonds;
who has endurance as his force and
strength for his army. (D)

A thousand-mile journey can be
made one step at a time.
People are constantly spoiling
projects that are only one step from
completion. (64-W)

3. SELF-CONTROL

Hinduism   Christianity

RIGHT SPEECH AND TRUTHFULNESS

To speak without ever causing pain to another, to be truthful, to say always what is kind and beneficial, and to study the scriptures regularly: this practice is called austerity of speech. (BG-S p. 118)

Truth alone succeeds, not untruth. By truthfulness the path of felicity is opened up, the path which is taken by the sages, freed from cravings, and which leads them to truth's eternal abode. (U-M)

What I say to you is: everyone who grows angry with his brother shall be liable to judgment; any man who uses abusive language toward his brother shall be answerable to the Sanhedrin, and if he holds him in contempt he risks the fires of Gehenna. . . . Say "yes" when you mean "yes," and "no" when you mean "no." Anything beyond that is from the evil one. (Matt. 5:22, 37)

Every idle word that men shall speak they shall give account thereof in the day of judgment. (Matt. 12:36)

The tongue no man can tame is an unruly devil. (James 3:8)

Love . . . rejoices not in iniquity, but rejoices in the truth. (I Cor. 13:4)

. . . be not against the truth. (James 3:14)

3. SELF-CONTROL

Buddhism   Taoism

RIGHT SPEECH AND TRUTHFULNESS

Beware of the anger of the tongue, and control thy tongue! Leave the sins of the tongue, and practise virtue with thy tongue! (D-232)

Speak the truth, do not yield to anger; give, if thou art asked for little; by these three steps thou wilt go near the gods. (D-224)

Him I call indeed a brahmana who utters true speech, instructive and free from harshness, so that he offends no one. (D)

Do not speak harshly to anyone; those who are spoken to will answer you in the same say. Angry speech is painful: blows for blows will touch you. (D)

The seventh perfection is: *Truth*. As the star of healing is balanced in the heavens, and swerves not from its path in its time and its season, so also shall you remain fixed on your path of truth. (*Sutta-Pitaka*; *Buddha-Vasma*: W p. 12)

As honest words may not sound fine,
Fine words may not be honest ones;
A good man does not argue, and
An arguer may not be good! (81-B)

The excellence of speech is judged by its truthfulness. (8-W)

Much talk means much exhaustion;
Better far it is to keep your thoughts! (5-B)

Indeed the Wise Man's office
Is to work by being still;
He teaches not by speech
But by accomplishment;
He does for everything,
Neglecting none;
Their life he gives to all,
Possessing none;
And what he brings to pass
Depends on no one else.
As he succeeds,
He takes no credit
And just because he does not take it,
Credit never leaves him. (2-B)

Hinduism

Christianity

ANGER

If a man shall learn, even while he lives and bears his body's chain to master lust and anger, he is blest. (BG-AV)

Let every man be swift to hear, slow to speak, slow to anger. (James 1:22)

Let not the sun go down on your wrath. (Eph. 4:26)

MODERATION

Call that true piety which most removes earthly aches and ills, where one is moderate in eating and in resting and in sport—measured in wish and act—sleeping betimes, and waking betimes for duty. (BG-AVI)

Let your moderation be known to all men. (Phil. 4:5)

Buddhism   Taoism

ANGER

He who holds back rising anger like a rolling chariot, him I call a real driver; other people are but holding the reins. (D-222)

Let a man leave anger, let him forsake pride. (D-221)

Requite anger with virtue.

MODERATION

Go not too far but learn to shun excess; for overblowing lost what blowing won. (*Jatakas* 60-W p. 35)

When entertained by another with food and drink, eat not too much, drink not too much. (*Jatakas* 477-W p. 40)

The wise reject all extremes. (29-W)

In serving heaven and in ruling men use moderation. (59-W)

To take all one wants is never as good as to stop when one should. (9-W)

Hinduism   Christianity

FREEDOM FROM WORLDLY DESIRES

Well I know that earthly treasure
lasts but till the morrow. (U-K)

The sages tell us that renunciation
means the complete giving up of all
actions which are motivated by
desire. And they say that non-
attachment means abandonment of
the fruits of action. (BG-S p. 120)

When he casts from him
Vanity, violence,
Pride, lust, anger
And all his possessions,
Totally free
From the sense of ego
And tranquil of heart:
That man is ready
For oneness with Brahman.
  (BG-S p. 128)

Absorbed in Brahman
He overcomes the world
Even here, alive in the world.
  (BG-S p. 59–60)

Stop hoping for worldly rewards.
  (BG-S p. 48)

The world is imprisoned in its own
activity except when actions are performed as worship of God. Therefore
you must perform every action
sacramentally, and be free from all
attachments to results. (BG-S p. 45)

Do not lay up for yourself an earthly
treasure. Moths and rust corrode;
thieves break in and steal. Make it
your practice instead to store up
heavenly treasure, which neither
moths nor rust corrode nor thieves
break in and steal. (Matt. 6:19–20)

Love not the world, neither the
things that are in the world. (I John
  2:15)

They are not of the world even as I
am not of the world. (John 17:16)

Buddhism   Taoism

FREEDOM FROM WORLDLY DESIRES

Come, look at this world, glittering like a royal chariot; the foolish are immersed in it, but the wise do not touch it. (D-171)

Riches destroy the foolish, if they look not for the other shore; the foolish by his thirst for riches destroys himself, as if he were [destroying] others. (D-355)

No sufferings befall the man who is not attached to name and form, and who calls nothing his own. (D-221)

. . . let a brother, as he dwells in the body, so regard the body that he, being strenuous, thoughtful, and mindful, may, whilst in the world, overcome the grief which arises from the body's cravings. (T p. 49; Buddha's Farewell Address)

He has gone beyond all that is worldly, yet he has not moved out of the world; in the world he pursues his course for the world's weal, unstained by worldly taints.
   (T p. 132; The Bodhisattva's Vow of Universal Redemption)

Cut down the whole forest [of desires], not a tree only! Danger comes out of the forest [of desires]. When you have cut down both the forest [of desires] and its undergrowth, then, Bhikshus, you will be rid of the forest and of desires!
   (D-283)

The secret waits for the insight
Of eyes unclouded by longing;
Those who are bound by desire
See only the outward container.
(1-B)

. . . let there be
A visible simplicity of life,
Embracing unpretentious ways,
And small self-interest
And poverty of coveting. (19-B)

The Wise Man does not hoard his
   things;
Hard-pressed, from serving other
   men,
He has enough and some to spare;
But having given all he had,
He then is very rich indeed. (81-B)

Hinduism	Christianity

RENUNCIATION

To nothing be slave, Nor desire possession Of man-child or wife, Of home or of household; Calmly encounter The painful, the pleasant; Adore me only. (BG-S p. 102)	For what is a man profited, if he shall gain the whole world, and lose his own soul? (Matt. 16:26)
	He that loveth father or mother more than me is not worthy of me; and he that loveth son or daughter more than me is not worthy of me. And he that taketh not his cross and followeth after me is not worthy of me. He that findeth his life shall lose it: and he that loseth his life for my sake shall find it. (Matt. 10:37–39)
When a man lacks lust and hatred, His renunciation does not waiver. He neither longs for one thing Nor loathes its opposite: The chains of his delusion are soon cast off. (BG-S pp. 56–57)	

Buddhism

Taoism

RENUNCIATION

The third perfection is: *Renunciation*. As a man in prison, suffering pain for long, knows that there is no pleasure for him but only to await release, so shall you look upon your existences on earth as prisons, and turn your face toward renunciation and await release. (*Sutta-Pitaka*; *Buddha-Vasma*: W p. 12)

Wise people do not call that a strong fetter which is made of iron, wood, or hemp; passionately strong is the care for precious stones and rings, for sons and a wife. (D-345)

Him I call indeed a brahmana who, after cutting all fetters, never trembles, is free from bonds and unshackled. (D)

If the student of the way wishes to understand the real mystery, he need only put out of his mind attachment to anything whatsoever. (T p. 199 from the teachings of the 9th-century A.D. Zen Master Hsi Yun)

The student learns by daily increment
The Way is gained by daily loss
Loss upon loss until
At last comes rest.

By letting go it all gets done;
The world is won by those who let it go!
But when you try and try,
The world is then beyond the winning. (48)

A loss sometimes benefits one
Or a benefit proves to be loss. (42-B)

Hinduism	Christianity

CONTROL OF THOUGHTS, DESIRES, AND ACTIONS

The wise control their minds. (U-S)

When a man lacks discrimination and his mind is uncontrolled, his senses are unmanageable, like the restive horses of a charioteer. But when a man has discrimination and his mind is controlled, his senses, like the well-broken horses of a charioteer, lightly obey the rein. (U-K)

As a man acts, so does he become. A man of good deeds becomes good, a man of evil deeds becomes evil. A man becomes pure through pure deeds, impure through impure deeds.

As a man's desire is, so is his destiny. For as his desire is, so is his will; as his will is, so his deed; and as his deed is, so is his reward, whether good or bad. (U-B)

A governed mind shall sometime feel the sense-storms sweep, and wrest strong self-control by the roots. Let him regain his kingdom, let him conquer this. That man alone is wise who keeps mastery of himself. (BG-AII)

The mind that gives itself to follow the senses sees its helm of wisdom torn away, and like a ship in waves of whirlwind drives to wreck and death. (BG-AII)

Be not conformed to this world; but be ye transformed by the renewing of your mind. (Rom. 12:2)

Let every man be swift to hear, slow to speak, and slow to wrath. (James 1:19)

What comes out of the mouth originates in the mind. It is things like this that make a man impure. From the mind stem evil designs. (Matt. 15:18–19)

Behold the ships which though they are so great and driven by fierce winds, yet are turned about, with a very small rudder at the will of the pilot. (James 3:4)

Buddhism   Taoism

Control of Thoughts, Desires, and Actions

All that we are is the result of what we have thought: it is founded on our thoughts; it is made up of our thoughts. If a man speaks or acts with an evil thought, pain follows him, as the wheel follows the foot of the ox that draws the carriage. . . . If a man speaks or acts with a pure thought, happiness follows him, like a shadow that never leaves him.
(D-1,2)

As the arrow-maker makes straight his arrow, a wise man makes straight his trembling and unsteady thought, which is difficult to guard and difficult to hold back.

It is good to tame the mind, which is difficult to hold in and flighty, rushing wherever it listeth; a tamed mind brings happiness. (D-35)

If a man's thoughts are unsteady, if he does not know the true law, if his peace of mind is troubled, his knowledge will never be perfect.
(D-38)

If one man conquer in battle a thousand times thousand men, and if another conquer himself, he is the greatest of conquerors. (D-103)

He who overcomes his fierce desire, difficult to conquer in this world; sufferings fall off him like water-drops from a lotus leaf. (D-336)

The softest of stuff in the world
Penetrates quickly the hardest;
Insubstantial, it enters
Where no room is.
By this I know the benefit
Of something done by quiet being;
In all the world but few can know
Accomplishment apart from work,
Instruction when no words are
  used. (43-B)

He who conquers others is strong;
He who conquers his own will is
  mighty. (33-W)

Hinduism   Christianity

CONTROL OF THE SENSES

With the help of the mind and the intellect, keep the senses from attaching themselves to objects of pleasure. They will then be purified by the light of the Inner Reality, and that light will be revealed. (U-S)

With earnest effort hold the senses in check. Controlling the breath, regulate the vital activities. As a charioteer holds back his restive horses, so does a persevering aspirant hold back his mind. (U-S)

When a man can still the senses
I call him illumined.
The recollected mind is awake
In the knowledge of the Atman*
Which is dark night to the ignorant:
The ignorant are awake in their
    sense-life
Which they think is daylight:
To the seer it is darkness.
    (BG-S p. 43)

. . . they that are after the flesh do mind the things of the flesh; but they that are after the spirit the things of the spirit. For to be carnally minded is death; but to be spiritually minded is life and peace. (Rom. 8:5–6)

---

*The spiritual essence in man.

Buddhism

Taoism

CONTROL OF THE SENSES

He who lives looking for pleasures only, his senses uncontrolled, immoderate in his food, idle, and weak, Mâra (the tempter) will certainly overthrow him, as the wind throws down a weak tree. (D-7)

He who lives without looking for pleasures, his senses well controlled, moderate in his food, faithful and strong, him Mâra will certainly not overthrow, any more than the wind throws down a rocky mountain. (D-8)

Can you govern your animal soul, hold to the One and never depart from it?
Can you throttle your breath, down to the softness of breath in a child?
Can you purify your mystic vision and wash it until it is spotless?
Can you love all your people, rule over the land without being known?
Can you be like a female, and passively open and shut heaven's gates?
Can you keep clear in your mind the four quarters of earth and not interfere?

Quicken them, feed them;
Quicken but do not possess them.
Act and be independent;
Be the chief but never the lord:
This describes the mystic virtue. (10-B)

Stop up your senses;
Close up your doors;
Be not exhausted
As long as you live.
Open your senses;
Be busier still:
To the end of your days
There's no help for you. (52-B)

4. REWARD AND PUNISHMENT

Hinduism   Christianity

REWARD AND PUNISHMENT

This body is called the Field, because a man sows seeds of action in it, and reaps their fruits. (BG-S p. 100)

Be not deceived; God is not mocked: for whatsoever a man soweth, that shall he also reap. (Gal. 6:7)

Listen carefully to what you hear. In the measure you give you shall receive. (Mark 4:24)

4. REWARD AND PUNISHMENT

Buddhism

Taoism

REWARD AND PUNISHMENT

Not in the sky, not in the midst of the sea, not if we enter into the clefts of the mountains, is there known a spot in the whole world where a man might be freed from an evil deed. (D-127)

A fool does not know what awaits him when he commits his evil deeds; but the wicked burns by his own deeds, as if burned by fire. (D)

If a man offend a harmless, pure, and innocent person, the evil falls back upon that fool, like light dust thrown up against the wind. (D-125)

Even an evildoer sees happiness so long as his evil deed does not ripen; but when his evil deed ripens, then does the evildoer see evil. (D-119)

Even a good man sees evil days so long as his good deed does not ripen; but when his good deed ripens, then does the good man see good things. (D-120)

Today too many men:
Care for no one other than themselves;
Seem to seek injustice;
Are boastful braggards.
These characteristics lead to death.
The man who is compassionate, just, humble,
Knows these virtues lead to life everlasting. (67-S)

The wise man knows the more he gives to others
The more he has left for himself. (81-S)

Those who do evil in the open light of day—men will punish them.
Those who do evil in secret—God will punish them.[3]

5. GOD

Hinduism	Christianity

GOD

Desiring that he should become many, that he should make of himself many forms, Brahman meditated. Meditating, he created all things.

Creating all things, he entered into everything. Entering into all things, he became that which has shape and that which is shapeless; he became that which can be defined and that which cannot be defined; he became that which has support and that which has not support; he became that which is conscious and that which is not conscious; he became that which is gross and that which is subtle. He became all things whatsoever: therefore the wise call him the Real.

Concerning which truth it is written: Before creation came into existence, Brahman existed as the Unmanifest. From the Unmanifest he created the manifest. From himself he brought forth himself. Hence he is known as the Self-Existent.
(U-T)

He alone is all this—what has been and what shall be. He has become the universe. Yet he remains forever changeless, and is the lord or immortality. (U-S)

Though he fills the universe, he transcends it. (U-S)

God that made the world and all things . . . .
He is not far from every one of us: For in him we live, and move, and have our being. (Acts 17:24–28)

There is one God and Father of all, who is above all and through all, and in you all. (Eph. 4:6)

I am the first and the last: . . . I am alive for evermore. (Rev. 1:17–18)

I am Alpha and Omega, the beginning and the ending, saith the Lord, which is, and which was, and which is to come, the Almighty. (Rev. 1:8)

5. GOD

Buddhism*   ### Taoism

GOD

There is, monks, an unborn, not become, not made, uncompounded, and were it not, monks for this unborn not become, not made, uncompounded, no escape could be shown here for what is born, has become, is made, is compounded. (T from the *Samyutta-Nikaya* of Theravada Buddhism)

There are ways but the Way is uncharted;
There are names but not nature in words:
Nameless indeed is the source of creation
But things have a mother and she has a name. (1-B)

The Way begot one,
And the one, two;
Then the two begot three
And three, all else.

All things bear the shade on their backs
And the sun in their arms;
By the blending of breath
From the sun and the shade,
Equilibrium comes to the world. (42-B)

The Way is a void,
Used but never filled:
An abyss it is,
Like an ancestor
From which all things come.

It blunts sharpness,
Resolves tangles;
It tempers light,
Subdues turmoil.

A deep pool it is,
Never to run dry!
Whose offspring it may be
I do not know:
It is like a preface to God. (4-B)

The Way is always still, at rest,
And yet does everything that's done. (37-B)

*The scriptures of Buddhism do not deal extensively with the nature of God. The Buddha did not encourage speculation along this line, but it seems clear from writings such as the very important Sermon at Benares, which speaks of Brahman and other Hindu concepts, that the basic cosmology of the Hindu religion was also recognized by the Buddha.

Hinduism

Christianity

Unmanifest to the senses, beyond all thought, infinite in form, is God. He is the doer of all good; he is forever tranquil; he is immortal. He is One, without beginning, middle, or end; he is all-pervading. He is infinite wisdom, and he is bliss. (U-K)

God is a spirit. (John 4:24)

Filled with Brahman are the things
   we see,
Filled with Brahman are the things
   we see not,
From out of Brahman floweth all
   that is:
From Brahman all—yet he is still
   the same. (U-I)

I am alike for all! I know not hate, I know not favor! (BG-A IX)

Your Father which is in
heaven . . . maketh his sun to rise
on the evil and on the good and sen-
deth rain on the just and the unjust.
   (Matt. 5:45)
God is no respecter of persons. (Acts
   10:34)
God is love: and he who dwells in
love dwells in God. (John 4:16)

. . . In this way you will come finally to the Lord, who is the light-
giver, the highest of the high. (BG-S
   p. 75)

The light is among you only a little
   longer
Walk while you have it or darkness
   will come over you:
The man who walks in the dark
   does not know where he is going.
While you have the light, keep faith
   in sons of light. (John 12:35–36)

He is all-knowing God, lord of the
   emperors,
Ageless, subtler far than mind's in-
   most subtlety,
Universal sustainer,
Shining sunlike, self-luminous.
   (BG-S p. 75)

I have come to the world as its light
to keep anyone who believes in me
from remaining in the dark. (John
   12:46)

I am the light of the world, no follower of mine shall ever walk in
darkness; no, he shall possess the
light of life. (John 8:12)

Buddhism   ## Taoism

O the great Way o'erflows
And spreads on every side!
All being comes from it;
No creature is denied.
But having called them forth,
It calls not one its own.
It feeds and clothes them all
And will not be their lord. (34-B)

The movement of the Way is a
    return;
In weakness lies its major
    usefulness,
From what-is all the world of things
    was born
But what-is sprang in turn from
    what-is-not. (40-B)

Hinduism

Christianity

The one absolute, impersonal existence, together with his inscrutable
Maya, appears as the divine Lord,
the personal God, endowed with
manifold glories. By his divine
power he holds dominion over all
the worlds. At the period of creation
and dissolution of the universe, he
alone exists. Those who realize him
become immortal. The Lord is One
without a second. Within man he
dwells, and within all other beings.
He projects the universe, maintains
it and withdraws it into himself.
   (U-S)

The whole universe came forth from
Brahman and moves in Brahman.
Mighty and awful is he, like to a
thunderbolt crashing loud through
the heavens. (U-K)

In the beginning was the Word, and
the Word was with God, and the
Word was God. . . . All things were
made by him; and without him was
not any thing made that was made.
   (John 1:1–3)

Him the sun does not illumine, nor
the moon, nor the stars, nor the
lightning—nor, verily, fires kindled
upon the earth. He is the one light
that gives light to all. He shining,
everything shines. (U-K)

. . . he that built all things is God.
   (Heb. 3:4)

God is light and in him is no darkness at all. (John 1:4)

The light that shines above the
heavens and above the world, the
light that shines in the highest
world, beyond which there are no
others—that is the light that shines
in the hearts of men. Truly has this
universe come forth from Brahman.
In Brahman it lives and has its being. Assuredly, all is Brahman. Let a
man, freed from the taint of passion,
worship Brahman alone. (U-C)

Let your light . . . shine before men.
   (Matt. 5:16)

What communion hath light with
darkness? . . . ye are the temple of
the living God; as God hath said, I
will dwell in them, and walk in
them. (II Cor. 6:14–16)

. . . in him we live, and move, and
have our being. (Acts 17:28)

Buddhism

Taoism

Something there is, whose veiled
    creation was
Before the earth or sky began to be;
So silent, so aloof and so alone,
It changes not, nor fails, but touches
    all:
Conceive it as the mother of the
    world.

I do not know its name;
A name for it is "Way";
Pressed for designation,
I call it Great.
Great means outgoing,
Outgoing, far-reaching,
Far-reaching, return. (25-B)

6. THE LAW

Hinduism   Christianity

THE LAW

Then he [Brahman] created the most
excellent law. There is nothing
higher than the law. The law is the
truth. Therefore it is said that if a
man speaks the truth he declares the
law, and if he declares the law he
speaks the truth. The law and the
truth are one. (U-B)

. . . it is easier for heaven and earth
to pass than one tittle of the law to
fail. (Luke 16:17)

The law is holy, and the commandment holy, and just and good. (Rom.
7:12)

. . . we know that the law is
spiritual. (Rom. 7:14)

There is one lawgiver, who is able to
save and to destroy. (James 4:12)

COMMENTS ON "THE LAW"

It would appear from what we read in these scriptures and from what we can
observe, that within our creation there are certain fundamental laws that govern
the dynamics of our world. When man lives and works in harmony with these
laws, the results are what we have come to call good for all concerned. When these
laws are violated, eventual pain and distress result. A full understanding of the
laws with all their ramifications is probably beyond man's ability at our present
state of development. That which has been passed down to us by the great religious leaders represents a simplification of the laws that govern our creation,
tailored to the needs and capacities of those to whom they were addressed. In section 4 of this chapter, "Reward and Punishment," the scriptures describe the working out of one aspect of the Law with respect to the results of man's actions.

6. THE LAW

Buddhism   Taoism

THE LAW

He who dwells in the law, delights in the law, meditates on the law, recollects the law, that Bhikshu will never fall away from the true law. (D-364)

He who drinks in the law lives happily with a serene mind; the wise man rejoices always in the law, as preached by the elect. (D-79)

The Bhikshu who controls his mouth, who speaks wisely and calmly, who teaches the meaning and the law, his word is sweet. (D-363)

The universe makes no rules—yet, we all obey its rules. (73-S)

What kind of man can remain patiently at rest and yet move other men to action? Only one kind of man: the man who lives by the Way of Nature. A man who knows the Way of Nature can give himself to others and always remain full. (15-S)

7. THE PATH (THE WAY)

Hinduism   Christianity

THE PATH (THE WAY)

Like the sharp edge of a razor, the sages say, is the path. Narrow it is, and difficult to tread! (U-K)

The path of liberation is subtle, and hard, and long. . . . By this path alone the wise, the knowers of Brahman, attain him while living, and achieve final liberation at death. (U-B)

Enter by the narrow gate. For wide is the gate and broad is the way that leads to destruction, and many there are who enter that way. How narrow the gate and close the way that leads to life! And few there are who find it. (Matt. 7:13–14)

7. THE PATH (THE WAY)

Buddhism

Taoism

THE PATH (THE WAY)

Avoiding these two extremes* the Tathagata† has gained knowledge of the Middle Path which produces insight and knowledge, and tends to calm, to higher knowledge, enlightenment, Nirvana. (T p. 29 from the Buddha's sermon at Benares)

Therefore, if students of the Way only regard seeing, hearing, feeling, and knowing as their [proper] activities, upon being deprived of these perceptions, their way towards [an understanding of] mind is cut off and they find nowhere to enter. . . . Exist independently of all that is above, below, or around you, for there is nowhere in which the Way cannot be followed. (T p. 197 from the teachings of Zen master Hsi Yun, A.D. 840)

The man who has learned the Way of Nature has learned to avoid excess and to live his life walking carefully along the middle road. (24-S)

If you work by the Way,
You will be of the Way;
If you work through its virtue,
You will be given the virtue;
Abandon either one
And both abandon you.

Gladly then the Way receives
Those who choose to walk in it;
Gladly too its power upholds
Those who choose to use it well;
Gladly will abandon greet
Those who to abandon drift. (23-B)

And so there is a proverb:
"When going looks like coming back,
The clearest road is mighty dark."
Today, the Way that's plain looks rough,
And lofty virtue like a chasm;
The purest innocence like shame,
The broadest power not enough,
Established goodness knavery,
Substantial worth like shifting tides.

The Way is obscure and unnamed;
It is a skilled investor, nonetheless,
The master of accomplishment. (41-B)

*That cojoined with passion and luxury and that cojoined with self-torture.
†The Perfect One, i.e. the Buddha.

<u>Hinduism</u>   <u>Christianity</u>

Buddhism

Taoism

The straightest, yet it seems
To deviate, to bend;
The highest skill and yet
It looks like clumsiness;
The utmost eloquence,
It sounds like stammering. (45)

If you can create things
Without feeling the need to own
them;
If you can aid mankind
Without waiting for reward;
If you can learn to act as a leader
While men still look upon you as a
brother;
Then you have learned to travel The
Way. (10-S)

8. THE SPIRITUAL NATURE OF HUMANITY

Hinduism

Christianity

THE LIGHT WITHIN*

The Atman† is the light:
The light is covered by darkness: . . .
When the light of the Atman
Drives out our darkness
That light shines forth from us,
A sun in splendour,
The revealed Brahman.‡
  (BG-S p. 59)

What is man's will
And how shall he use it?
Let him put forth its power
to uncover the Atman,
Not hide the Atman.
  (BG-S p. 63)

The yogi experiences directly the truth of Brahman by realizing the light of the Self within. He is freed from all impurities—he the pure, the birthless, the bright. (U-S)

Be devoted to the eternal Brahman. Unite the light within you with the light of Brahman. Thus will the source of ignorance be destroyed and you will rise above karma. (U-S)

In the beginning was the Word, and the Word was with God, and the Word was God. In him was life; and the life was the light of men. And the light shineth in darkness; and the darkness comprehended it not.
  (John 1:1–5)

No man when he hath lighted a candle, putteth it in a secret place, neither under a bushel, but on a candlestick, that they which come in may see the light. The light of the body is the eye; therefore when thine eye is single, thy whole body also is full of light; but when thine eye is evil, thy body also is full of darkness.
Take heed therefore that the light which is in thee be not darkness.
If thy whole body therefore be full of light, having no part dark, the whole shall be full of light as when the bright shining of a candle doth give thee light. (Luke 11:33–39)

Let your light so shine before men, that they may see your good works, and glorify your Father which is in heaven. (Matt. 5:16)

see also Matt. 5:14–15
         Matt. 6:22–23

---

*The light within man as a reported visible phenomenon for some saints, mystics, and others is discussed in chapter 18, "The Message of the Teachings and Daily Life."
†Atman—The spiritual essence in man.
‡Brahman—God.

8. THE SPIRITUAL NATURE OF HUMANITY

Buddhism   Taoism

THE LIGHT WITHIN

. . . so let your light shine before the world that you, having embraced the religious life according to so well-taught a doctrine and a discipline, are seen to be forbearing and mild.
(*Maha-Vagga, Sacred Books of the East,* vol. XVII)

Good people shine from afar, like the snowy mountains. (D-304)

Those whose minds are well-grounded in the (seven) elements of knowledge, who without clinging to anything, rejoice in freedom from attachments, whose appetites have been conquered, and who are full of light, are free, even in this world. (D-89)

This indeed is
Subtle Light;
The gentle Way
Will overcome
The hard and strong. (36-B)

Stop up your senses;
Close up your doors; . . .
You are bright, it is said,
If you see what is small; . . .
By the use of its light,
Make your eyes again bright
From evil to lead you away.

This is called "practicing constancy." (52-B)

Hinduism	Christianity

THE SELF

The Lord God, all-pervading and om-nipresent, dwells in the heart of all beings. Full of grace, he ultimately gives liberation to all creatures by turning their faces toward himself. (U-S)

Ye are the temple of God. (I Cor. 3:16)

And the Word was made flesh, and dwelt among us, . . . full of grace and truth. (John 1:14)

He is the innermost Self. He is the great Lord. He it is that reveals the purity within the heart by means of which he, who is pure being, may be reached. He is the ruler. He is the great Light, shining forever. (U-S)

In Him was life; and the life was the light of men. (John 1:4)

He is within all persons as the Inner Self, facing in all directions.* (U-S)

The kingdom of God is within you. (Luke 17:21)

Pure like crystal water is that Self, the only seer, the One without a second. He is the kingdom of Brahman—man's highest goal, supreme treasure, greatest bliss. (U-B)

The self is described as *not this, not that*. It is incomprehensible, for it cannot be comprehended; undecay-ing, for it never decays; unattached, for it never attaches itself; unbound, for it is never bound. By whom, O my beloved, shall the Knower be known? (U-B)

He that has known the glory of the self within the ephemeral body—that stumbling block to enlightenment—knows that the Self is one with Brahman, Lord and creator of all. (U-B)

Is it not written in your law, I said, Ye are gods? (John 10:34)

---

*As discussed in chapter 18, there are descriptions by those who have experienced certain higher forms of consciousness of being able to "see" in all directions at one time.

Buddhism   Taoism

THE SELF

Ordinary people look outwards,   Touch ultimate emptiness;
while followers of the Way look into   Hold steady and still.
their own minds, but the real
Dharma is to forget both the exter-   This, I say, is the stillness:
nal and the internal. The former is   A retreat to one's roots;
easy enough, the latter is very   Or better yet, return
difficult. Men are afraid to forget   To the will of God,
their own minds, fearing to fall   Which is, I say, to constancy.
through the void with nothing to   The knowledge of constancy
which they can cling. They do not   I call enlightenment and say
know that the void is not really void   That not to know it
but the real realm of the Dharma.   Is blindness that works evil.
This spiritually enlightened nature is   (16-B)
without beginning or end, as old as
space, neither subject to birth nor
destruction. (T p. 199 from teachings of the Zen Master Hsi Yun)

Hinduism

Christianity

Smaller than a grain of rice is the Self; smaller than a grain of barley, smaller than a mustard seed, smaller than a canary seed, yea, even smaller than the kernel of a canary seed. Yet again is that Self within the lotus of my heart, greater than the earth, greater than the heavens, yea, greater than all the worlds. (U-C)

The kingdom of heaven is like to a grain of mustard seed, which a man took and sowed in his field.* Which indeed is the least of all seeds; but, when it is grown it is the greatest among herbs, and becometh a tree, so that the birds of the air come and lodge in the branches thereof. (Matt. 13:31–32)

Like two birds of golden plumage, inseparable companions, the individual self and the immortal Self are perched on the branches of the self-same tree. The former tastes of the sweet and bitter fruits of the tree; the latter, tasting of neither, calmly observes. (U-M)

He who knows that the individual soul, enjoyer of the fruits of action, is the Self—ever present within, lord of time, past and future—casts out all fear. For this Self is the immortal Self. (U-K)

The Self, whose symbol is OM, is the omniscient Lord. He is not born. He does not die. He is neither cause nor effect. This Ancient One is unborn, imperishable, eternal; though the body be destroyed, he is not killed. (U-K)

Both the individual self and the Universal Self have entered the cave of the heart, the abode of the Most High. (U-K)

With the heart man believeth unto righteousness. (Rom. 10:10)

---

*The kingdom of God is within you (Luke 17:21). This body is called the field (Bhagavad Gita).

Buddhism

Taoism

All the Buddhas and all sentient beings are nothing but universal mind,
besides which nothing exists. This
mind, which always has existed, is
unborn and indestructible. . . .
Our original Buddha-nature is, in all
truth, nothing which can be appre-
hended. It is void, omnipresent,
silent, pure; it is glorious and mysterious peacefulness, and that is all
which can be said. You must yourself awake to it, fathoming its
depths. . . . This pure mind, the
source of everything, shines on all
with the brilliance of its own perfection, but the people of the world do
not awake to it, regarding only that
which sees, hears, feels, and knows
as mind. (T pp. 195–97 from the
teachings of the Zen Master Hsi
Yun)

Hinduism

Know this Atman
Unborn, undying,
Never ceasing,
Never beginning,
Deathless, birthless,
Unchanging forever.
How can it die
The death of the body?
   (BG-S p. 37)

For like the ether,
Pervading all things,
Too subtle for taint,
This Atman also
Inhabits all bodies
But never is tainted.
   (BG-S p. 105)

Christianity

Are you not aware that you are the temple of God, and that the Spirit of God dwells in you? (I Cor. 3:16)

. . . You are the temple of the living God. (II Cor. 6:16)

You must know that your body is the temple of the Holy Spirit, who is within—the Spirit you have received from God. (I Cor. 6:19)

SPIRITUAL SIGHT

He who with spiritual eye directly perceives the self-effulgent Being, the lord of all that was, is, and shall be—he indeed is without fear, and causes fear in none. (U-B)

Knowing their moods and notions, he is invisible always to the ignorant, but his sages see him with the eye of wisdom. (BG-S p. 112)

. . . when thine eye is single* thy whole body also is full of light.
   (Luke 11:34)

---

*The single eye in this passage is believed by many to refer to the spiritual or third eye, which is said to be a force center in man's subtle body located between the eyebrows (see chapter 5). "With the eye of the inner vision can God be seen, even when man is occupying a body of flesh. Not with the physical eye can Deity be seen, though the hallmark of divinity is everywhere. There is an eye which can be developed and used, and which will enable its possessor to see God, working on the inner side of Life, within himself and within all forms, for 'when thine eye is single, thy whole body is full of light.' In that light shall we see Light, and so see God." (From *Esoteric Psychology I*, by Alice A. Bailey, p. 182)

Buddhism   Taoism

SPIRITUAL SIGHT

With his heart thus serene . . .
with the pure Heavenly Eye, sur-
passing that of man, he sees beings
as they pass away from one form of
existence and take shape in another.
(T p. 106. From the words of the
Buddha as recorded in the *Sam-
manaphala Suttanta*)

You can see the whole world
Without leaving your room.
You can see the universe
Without even looking out your
    window.
In fact, it is often true
That the farther one travels
The less one sees.
By looking inside himself,
The wise man sees with his
    heart and his mind,
And his heart and his mind see
    everywhere. (47-S)

Hinduism   Christianity

MEDITATION

The eyes do not see him, speech cannot utter him, the senses cannot reach him. He is to be attained neither by austerity nor by sacrificial rites. When through discrimination the heart has become pure, then, in meditation, the Impersonal Self is revealed. The subtle Self within the living and breathing body is realized in that pure consciousness wherein is no duality. (U-M)

The self resides within the lotus of the heart. Knowing this, devoted to the self, the sage enters daily that holy sanctuary. (U-C)

This Brahman, this Self, deep-hidden in all beings, is not revealed to all; but to the seers, pure in heart, concentrated* in mind—to them he is revealed. (U-K)

None beholds him with the eyes, for he is without visible form. Yet in the heart is he revealed, through self-control and meditation. Those who know him become immortal. When all the senses are stilled, when the mind is at rest, when the intellect wavers not—then, say the wise, is reached the highest state. This calm of the senses and the mind has been defined as yoga. He who attains it is freed from illusion. (U-K)

Be still and know that I am God. (Ps. 46:10)

God is a Spirit; and they that worship him must worship him in spirit. (John 4:24)

I was in the Spirit on the Lord's day. (Rev. 1:10)

Meditate on these things. (I Tim. 4:15)

Let the words of my mouth and the meditation of my heart, be acceptable in thy sight, O Lord. (Ps. 19:14)

. . . the meditation of my heart shall be of understanding. (Ps. 49:3)

I die daily. (I Cor. 15:31)

*Meditation is defined by the Indian sage Patanjali as "sustained concentration."

Buddhism   Taoism

MEDITATION

He who gives himself to vanity, and
does not give himself to meditation,
forgetting the real aim [of life] and
grasping at pleasure, will in time
envy him who has exerted himself
in meditation. (D-209)

The wise people, meditative, steady
always possessed of strong powers,
attain to Nirvana, the highest happiness. (D-23)

The disciples of Gautama are always
well awake, and their minds day and
night always delight in meditation.
  (D-301)

Those who know do not talk,
And talkers do not know.

Stop your senses,
Close the doors;
Let sharp things be blunted,
Tangles resolved,
The light tempered,
And turmoil subdued;
For this is mystic unity
In which the Wise Man is moved
Neither by affection
Nor yet by estrangement
Or profit or loss
Or honor or shame.
Accordingly, by all the world,
He is held highest. (56-B)

Touch ultimate emptiness,
Hold steady and still. (16-B)

9. QUALITIES TO BE GAINED

Hinduism

Christianity

FAITH

The faith of each believer . . . conforms itself to what he truly is. (BG-A XVII)

Cling in faith and love and reverence to me, so shalt thou come to me. (BG-A XVIII)

Take refuge utterly in him [the Lord]. By his grace you will find supreme peace, and the state which is beyond all change. (BG-S p. 129)

Thou art the refuge of those who surrender themselves to thee. Reveal thyself to me. Make me thine own. I take my refuge in thee. (U-T)

Faith is the substance of things hoped for, the evidence of things not seen. (Heb. 11:1)

Ask, and it shall be given to you; seek and you will find; knock, and it will be opened to you. (Matt. 7:7)

And Jesus, answering, saith unto them, have faith in God. For verily I say unto you, that whosoever shall say unto this mountain, Be thou removed, and be cast into the sea; and shall not doubt in his heart, but shall believe that those things which he saith shall come to pass; he shall have whatsoever he saith. (Mark 11:22–23)

God is our refuge and strength. (Ps. 46:1)

Therefore I say unto you, take no thought for your life, what ye shall eat, or what ye shall drink; nor yet for your body, what ye shall put on. Is not the life more than meat, and the body more than nourishment? Behold the fowls of the air; for they sow not, neither do they reap, nor gather into barns; yet your heavenly Father feedeth them. . . . Seek ye first the kingdom of God . . . and all these things shall be added unto you. (Matt. 6:25–33)

9. QUALITIES TO BE GAINED

Buddhism

Taoism

FAITH

If a man's faith is unsteady, if he does not know the true law, if his peace of mind is troubled, his knowledge will never be perfect. (D-38)

Little faith is put in those who have little faith. (23-W)

The wise man bends to the will of the way of nature. (22-S)

Hinduism	Christianity

COURAGE

He who seeks freedom
Thrusts fear aside,
Thrusts aside anger
and puts off desire. (BG-S p. 62)

And fear not them which kill the body, but are not able to kill the soul. (Matt. 10:28)

There is no fear in love; but perfect love casteth out fear. (I John 4:18)

God hath not given us the spirit of fear; but of power, and of love, and of a sound mind. (I Tim. 1:7)

Wherefore take unto you the whole armour of God, that ye may be able to withstand in the evil day, and having done all, to stand. (Eph. 6:13)

SELFLESSNESS

Work done with anxiety about results is far inferior to work done without such anxiety, in the calm of self-surrender. Seek refuge in the knowledge of Brahman. They who work selfishly for results are miserable. (BG-S p. 41)

To unite the heart with Brahman and then to act: that is the secret of non-attached work. In the calm of self-surrender, the seers renounce the fruits of their actions, and so reach enlightenment. (BG-S p. 41)

If anyone wishes to walk in my footsteps let him renounce self. (Mark 8:34)

Take heed and beware of covetousness; for a man's life consisteth not in the abundance of the things which he possesseth. (Luke 12:15)

CONTENTMENT

When you have the golden gift of contentment you have everything. (Hitopadesa W)

I have learned in whatever state I am in, with that to be content. (Phil. 4:11)

. . . be content with such things as ye have. (Heb. 13:5)

Buddhism

Taoism

COURAGE

The fifth perfection is: *Courage*. As the lion, king of beasts, whether when lying down or standing up, lacks no courage, but is ever high-hearted, so also shall you in each of your individual-existences hold fast to your courage. (*Sutta-Pitaka; Buddha-Vasma*: W p. 12)

"What all men fear, I too must fear"—How barren and pointless a thought! (20-B)

Once grasp the great Form without form and you roam where you will with no evil to fear. Calm, peaceful, at ease. (35-B)

SELFLESSNESS

Unhappiness is caused by selfish craving. (T p. 28. Second Noble Truth)

I suffer most because
Of me and selfishness.
If I were selfless, then
What suffering would I bear?
(13-B)

. . . let there be a visible simplicity of life, embracing unpretentious ways and small self-interest and poverty of coveting. (19-B)

CONTENTMENT

Him I call indeed a brahmana who has traversed this miry road, the impossible world, difficult to pass, and its vanity; who has gone through and reached the other shore, is thoughtful, steadfast, free from doubts, free from attachment, and content. (D)

He who is satisfied with his lot is rich. (33-W)

There is no calamity greater than discontent. (46-W)

It is wealth to be content;
It is willful to force one's way on others. (B)

Hinduism   Christianity

SERENITY IN THE FACE OF PLEASURE OR PAIN

A serene spirit accepts pleasure and pain with an even mind, and is unmoved by either. He alone is worthy of immortality. (BG-S p. 36)

Perform every action with your heart fixed on the Supreme Lord. Be eventempered in success or failure, for it is this evenness of temper which is meant by yoga. (BG-S p. 40)

You, Arjuna, must overcome the three gunas. You must be free from the pairs of opposites.* Poise your mind in tranquility. Take care neither to acquire nor to hoard. Be established in the consciousness of Atman always. (BG-S p. 40)

The sense of individuality in us is said to cause our experience of pleasure and pain. (BG-S p. 103)

I know how to live humbly and I know how to live in abundance . . . to be filled and to be hungry, to have abundance and to suffer want. I can do all things in him who strengthens me. (Phil. 4:12–13)

*Heat and cold, pleasure and pain, etc.

Buddhism   Taoism

SERENITY IN THE FACE OF PLEASURE OR PAIN

As a solid rock is not shaken by the wind, wise people falter not amidst blame and praise. (D-81)

Whether touched by happiness or sorrow, wise people never appear elated or depressed. (D 83)

The tenth perfection is: Serenity. As indeed the earth looks with serenity on all the pure and impure that are cast upon it, even so shall you approach with serenity both joy and sorrow—if you are to attain wisdom. (*Sutta-Pitaka; Buddha-Vasma*: W p. 12)

Which is dearer, fame or self?
Which is worth more, man or pelf?
Which would hurt more, gain or
    loss?

The mean man pays the highest
    price;
The hoarder takes the greatest loss;
A man content is never shamed,
And self-restrained, is not in danger:
He will live forever. (44-B)

No sin can exceed
Incitement to envy;
No calamity's worse
Than to be discontented;
Nor is there an omen
More dreadful than coveting.
But once be contented,
And truly you'll always be so.
    (46-B)

Hinduism   Christianity

HUMILITY

Therefore I tell you:
Be humble, be harmless,
Have no pretension. (BG-S p. 101)

The doer without desire,
Who does not boast of his deed,
Who is ardent, enduring,
Untouched by triumph,
In failure untroubled:
He is a man of sattwa.
  (BG-S p. 123)

Religion shown in act of proud display . . . is . . . rash and vain.
  (BG-A XVII)

Whoever shall exalt himself shall be abased; and he that shall humble himself shall be exalted. (Matt. 23:12)

God resists the proud and gives grace to the humble. (I Pet. 5:5)

Many that are first, shall be last; and the last shall be first. (Matt. 19:30)

Charity . . . is not pretentious, is not puffed up. (I Cor. 13:4)

When thou doest thine alms, do not sound a trumpet before thee as the hypocrites do. And when thou prayest thou shalt not be as the hypocrites are: for they love to pray standing in the synagogues and in the corners of the streets, that they may be seen of men. (Matt. 6:2–5)

Buddhism	Taoism

HUMILITY

Let a man leave anger, let him forsake pride. (D-221)

The Wise Man chooses to be last
And so becomes the first of all;
Denying self, he too is saved.
For does he not fulfillment find
In being an unselfish man? (7-B)

The Wise Man, therefore, while he is alive,
Will never make a show of being great;
And that is how his greatness is achieved. (34-B)

. . . the Wise Man cherishes the One,
As a standard to the world:
Not displaying himself,
He is famous;
Not asserting himself,
He is distinguished;
Not boasting his powers,
He is effective;
Taking no pride in himself,
He is chief.
Because he is no competitor,
No one in all the world
Can compete with him. (22-B)

A man of highest virtue
Will not display it as his own;
His virtue then is real.
Low virtue makes one miss no chance
To show his virtue off;
His virtue then is nought.
High virtue is at rest;
It knows no need to act.
Low virtue is a busyness
Pretending to accomplishment.
(38-B)

Hinduism   Christianity

SAFETY IN THE FACE OF DANGER

When a man has no lust, no hatred,
a man walks safely among the things
of lust and hatred. (BG-S p. 43)

And who is he that will harm you, if
ye be followers of that which is
good? (I Pet. 3:13)

Behold, I give unto you power to
tread on serpents and scorpions, and
over all the powers of the enemy;
and nothing shall by any means hurt
you. (Luke 10:19)

And these signs shall follow them
that believe . . . they shall take up
serpents; and if they drink any
deadly thing it shall not hurt them.
    (Mark 16:17–18)

Buddhism   Taoism

SAFETY IN THE FACE OF DANGER

He who has no wound on his hand
may touch poison with his hand;
poison does not affect one who has
no wound; nor is there evil for one
who does not commit evil. (D-124)

As I have heard, the man who
  knows
On land how best to be at peace
Will never meet a tiger or a buffalo;
In battle, weapons do not touch his
  skin.
There is no place the tiger's claws
  can grip;
Or with his horn, the buffalo can
  jab;
Or where the soldier can insert his
  sword.
Why so? In him there is no place of
  death. (50-B)

Rich in virtue, like an infant,
Noxious insects will not sting him;
Wild beasts will not attack his flesh
Nor birds of prey sink claws in him.
  (55-B)

Hinduism	Christianity

WISDOM

That man alone is wise who keeps the mastery of himself. (BG-A II)

Cut . . . with the sword of wisdom . . . this doubt that binds thy heart! Cleave the bond born of thy ignorance. Be bold and wise. (BG-A IV)

Be wise as serpents and harmless as doves. (Matt. 10:16)

Buddhism

Taoism

WISDOM

By rousing himself, by earnestness, by restraint and control, the wise man may make for himself an island which no flood can overwhelm.
(D-25)

When the learned man drives away vanity by earnestness, he, the wise, climbing the terraced heights of wisdom, looks down upon the fools; free from sorrow he looks upon the sorrowing crowd, as one that stands on a mountain looks down upon them that stand upon the plain.
(D-28)

He who understands others is wise;
He who understands himself is enlightened. (33-W)

The wise man is square but not
   sharp;
Straight but not severe;
Bright but not dazzling. (58-W)

The wise man sets no high value on a thing simply because it is hard to get. (64-W)

The Wise Man's mind is free
But tuned to people's need:
   "Alike to good and bad
   I must be good,
   For Virtue is goodness.
   To honest folk
   And those dishonest ones
   Alike, I proffer faith,
   For Virtue is faithful."

The Wise Man, when abroad,
Impartial to the world,
Does not divide or judge.
But people everywhere
Mark well his ears and eyes;
For wise men hear and see
As little children do. (49-B)

Hinduism	Christianity

PERFECTION

Learn from me now,
O son of Kunti,
How man made perfect
Is one with Brahman. (BG-S p. 127)

The Lord is everywhere and always perfect. (BG-S p. 59)

Control the vital force. Set fire to the Self within by the practice of meditation. Be drunk with the wine of divine love. Thus shall you reach perfection. (U-S)

Be ye perfect as your father in heaven is perfect. (Matt. 5:48)

. . . just men made perfect. (Heb. 12:23)

The mystery which hath been hid from ages and from generations, but now is made manifest to his saints. . . which is Christ in you, the hope of glory; whom we preach, warning every man and teaching every man in all wisdom, that we may present every man perfect in Christ Jesus. (Col. 1:26–28)

PEACE

Votaries renouncing fruit of deeds gain endless peace. (BG-A V)

Near to renunciation—very near— dwelleth eternal peace. (BG-A XII)

No peace is here or otherwhere—no hope, nor happiness for those who doubt. (BG-A IV)

The fruit of the Spirit is love and peace. (Gal. 5:22)

For the kingdom of God is not meat and drink; but righteousness, and peace, and joy in the Holy Ghost. (Rom. 14:17)

. . . the peace of God, which passeth all understanding. (Phil. 4:7)

Buddhism   Taoism

PERFECTION

The ten perfections are: giving, duty, renunciation, insight, courage, patience, truth, resolution, lovingkindness, serenity. (*Sutta-Pitaka;
Buddha-Vasma*)

The saying of the men of old
Is not in vain:
"The crooked shall be made
   straight."*
To be perfect, return to it. (22-B)

PEACE

As they who dig deep and untiringly even in the sand will find water, so the wise in perseverance strong find in their hearts peace. (*Jatakas* 2-W
   p. 34)

The last two elements of the eight-fold path:

Right Contemplation of the noble truths in calmness and detachment.

Right Concentration will then follow and lead to the path of perfect peace.
   (*Vinaya-Pitaka; Maha-Vagga:* W
   p. 10)

The goal of the way is peace. (9-W)

*This phrase is found in Isaiah 40:4, which reads "The crooked shall be made straight, and the rough places plain; and the glory of the Lord shall be revealed." This is further commented on in chapter 9, "Symbolic Writing and Allegory."

2. The Golden Rule and Moral Laws

THE GOLDEN RULE

Therefore all that you wish men to do to you, even so do you also to them; for this is the Law and the Prophets. (Matt. 7:12)

This statement by Jesus Christ, referred to by Christians as the Golden Rule, is found in one form or another in all the major religions.

About 500 years before the birth of Jesus, Confucius stated it, as related in the following from the Analects:

Confucius was asked, "Is there one word which may serve as a rule of practice for all one's life?" And he replied, "Is 'Reciprocity' not such a word? Do not to others what you do not want done to yourself."

This rule was given even earlier in the Hindu Vedas. From the Mahabharata we read:

Do not to others what you do not wish done to yourself; and wish for others too what you desire and long for, for yourself—this is the whole of Dharma,* heed it well.

In the Dhammapada, the Buddhist Book of Proverbs, we find written:

All men shrink from suffering, and all love life; remember that you too are like them; make your own self the measure of the others, and so abstain from causing hurt to them.

From Taoist writings:

Pity the misfortunes of others; rejoice in the well-being of others; help those who are in want; save men in danger; rejoice at the success of others; and sympathize with their reverses, even as though you were in their place.[1]

Muhammad said:

*Dharma—the unique Law of Moral Order which each individual must discover for him- or herself.

Do to all men as you would wish to have done unto you; and reject for others what you would reject for yourselves. (*Hadith*)

The essence of the Golden Rule is contained in the scriptures of Judaism in the statement in Leviticus 19:18, "Thou shalt love thy neighbor as thyself."

The Palestinian sage Hillel was challenged by a pagan to tell all about Judaism in the time a man might stand on one foot. He replied:

That which is hurtful to thee do not to thy neighbor. This is the whole doctrine. The rest is commentary. Now go forth and learn.

Long before the birth of Jesus in the same area of the world, Zarathustra, the founder of Zoroastrianism, the religion of the early Persians and the present Parsees in India, said:

That which is good for all and any one—
For whomsoever—that is good for me.
What I hold good for self, I should for all.
Only Law Universal is true Law.

MORAL LAWS—COMMANDMENTS

The well-known Ten Commandments of Judaism and Christianity have formed and continue to form the basis of right conduct in many lands. These commandments can be divided into two categories: respect for authority and moral laws. The first four commandments concern resepct for the authority of God and parents.

The other six—the moral laws, listed below—deal with how we are to control and conduct ourselves in dealing with our fellow men:
Thou shalt not kill.
Thou shalt not commit adultery.
Thou shalt not steal.
Thou shalt not bear false witness against thy neighbor.
Thou shalt not covet thy neighbor's house.
Thou shalt not covet thy neighbor's wife, nor his manservant, nor his maidservant, nor his ox, nor his ass, nor anything that is thy neighbor's.

These teachings of Moses are, of course, also acknowledged by Muslims to be inspired works. Muhammad reiterated them in various places in his own teaching. In Hinduism and Buddhism we have commandments with essentially the same moral teachings.

In the very ancient writings of the sage Patanjali, whose teachings form a basic outline of spiritual development for Hindu seekers of union with God, we find the following five "commandments" enjoined:[2]

Harmlessness
Truth to all beings
Abstention from theft
Abstention from incontinence
Abstention from avarice (covetousness)

Buddhists follow ten commandments, the first five of which apply to all Buddhists, the last five only to monks. The first five Buddhist commandments are:

Do not destroy life.
Do not take what is not given you.
Do not commit adultery.
Tell no lies and deceive no one.
Do not become intoxicated. (*Vinaya-Pitaka; Maha-Vagga*)

3. Religions of the Near East: Judaism and Islam

JUDAISM

The great patriarchs and prophets of the Old Testament provided the world with a major spiritual impulse whose effects are still with us today. Their writings continue to inspire many, and they form the basis for the system of laws by which a great part of the world is governed.

The religion they founded, Judaism, is still practised today by many of their racial descendants throughout the world. Central to Jewish belief is the book called the Torah, which consists of the first five books of Judaic scripture: Genesis, Exodus, Leviticus, Numbers, and Deuteronomy (the books attributed to Moses). Augmenting the Torah in documenting that which guides Jewish belief are the other books of what Christians call the Old Testament, including Psalms, Proverbs, Job, and the books of the prophets. To this are added writings of the early rabbis that come under the name Talmud, and the sum total of teaching and interpretation to which the Jew gives the title of Tradition.

Although not large numerically compared with other religious groups, the Jews exert influence beyond their numerical strength. One factor that no doubt contributes to this influence is the attitude of Judaism, which views the process of study and learning as sacred pursuits. This has been an incentive for Jews in all nations to stress intellectual development and thereby prepare themselves for significant contributions to mankind in many fields.

Other precepts given major emphasis in Judaism are: love of God and man, justice, and charity. These have also had great significance in molding the character of the Jews throughout the world.

The importance of love of God and man is heralded by two passages from the Torah well known to every Jew:

> You shall love the Lord your God with all your heart and with all your soul and with all your might. (Deut. 6:5)

> Thou shalt love thy neighbor as thyself. (Lev. 19:18)

These words are of course familiar to Christians also. They are repeated in the New Testament (Matt. 37:39). Jesus, in response to the question, "Which is the great commandment in the law?" put by one of the Pharisees, answers with these two passages.

Regarding the relationship of Judaism to other religions, it may be viewed as forming the foundation for two of the largest religions in the world today, Christianity and Islam. Further, this link and the validity of Judaism are acknowledged by both Christians and Muslims. This is attested to in the recorded words of the founders of both of these religions.

The next logical question is: what is the view of Judaism toward other religions? Rabbi Milton Steinberg provides the following view in his book *Basic Judaism*:[1]

> To the Jewish traditionalist Judaism is religion *par excellence*, the true faith.
>
> Other religions, however, are not necessarily or totally false. On the contrary, they may be true in part, according to the degree in which they approximate Judaism.
>
> Modernists refuse to look on the diverse communions as though they were so many systems of propositions of which only one can be true while all others must be false. They conceive of them rather as one thinks of different individuals or cultures, each possessed of verities peculiar to itself. . . .
>
> In this light, it is good, not regrettable, that religions are plural, just as it is advantageous to the world that there are many persons and civilizations. . . .
>
> For the Jewish modernist Judaism is wonderfully dowered with merits. . . .
>
> But any religion may share some of these qualities, or display still others which Judaism lacks.
>
> Brahmanism has gone much further in exploring the mystic way and in evolving the techniques of discipline.
>
> Quakerism has worked out in greater detail the ethics of peaceableness.
>
> Roman Catholicism is more elaborate and dramatic ritually.
>
> The end of the matter is this: the Jewish modernist prefers not to put religions in contrast with one another. He is content that each has its share of verity and worth. . . . As for himself, he is at peace in Judaism.

The Judaic Tradition holds that humanity is indeed divine, and in the following two statements by Rabbi Steinberg this view is depicted:

> The life of reason is necessary further as a means whereby men may reveal the Divinity lodged in them.
>
> The divine spark in man cannot forever be obscured.

These words might well be compared with those listed under "The Spiritual Nature of Humanity" in chapter 1, especially under the section titled "The Self."

With respect to Christianity, Jews will generally accept that Jesus was a gifted and exalted teacher but do not accept him as the awaited Messiah.

Representative Judaic scripture is listed under some of the topical headings used in chapter 1 after the following discussion of Islam.

ISLAM

With over 400 million followers, Islam is today the second largest religion in the world, surpassed only by Christianity in numbers of the faithful.

Islam was founded by Muhammad, an Arab born in Mecca in A.D. 570. Muhammad was a prophet, inspired while in trance during periods of meditation. That which was transmitted through him was memorized or written down by his followers and compiled after his death in the scripture called the Koran. He was a reformer in a land that badly needed reform. He was also ultimately a great leader who governed his followers well and led them in defense of their principles against the many attacks of those who wanted things to remain as they were. He succeeded in spreading his teachings throughout all Arabia.

It is important to recognize the significance of Muhammad's accomplishment. Arabia before Muhammad began to preach was a land of cruel idolatry, with idols to be worshipped for every day of the year, human beings offered in sacrifice to idols, and worshippers consuming human flesh. Lust, licentiousness, and wars were the order of the day, and gambling and drunkenness were widespread.

Muhammad's efforts resulted in a complete change, to belief in one God, in the equality of all men and women before God and the law, an emphasis on truthfulness, justice, kindness, and charity, and the prohibition of drunkenness and adultery.

After Muhammad's death, his followers accomplished the spread of Islam throughout North Africa and the Middle East to northern Spain and as far east as India. They established a civilization with centers of learning that excelled in philosophy, mathematics, and medicine. Islam succeeded in preserving much of the knowledge of the classical world through the Middle Ages when culture and learning were at a low ebb in Europe.

Islam's view of Muhammad's role is spelled out clearly in the Koran, "Muhammad is but a messenger, messengers [the like of whom] have passed away before him." (III, 144)[2]

The Koran also comments on the two other religions that the Arabs were in contact with, as is indicated by the following (the reader should be aware that the Koran consists not of the words of Muhammad but of words transmitted to him while in a meditative trance.):

Lo! We inspire thee as We inspired Noah and the prophets after him, as We inspired Abraham and Ishmael and Isaac and Jacob and the tribes, and Jesus and Job and Jonah and Aaron and Solomon, and We inspired unto David the Psalms. (IV 164)

He hath ordained for you that religion which he commended unto Noah, and that which We inspire in thee [Muhammad], and that which We commended unto Abraham and Moses and Jesus, saying: Establish the religion, and be not divided therein. (XLII 13)

He hath revealed unto thee [Muhammad] the Scripture with truth, confirming that which was [revealed] before even as He revealed the Torah and the Gospel. (III 3)

Say [O Muhammad]: We believe in Allah and that which is revealed unto us and that which was revealed unto Abraham and Ishmael and Isaac and Jacob and the tribes, and that which was vouchsafed unto Moses and Jesus and the Prophets from their Lord. We make no distinction between any of them, and unto Him we have surrendered. (III 84)

The Muslim view of Jesus differs from that of the Jews. As shown in the passages that follow, the Koran states that Jesus is the Messiah predicted in the Old Testament. However, while the Koran gives a special status to Jesus, it denies the contention of some Christians that Jesus is identical with God, pointing out that Jesus never made this claim for himself: rather it was made by others who came after him. A point of view that could reconcile these two differing claims is discussed in the last section of chapter 9.

Of those messengers, some of whom We have caused to excel others, and of whom there are some unto whom Allah spake, while some of them He exalted [above others] in degree; and We gave Jesus, son of Mary, clear proofs [of Allah's sovereignty] and We supported Him with the holy Spirit. (II 253)

(And remember) when the angels said: O Mary! Lo! Allah giveth thee glad tidings of a word from Him, whose name is the Messiah, Jesus son of Mary, illustrious in the world and the Hereafter, and one of those brought near [unto Allah]. (III 45)

They surely disbelieve who say: Lo! Allah is the Messiah, son of Mary. The Messiah [himself] said: O Children of Israel worship Allah, my Lord and your Lord. (V 72)

It was Muhammad's view that people should be free to accept or not accept the teachings of Islam or any other religion according to their own conscience and free will. The Koran states: "There is no compulsion in religion" (II 256). This was not necessarily the view of some of the more zealous followers of Islam who came after Muhammad. It is important to note that the definition of Islam is *to surrender to the will of God*—and so the pharse "There is but one religion, Islam" is actually not in conflict with the Koran's acceptance of the validity of Judaism and Christianity, since these religions teach surrender to the will of God.

For comparative purposes, Muslim teachings in several subject areas are listed below.

LIGHT

Allah is the Protecting Friend of those who believe. He bringeth them out of darkness into light. (II 257)

Compare this with the prayer of the Upanishads:

Lead me from the unreal to the real,
Lead me from darkness to light.
Lead me from death to immortality. (Brihadaranyaka Upanishad)

THE PATH

The opening of the Koran reads:

Praise be to Allah, Lord of the Worlds,
The Beneficent, the Merciful.
Owner of the Day of Judgment,
Thee (alone) we worship; thee (alone) we ask for help.
Show us the straight path,
The path of those whom Thou hast favored. (I 1–6)

MEDITATION

Even before his enlightenment, it was Muhammad's practice to set aside a month every year during which he retired with his family to a cave in the desert for meditation. It was in one of these meditation periods that he had the vision that initiated his ministry. Those words that came to Muhammad while in a state of trance at various times and places are held sacred by Muslims and have been recorded (following Muhammad's death) in the Koran—the sacred book. The words uttered by Muhammad when no physical change was apparent in him are preserved for us in the *Hadith*.

ANGELS

The Koran refers to angels, including the angels Gabriel and Michael. Angels are mentioned also in the scriptures of Christianity, Judaism, and Hinduism.

A BRIEF SCRIPTURAL COMPARISON

The scriptures of Judaism and Islam are compared in the following selections for some of the same topical headings used in chapter 1. A comparison with the scriptures in chapter 1 will show that most of the same basic teachings appear in the scriptures of all six of these religions.

Judaism	Islam

COMPASSION (MERCY)

Sow in righteousness, reap in mercy. (Hos. 10:12)

Did He not find you an orphan and give you a home? Did He not find you lost and show you the way? Did He not find you needy and enrich you? Therefore the orphan oppress not. Therefore the beggar drive not away. (Koran 93:6–10)[3]

Muhammad was asked to curse the infidels, and He answered: "I was not sent to curse the infidels but to have mercy on mankind." (*Hadith*–325)[4]

CHARITY

If your brother becomes poor and cannot maintain himself, you shall maintain him. (Lev. 25:35)

Open wide your hand to your brother, to the needy and to the poor. (Deut. 15:11)

When people ask what they should spend in charity, say "All that you have left over above your needs." (Koran 2:216)

If you give alms publicly, it is well; but it is better to give them secretly. Allah knows what you do. (Koran 2:273)

DUTY

Whatever your hand finds to do, do it with all your might. (Eccles. 8:9)

He who is fit and able to work for himself and others and does not, God is not gracious to him. (*Hadith*–262)

Judaism   ## Islam

RIGHT SPEECH AND TRUTHFULNESS

Death and life are in the power of the tongue and those who indulge it shall eat its fruit. (Prov. 18:21)

A soft answer turns away wrath, but harsh words stir up anger. (Prov. 15:1)

In many words there is room for sin, but he who controls his lips is wise. (Prov. 10:19)

Truth hath come and falsehood hath vanished away. Lo! falsehood is ever bound to vanish. (Koran XVII 81)

Muhammad was asked: "What is the essence of Islam?" And he replied: "Purity of speech and charity." (Hadith-243)

ANGER

He who is slow to anger has great understanding, but he who becomes easily angered exalts folly. (Prov. 14:29)

He who cannot control his temper is like a city without defenses. (Prov. 25:28)

Muhammad was asked for advice, and he said, "Be not angry." (Hadith-80)

He is not strong who throws others down but he is strong who controls his anger. (Hadith-82)

REWARD AND PUNISHMENT

The merciful man doeth good to his own soul: but he that is cruel troubleth his own flesh. . . . to him that soweth righteousness shall be a sure reward. (Prov. 11:17-18)

Whatever good you do for others, you send it before your own souls and shall find it with Allah who sees all you do. (Koran 2:104)

Every soul will be rewarded according to its merit. (Koran 3:182)

Judaism	Islam

GOD

Hear, O Israel: the Lord our God is One. (Deut. 6:4)

In the beginning God created the heaven and the earth. . . . And God said, Let there be light: and there was light. And God saw the light that it was good: and God divided the light from the darkness. (Gen. 1:1–4)

Your God is one God; there is no God save Him, the Beneficent, the Merciful. (Koran II 163)

Allah in the east, Allah in the west; wherever you turn, there is Allah's face. (Koran 2:109)

Praise be to Allah, Who hath created the heavens and the earth, and hath appointed darkness and light. (Koran VI 1)

Allah is the Light of the heavens and the earth. (Koran XXIV 35)

Unto Allah belongeth whatsoever is in the heavens and whatsoever is in the earth; and unto Allah all things are returned.* (Koran III 109)

FAITH

Cast your burden upon the Lord, and he will sustain you. (Ps. 55:22)

If Allah is your helper none can overcome you, and if he withdraw His help from you, who is there who can help you? In Allah let believers put their trust. (Koran III 160)

CONTENTMENT

Who is rich? He who is satisfied with his lot. (*The Sayings of the Fathers*)

Riches do not come from an abundance of goods but from a contented mind. (*Hadith–69*)

---

*The passages on God from the Koran might be compared with the following from the Hindu Svetasvatara Upanishad: "The Lord is One without a second. Within man he dwells, and within all other beings. He projects the universe, maintains it, and withdraws it unto himself."

Judaism	Islam

HUMILITY

When pride comes, then comes shame; but with the lowly is wisdom. (Prov. 11:2)

A man's pride shall bring him low, but the humble in spirit shall obtain honor. (Prov. 29:23)

Pride goes before destruction and a haughty spirit before a fall. (Prov. 16:18)

The person who has one atom of pride in his heart will not enter Paradise. (*Hadith*–37)

Successful indeed are the believers who are humble in their prayers, and who shun vain conversation. (Koran XXIII 1–3)

WISDOM

How much better it is to get wisdom than gold; to get understanding rather than silver. (Prov. 16:16)

Wisdom is better than strength. (Eccles. 9:16)

God created nothing better than Reason. (*Hadith*–372)

Who are the learned? They who practice what they know. (*Hadith*–294)

PEACE

There is no peace for the wicked. (Isa. 48:22)

Acquaint thyself with [God] and be at peace. (Job 22:21)

. . . seek peace and pursue it. (Ps. 34:14)

They shall beat their swords into plowshares, and their spears into pruning hooks; nation shall not lift up sword against nation, neither shall they learn war any more. (Isa. 2:4)

Shall I tell you what are better acts than fasting, charity and prayers? Making peace between enemies are such acts; for enmity and malice tear up the heavenly rewards by the roots. (*Hadith*–340)

4. CONFUCIANISM

The teachings of Confucius, who lived from 551 to 479 B.C., have been a key factor in molding Chinese civilization. Even in recent times the followers of Confucianism have been estimated to be approximately 300 million, and almost all Chinese have been exposed to his teachings.

Although Confucianism is considered to be both a philosophy and a religion, Confucius himself spoke very little about the deity and things of the spirit. He was a practical philosopher who set down a system of morals which could be readily understood and indeed was taught to schoolchildren in China for hundreds of years.

Confucius did not claim to be an original thinker, indicating that he obtained his knowledge from study of the ancient Chinese classics. He is quoted as saying, "I am a transmitter, and not a creator," which is something of an understatement for a man who simplified a vast body of material into a brief, useful set of statements by which, for over 2,000 years, a great nation could train its citizens and leaders to live usefully and morally.

Confucius and Lao-tzu, the author of the Tao Te Ching, met when Confucius was thirty-four and Lao-tzu eighty-five. Lao-tzu was the keeper of the state archives, a rather secluded post, and yet was well known as a wise man and philosopher who had many followers. The report of this meeting points up the difference in the makeup of these two great teachers of China. Confucius was a devoted student of the Chinese classics and at the time of the meeting was working toward getting a system of ancient rituals and ceremonies incorporated into the constitution of the state.

He was told by Lao-tzu that "ancient ceremonies and old-time forms cannot revive China. Obedience to the letter must give way to the life of the spirit."[1]

Confucius was asked by Lao-tzu if he had learned the Divine Way (the Tao). When Confucius replied that he had not but that he had been a seeker for many years, he was told, "You cannot seize it by pursuing it. It will come itself into your heart if you give it a sanctuary there."[2] The Analects report that Confucius later taught that "What the superior man seeks is in himself; what the small man seeks is in others."

Confucius, who had dressed in his finest for the meeting, was also told to abandon vain display, advice he probably took to heart since we find written in the Analects, "The scholar who is intent upon learning the truth, yet is ashamed of his poor clothes and food, is not worthy to be discoursed with."

In commenting on the discussion with Lao-tzu to his disciples, Confucius is reported to have said:

> When I meet a man whose thoughts fly about lightly as a bird, I can wing him with an arrow. When I meet one whose mind ranges like the running deer, I am the hound to bring him down. Even if he dives deep like a fish, I am the angler to land him. But when I meet this one whose thoughts mount on the wind and rush through the heavens like the Dragon into infinity itself, what can I do? I can only listen and wonder with troubled and perplexed mind."[3]

In contrasting Confucius and Lao-tzu, we are comparing the philosopher who relies heavily on what he has read, heard, and seen to form his opinion with the introspective sage who draws his knowledge from a deeper source. The teachings of the men reflect this.

The works of Confucius are relatively down-to-earth and readily understood by many. Those of Lao-tzu, while quite practical in many respects, also reach to heights of mystical insight that few can fully comprehend.

Nevertheless, there are a great many parallels that can be drawn in the teachings of the two men as illustrated by the brief listing of the teachings of Confucius that follow. The selections are from the Analects[4] and are arranged under the topical headings used in chapter 1 to facilitate comparison with other religions.

Love

Fan Ch'ih asked about humanity. Confucius said: "Love men."

Faultfinding

The superior man makes the most of other people's good qualities, not the worst of their bad ones. (XII)

Excuse small faults. (XIII)

The superior man is exacting with himself; the inferior man is exacting with others. (XV)

GOODNESS AND RIGHTEOUSNESS

Better than the one who knows what is right is the one who loves what is right. (VI)

Fix your mind on truth; hold firm to virtue; rely on loving-kindness; and find your recreation in the Arts.

A superior man in dealing with the world is not for anything or against anything. He follows righteousness as the standard.

CHARITY

A man without charity in his heart, what has he to do with ceremonies? A man without charity in his heart, what has he to do with music? (III)

The superior man helps those whose need is urgent and not the rich to be richer. (V)

DUTY

Is not putting duty first and success second a way of raising the standard of virtue? (XII)

SELF-CONTROL

The superior man is always calm. (VII)

The superior man must be mindful of nine things: to be clear in vision, quick to listen, genial in expression, respectful in manners, true in utterances, serious in duty, inquiring in doubt, self-controlled in anger, just and fair when the way to success is open before him. (XVI)

RIGHT SPEECH AND TRUTHFULNESS

When truth and right go hand in hand a statement will bear repetition. (I)

MODERATION

The superior man when eating craves not to eat to the full. (I)

Freedom from Worldly Desires

The constant chase for gain is rich with ill-will. (IV)

The superior man seeks what is right; the inferior one what is profitable. (IV)

With coarse food to eat, water to drink, and a bent arm for a pillow, happiness may still be found. (VII)

The superior man thinks of virtue; the inferior man thinks of possessions. (IV)

God

Does Heaven ever speak? The four seasons come and go, and all creatures thrive and grow. Does Heaven ever speak! (XVII)

The Law

He who does not recognize the existence of a Divine Law cannot be a superior man. (XIX)

The Way

The superior man seeks the Way and not a mere living. (XV)

The Spiritual Nature of Humanity

Heaven produced the good that is in us. (VII)

Selflessness

If a man can subdue his selfishness for one full day everyone will call him good. (XII)

HUMILITY

Sorrow not because men do not know you; but sorrow that you know not men. (I)

In ancient times people were reluctant to speak, fearing that their deeds would not be as good as their words. (IV)

These are the four essential qualities of the superior man: he is humble, he is deferential to superiors, he is generously kind, and he is always just. (V)

The superior man can be dignified without being proud; the inferior man can be proud without being dignified. (XIII)

5. The Esotericists

Throughout recorded history we find that there have always been groups and individuals who focus more intently on the hidden or intangible aspects of existence than the average religious or materialistic people of their time. They think in terms of causes as well as effects and seek to penetrate to that which is behind what we see and experience in the world around us.

Seekers after truth who are motivated in this way have been termed *esotericists*, and while the term is most generally applied to those who think along religious or philosophical lines, the most advanced and creative members of our modern scientific community also fall under the definition of esotericists. Science will be discussed in a later chapter; here we will concentrate on those esotericists whose thinking is related more directly to religious concepts. With this restriction in mind we then ask:

WHO ARE THE ESOTERICISTS?

There are groups that fit the description of esotericists paralleling all major religions. Associated with Judaism, for example, are the Essenes and the Kabbalists. Related to Christianity are the Gnostics and the Rosicrucians. Islam has its Sufis and Hinduism has its Yogis. Buddhist esotericism in Tibet is described by Dr. W. Y. Evans-Wentz in a series of four books that include translated documents on the subject,* and Taoism also has its esoteric branches.

Others from ancient times who fit the definition of esotericists and for whom we have some written records are Hermes and certain of his followers for whom he wrote *The Book of Toth*; Pythagoras and the school founded by him; and also Plato and his followers. Going back to even earlier times the archeological investigations of James Churchward led him to the conclusion that not only the esoteric tradition, but indeed advanced civilization, far predates recorded history. This is further borne out by the

*The titles in this series are *The Tibetan Book of the Dead*, *Tibetan Yoga and Secret Doctrines*, *Tibet's Great Yogi Milarepa*, and *The Tibetan Book of the Great Liberation*. They are published by Oxford University Press.

mythology and folklore of ancient times. Written records such as the Egyptian Book of the Dead and the records in stone left by the builders of Stonehenge, and the many pyramids in South and Central America, as well as the Egyptian pyramids, reveal to the investigator with insight that ancient esotericists left a clear record of their importance and influence.

It is recorded that there were what are called "Mystery Temples" in Egypt, Greece, Rome, Chaldea, and Persia, which were the centers of esoteric teaching. In the British Isles the Druids, whom some believe to be responsible for the building of Stonehenge, maintained the mystery teachings, and in Scandinavia and Germany the ancient leader Odin was said to have established the mysteries.

Through the Middle Ages esoteric teachings were given under the guise of alchemy, and one of the more prominent of the alchemists was the Swiss physician Paracelsus. He was a renowned healer who set the stage for modern medicine. The King Arthur legend and stories, such as Parsifal and the Holy Grail, are said to be blinds or disguises for esoteric teaching. The writings of Sir Francis Bacon indicate that in addition to setting the stage for modern scientific investigation, he was what can be termed an esotericist.*

In more recent times there have been a number of writers and teachers who have given modern presentations of various aspects of the esoteric teaching. The two most profound and far-reaching of these are Helena Petrovna Blavatsky and Alice A. Bailey. Blavatsky's most significant work is *The Secret Doctrine*, first published in 1888. It is a treatise on the origins of the solar system and of man; it consists of extensive commentaries on material said to be from a very ancient document covering these subjects in summary form. She also explores in depth many related topics in the book's 1,474 pages.

The introduction to *The Secret Doctrine* makes the following statement relative to the material presented:

> It is perhaps desirable to state unequivocally that the teachings, however fragmentary and incomplete, contained in these volumes, belong neither to the Hindu, the Zoroastrian, the Chaldean, nor the Egyptian religion, neither to Buddhism, Islam, Judaism nor Christianity exclusively. The Secret Doctrine is the essence of all these.

In another place Blavatsky has the following to say concerning religion:

---

*Manly P. Hall in *The Secret Teachings of All Ages* calls Sir Francis Bacon "a link in that great chain of minds which has perpetuated the secret doctrine of antiquity from its beginning." He states that Bacon was "Father of modern science, remodeller of modern law, editor of the modern Bible, patron of modern democracy, one of the founders of modern Freemasonry," a Rosicrucian and possibly founder of that order. The translator's manuscript of what is now referred to as the King James Bible was turned over to Bacon by the king for checking, editing, and revision, and it remained in his hands for almost a year (pp. 165–68).

The function of religion [should be] to comfort and encourage humanity in its life-long struggle with sin and sorrow. This it can do only by presenting mankind with noble ideals of a happier existence after death, and of a worthier life on earth, to be won in both cases by conscious effort.[1]

H. P. Blavatsky was also founder of the Theosophical Society, which is still in existence and publishes many books on topics related to esoteric philosophy and religion.

It is difficult to assess the total effect of Blavatsky and the Theosophical movement but it is clear that with respect to bringing esoteric teachings before a much larger percentage of the population it certainly represents a most significant pioneering effort. A number of influential thinkers were intimately acquainted with the writings of Blavatsky, including, among authors: D. H. Lawrence, T. S. Eliot, Henry Miller, Sir Arthur Conan Doyle, Jack London, H. G. Wells, Sir Edwin Arnold, and the leaders of Ireland's literary revival: Yeats, George Russell, James Stephens, and James Joyce. Artists versed in theosophy include Gauguin, Mondrian, Kandinsky, Malevich and Paul Klee. Scientists who were very familiar with Theosophy include Einstein, Gustaf Stromberg, Camille Flammarion, Sir William Crookes, and Thomas Edison. Social historians Lewis Mumford and Theodore Roszak are also well versed in theosophical literature.[2]

Madame Blavatsky, Colonel Henry S. Olcott, and other Theosophists are credited with effecting a major revival of public interest in Hinduism in India. Colonel Olcott was especially successful in reviving Buddhism in Ceylon (now Sri Lanka) and Burma and also made an influential lecture tour of Japan at the invitation of a national committee of Buddhist priests.

Theosophists also had a very major early influence on Mahatma Gandhi, the leader of the nonviolent movement for Indian independence. Gandhi states in his autobiography that he was encouraged to read the Bhagavad Gita, which had such a profound influence on his life, not in his native India but in England. Those who encouraged him were Theosophists. He was later introduced to Madame Blavatsky and Mrs. Annie Besant,* and was led to a greater interest in Hinduism by reading Madame Blavatsky's book *A Key to Theosophy*.

Alice Bailey wrote and published twenty-four books that cover a whole spectrum of subjects from the esoteric viewpoint. These books were written over a thirty-year period beginning in late 1919. The material is a bit more attuned to the present-day reader than the works of Blavatsky and is no less impressive in content. One large volume, entitled *A Treatise on Cosmic Fire* (in excess of 1300 pages), which Mrs. Bailey dedicated to Blavatsky, fulfills a prediction by Blavatsky that a person would appear

---

*Who became president of the Theosophical Society.

in the twentieth century to provide the psychological key to the Cosmic Creation, thereby supplementing her own book *The Secret Doctrine.* The source that Mrs. Bailey claims for the material in her books will be discussed later in this chapter.

A third writer of major significance in this field is Helena Roerich, who has written a series of books published by the Agni Yoga society in New York. Her works do not generally follow a narrative or descriptive style but are rather collections of statements of an informative or inspirational nature on various subjects.

The works of all three of these authors are better approached by those not familiar with the concepts involved if some writings of a more basic and explanatory nature are read first. Examples of such basic treatments are *The Rosicrucian Cosmo-Conception* by Max Heindel and *Theosophy Simplified* by C. W. Leadbeater.

Other modern-day esotericists* who have contributed significantly to the store of written material in this area include Annie Besant, who was Blavatsky's pupil and highly talented in her own right; Dr. Rudolf Steiner; and Geoffrey Hodson. All of the writers mentioned thus far in this chapter are reported to have been accomplished in the higher forms of psychism, and some of their writings are said to be the result of psychic observations or telepathic communications.

Manly Palmer Hall, founder of the Philosophical Research Society in Los Angeles, has produced a large number of books on esoteric subjects. His *Secret Teachings of All Ages* is a comprehensive review of Western and Near Eastern esotericism from early Egyptian times through the American Revolution and includes Christian, Judaic, and Islamic esotericism.

Modern-day individuals from the East who have contributed significant material include Swami Vivekananda, founder of the Vedanta society in the United States, his teacher Sri Ramakrishna, and Sri Aurobindo and Mirra, the Mother, who jointly founded an ashram in Pondicherry, India, which has been visited by many Europeans and Americans.

In addition to the works by Evans-Wentz mentioned earlier, esoteric Buddhism has also been researched and reviewed in a series of books by Sir John Woodruff, who wrote under the pen name Arthur Avalon.

. The esotericists use the term *Ancient Wisdom* or *Ageless Wisdom* to describe their teachings, which they claim to be of very early origin, of a fundamental nature, and universally taught by esotericists in all times and places. It is interesting to note that St. Paul, whom the esotericists regard as a high "initiate" and therefore intrinsically aware of a portion of this teaching, speaks also of such a wisdom

> There is, to be sure, a certain wisdom which we express among the spiritually mature. It is not a wisdom of this age, however, nor of the rulers of this

*The term *occultist* is used somewhat interchangeably with *esotericist.*

age, who are men headed for destruction. No, what we utter is God's wisdom: a mysterious, a hidden wisdom. God planned it before all ages for our glory. . . . Of this wisdom it is written:

"Eye has not seen, ear has not heard, nor has it so much as dawned on man what God has prepared for those who love him."

Yet God has revealed this wisdom to us through the Spirit. The Spirit scrutinizes all matters, even the deep things of God. (I Cor. 2:6–10)[3]

WHAT THE ESOTERICISTS TEACH

The basic teachings of the esotericists will be briefly summarized here, and in later chapters their teachings will be related to those of the major world scriptures and modern science.

1. ALL IS ENERGY

The esotericists agree with the proposition of all the great religions that there is a hidden world in addition to our visible, tangible one. They further maintain, and our modern scientists agree, that all manifestation is energy. In addition, they teach that energy can be controlled by thought, in agreement with the statement of the Hindu scriptures: "God meditated* and the worlds were formed." Back of each visible structure or form in all of the kingdoms of nature is said to be an invisible pattern of energies and forces that serves to direct the formation of the form.

In the Brihadaranyaka Upanishad we find: "Primal energy is Brahman." Brahman in the Hindu scriptures is God in manifestation. This can be compared with the Christian recognition of God as "Light"† (which is synonymous with energy in scientific terms).

In the view of the esotericists, both creation and evolution play a part in the formation and continuation of our world. However, they regard the explanation provided by most churchmen and scientists as not comprehensive enough to provide a valid description of the process.

2. MAKEUP OF THE INVISIBLE AND VISIBLE UNIVERSE

The esoteric teaching separates the matter of our solar system into seven major divisions of differing degrees of density called *planes*, and each of these planes is divided into seven subplanes. The physical world we are accustomed to is said to be constituted from the three most dense subplanes of matter, which are the solid, liquid, and gaseous elements of the major division called the *physical plane*. Table 1 shows this graphically and gives the names for the levels of matter used by different esoteric writers. The higher the plane in the table, the more rarefied the matter it contains and the higher its rate of vibration. In referring to the table, one must not think of the so-called planes as physically separated; rather,

---

*Meditation is defined by the Hindu sage Patanjali as sustained concentrated thought.
†From the New Testament and the Nicene Creed.

they interpenetrate each other. We do not normally observe the "higher" or more rarefied planes above the three lowest subplanes of the physical because our consciousness is not developed to the degree that enables this visibility.

These planes or levels are alluded to in various scriptures. The Koran[4] states: "He it is Who Created for you all that is in the earth. Then turned He to the heaven, and fashioned it as seven heavens." In II Corinthians 12:2-4, St. Paul writes, "I knew a man in Christ above fourteen years ago (whether in the body, I cannot tell; or whether out of the body, I cannot tell: God knoweth) such an one caught up to the third heaven. . . . he was caught up into paradise, and heard unspeakable words, which it is not lawful for a man to utter." In Hinduism and Buddhism the idea of higher levels of consciousness is accepted teaching.

3. THE CONSTITUTION OF MAN

The esotericists, along with the great religions, hold that there is much more to man than that which is visible to our physical eyes. Man is held to have potential for divinity and is termed an "animal plus a living God" by H. P. Blavatsky.[8] Similarly in John 10:34 we read: "Jesus answered them, Is it not written in your law, I said, Ye are gods?" Genesis 2:3 states that "Man became a living soul," and St. Paul writes: "The first man is of the earth, earthy; the second man is the Lord from heaven." In the Bhagavad Gita we read, "He sees indeed who sees in all alike the living lordly soul, supreme, imperishable amid the perishing."

We see diagramed in Figure 1 the contention of the esotericists that man in his essential nature is a spark of the divine, termed a *monad*—threefold in nature and therefore in the image of God and represented on lower planes of the solar system by what is called the *spiritual triad*.* This spiritual man is linked by the soul to the lower man represented by what are termed the *personality vehicles*, composed of mental, emotional, and physical matter.

This view of man's constitution provides a possible explanation of the statement of Christ that "The Kingdom of God is within you" (Luke 17:21) and is consistent with Paul's mention of man's spirit, soul, and body in I Thessalonians 5:23.

The permanent atoms (sometimes called *seed atoms*) related to the mental, emotional, and etheric vehicles remain throughout the life, even though, as in the case of the physical body, other atoms may be replaced with time. These permanent atoms are strung along a line of energy called the *sutratma*, or silver cord.

*The esotericists state the correspondence to the Christian trinity as:
  Will or Power—Father
  Love Wisdom—Son
  Active Intelligence—the Holy Spirit

TABLE 1. SEVEN PLANES OF THE SOLAR SYSTEM

PLANE	SOURCE OF TERMINOLOGY		
	Dr. Annie Besant and Alice Bailey[5]	H. P. Blavatsky[6] (Eastern)	Max Heindel[7] (Rosicrucian)
7	Divine (Adi or Plane of the Logos)	Maha Paranirvanic	World of God
6	Monadic (Anupadaka)	Paranirvanic	World of Virgin Spirit
5	Spiritual (Atmic Plane)	Nirvanic	World of Divine Spirit
4	Intuitional (Buddhic Plane)	Buddhic	World of Life Spirit
3	Mental (Manasic Plane)	Manasic	World of Thought
2	Emotional (Astral Plane)	Astral	Desire World
Etheric Physical 1 Dense Physical	1st Ether 2nd Ether 3rd Ether Physical 4th Ether (Physical Plane) Gaseous Liquid Solid	Physical	Physical World

VEHICLES OF MANIFESTATION

The esoteric teachings hold that the physical body, which is constructed of the three lower levels of physical-plane matter (solid, liquid, and gaseous), and which we can sense with the faculties developed in the average human, is interpenetrated by other bodies of increasingly more rarefied matter. Referring to Figures 1 and 2, we see that the most dense of these is called the *etheric body* and that it consists of matter of the physical-plane ethers, the four highest subplanes of the physical plane.

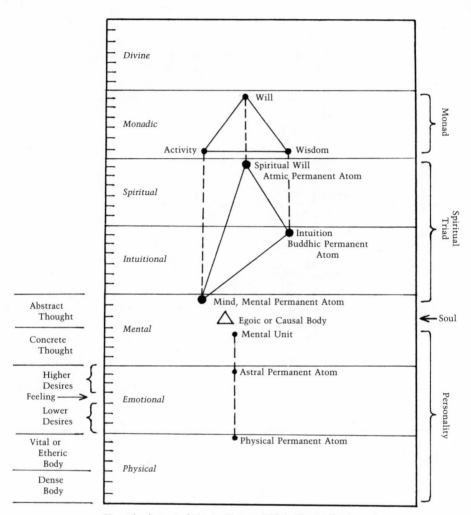

Diagram based on p. xiv of *Initiation, Human and Solar* by Alice A. Bailey. Annotation on left of diagram from p. 16 of *The Rosicrucian Cosmo-Conception* by Max Heindel.

Fig. 1. The Constitution of Man

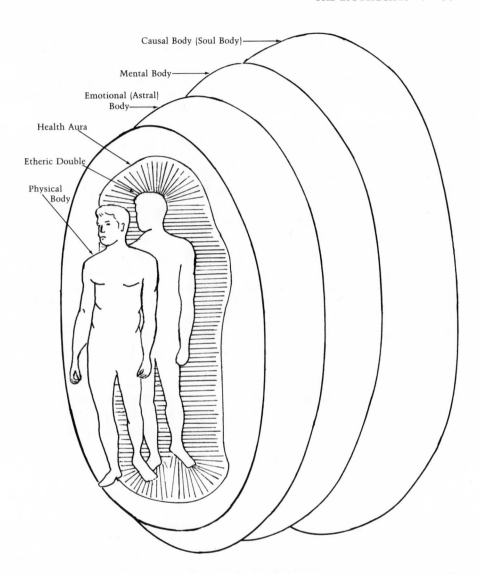

Causal Body (Soul Body)
Mental Body
Emotional (Astral) Body
Health Aura
Etheric Double
Physical Body

Normally interpenetrating bodies shown separated and planar rather than ovoid and overlapping for ease of illustration.

Fig. 2. Man's Vehicles of Manifestation

The Etheric Body

The etheric body is said to be the invisible scaffolding on which the dense physical body is built, having the same basic shape as the physical body. It is also called the *vital body* or *energy body*, being the vehicle through which the vital force or life force† and other energies and forces are transmitted to the physical body. In a healthy individual, the energy field of the etheric body extends outward from the physical body some distance. This forms an aura that many clairvoyants have reported observing. British physician Walter J. Kilner reported in his book *The Human Atmosphere* his observations of the human aura through lenses colored with coal tar dye. Some believe the vital aura accounts for the emanations captured in Kirlian photography. Kirlian photographic techniques were invented in the Soviet Union and utilize a pulsed electrical discharge applied to an object that is placed on the film used to obtain the photograph. The resulting pictures show parts of the human body surrounded by a corona.

Dr. Thelma Moss, a psychologist at the University of California, Los Angeles, has used Kirlian photography to study the effects produced by psychic healers. Photographing the coronas surrounding the finger pads of healers and their patients before and after the healing process, Dr. Moss found that the corona of the healer decreased in size and uniformity after the healing, while that of the patient increased, suggesting that an energy transfer had taken place (see Fig. 3).

It is interesting to compare drawings made to depict observations of the etheric aura by clairvoyants in Figure 4 with the enlarged Kirlian photograph in Figure 5, supplied by Dr. Moss, which shows the coronas around the finger pads of two people who placed their fingers adjacent to each other.

The condition of the vital body is said to be an important factor in health, and clairvoyants have said that the etheric aura appears diminished in a person who is ill, especially in the region of some bodily disorder. This same observation has been reported by Dr. Kilner in his book.

Some psychic healers are able to detect areas of disorder simply by passing their hands close to a person's body. Dolores Krieger, Ph.D., R.N., a professor of nursing at New York University, is a very successful psychic healer who runs a fully accredited N.Y.U. course at the master's level to teach what is termed the therapeutic touch, or the laying on of hands, for healing purposes. She describes sensing a point of disorder in a body by detecting what appears to her as a change in energy radiated in that area. When energy is directed out through the hands of a healer, the person being treated usually reports a warmth or tingling sensation in the area of

---

†This vital force is also referred to by the Hindu name *prana*.

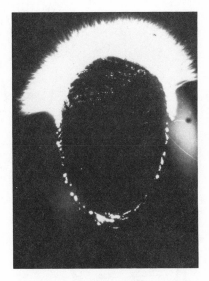

B
E
F
O
R
E

HEALER   PATIENT

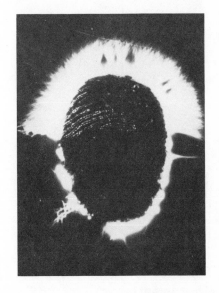

A
F
T
E
R

Fig. 3. Kirlian Photographs of Finger Pads
Before and After Psychic Healing

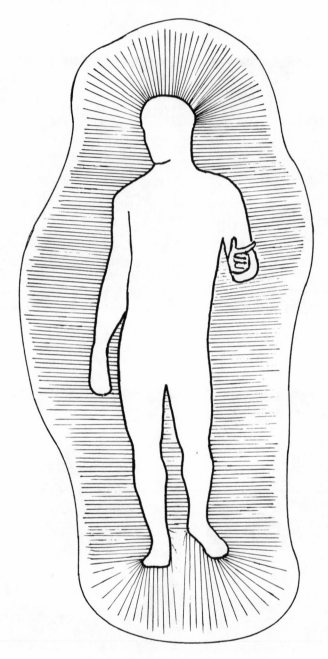

Fig. 4. Clairvoyant's Description of
Etheric Aura from 1902 Drawing

See *Man Visible and Invisible* by C. W. Leadbeater, Plate XXIV.

Fig. 5. Kirlian Photograph Showing Coronas
from Fingers of Two People

the disorder. It is not necessary for the healer to make physical contact for this to occur; simply placing the hands close to the skin is sufficient.

The fact that there is more at work here than the power of suggestion is borne out by a series of experiments conducted by Dr. Bernard Grad of McGill University's Allan Memorial Institute in Montreal. He studied the effects of the well-known healer Oskar Estebany on wounded laboratory mice and on barley seeds subjected to a salt solution to simulate a sick condition. In those experiments the animals treated by Estebany healed more quickly, and the barley seeds that came under his influence sprouted more quickly and grew taller, greener plants.

It is claimed by clairvoyants that the etheric body has seven major force centers or vortices—five arranged up the spinal column and two in the head. They are related to the ductless glands in the physical body. These are also referred to by the Eastern term *chakras*. The force-center designations, along with their corresponding ductless glands, are as follows:

Center	Ductless Gland
Base of Spine	Adrenal
Sacral	The gonads
Solar plexus	Pancreas
Heart	Thymus
Throat	Thyroid
Between the eyebrows	Pituitary body
Top of head	Pineal gland

These force centers and their significance are discussed further in chapter 9, "Symbolic Writing and Allegory."

It has been reported by clairvoyants that when death takes place, the etheric body separates from the physical body, and at the moment of death the final connecting strand, which appears to clairvoyant sight as a thin silvery cord,* is detached, completing the separation. Following death, the etheric body eventually disintegrates, as does the physical body, and the life of the individual passes on to the more refined astral and mental bodies.

Possibly it is this process of separation of the etheric from the physical body at death that is referred to in the following from Ecclesiastes in the Old Testament: ". . . man goeth to his long home, and the mourners go about the streets: Or ever the silver cord be loosed, or the golden bowl be broken. . . . Then shall the dust return to the earth as it was; and the spirit shall return to God who gave it" (Eccles. 12:5-7). The golden bowl in the passage is said to refer to the etheric body, which is reported by some clairvoyants to give off a golden glow. The term *bowl* is particularly

*The previously mentioned sutratma.

appropriate, if it is considered that the etheric body forms a mold for the dense physical.

The following passage from the Brihadaranyaka Upanishad describes the process of death and the separation of the higher vehicles from the lower:

> When his body grows weak and he becomes apparently unconscious, the dying man gathers his senses about him and completely withdrawing their powers descends into his heart. No more does he see form or color without.
> He neither sees, nor smells, nor tastes. He does not speak, he does not hear. He does not think, he does not know. For all the organs detaching themselves from his physical body, unite with his subtle body. Then the point of his heart, where his nerves join, is lighted by the light of the Self, and by that light he departs either through the eye, or through the gate of the skull, or through some other aperture of the body. When he thus departs, life departs; and when life departs, all the functions of the vital principle depart. The Self remains conscious, and conscious, the dying man goes to his abode. The deeds of this life and the impressions they leave behind, follow him.[9]

In 1906 Dr. Duncan McDougall at Massachusetts General Hospital in Boston ran a series of experiments with dying people in which the person and the bed they occupied were placed on a balance (which could detect changes of two-tenths of an ounce) and counterbalanced with weights.[10] It was observed that at the moment of death there was a sudden decrease in weight, causing the person and bed to rise rapidly on the balance. The etheric body, though invisible to the sight of the average person, is composed of physical matter, and these experiments suggest the possibility that it may have measurable weight. There is no record of other similar experiments with dying humans conducted since that time. Dr. McDougall's experiments included only six patients, and although all tests appeared to show a weight loss, he considered only four of the tests experimentally valid because of inadequate time to accurately adjust the balance in two of the cases.

Dr. Elisabeth Kübler-Ross,[11] a Swiss-born psychiatrist, and Raymond Moody, a Georgia physician, have independently done many case studies on dying and on revived "dead" persons and are both convinced that life goes on in a separated existence after physical death. Dr. Kübler-Ross has herself had several out-of-body experiences.

Dr. Moody, in his book *Life after Life*,[12] gives a model description of clinical "death" followed by resuscitation that is distilled from about fifty cases. It reads in part:

> A man . . . hears himself pronounced dead by his doctor . . . and . . . finds himself moving through a long dark tunnel. After this, he suddenly finds himself outside his own physical body but still in the immediate physical environment, . . . he notices that he still has a "body," but of a very different nature and with very different powers from the physical body he has left behind.

Dr. Moody quotes in his book the following description, given by a man near death, of the body he occupied after vacating his physical body:

> It was another body . . . but not another regular human body . . . It was not exactly like a human body, but it wasn't any big glob of matter, either. It had form to it, but no colors. And I know I still had something you could call hands . . . I can best describe it as an energy pattern. If I had to put it into words I would say that it was transparent, a spiritual as opposed to a material being, yet, it definitely had different parts.

Two of the interviews quoted in Dr. Moody's book likened the sensation of leaving the physical body to going through a deep, dark valley, and the following description is interesting because of its biblical reference:

> Suddenly, I was in a very dark, very deep valley. It was as though there was a pathway, almost a road through the valley, and I was going down the path. . . . Later, after I was well, the thought came to me, "Well, now I know what the Bible means by 'the valley of the shadow of death,' because I've been there."

For those interested in looking into this further, a rather detailed description of the sequence of events in death and the etheric separation from an esoteric point of view is found on pages 472–78 of *Esoteric Healing* by Alice A. Bailey.

The Emotional (Astral) Body

The emotional body is the vehicle of manifestation that a man appropriates from matter of all seven of the different graded subplanes that make up the emotional plane. The emotional body interpenetrates the physical and etheric bodies and is man's vehicle of emotional sensitivity. It is interposed between the etheric body and the mental body from the viewpoint of grades of matter and forms a connecting link between these two. As a man progresses in controlling his thoughts and emotions and eliminating the baser emotions from his life, the astral body is said to be modified so that it is made up of an increasing proportion of matter of the higher subplanes of the emotional plane and a decreasing proportion of lower subplane matter.

The emotional body has been described by clairvoyants to be an ovoid of cloudy matter surrounding a more compact form in the shape and size of the physical body and to have varying colors to astral sight, depending on the emotions expressed. The baser emotions result in dark, muddy hues, and the higher emotions produce bright, delicate colors. Color plates from paintings showing examples of the astral and mental bodies as a clairvoyant observed them can be found in *Man, Visible and Invisible*, by the Theosophical writer C. W. Leadbeater.

The astral plane is also referred to as the *plane of illusion*. It responds to man's emotional nature and on it are found the distorted forms created by man's fear, lust, and anger as well as the more positive desire forms related to man's higher aspirations. It is well known that some are easily carried away in undesirable directions by their emotions, and a prime requisite for maturity and growth is control of the emotions by the mind.

Clairvoyants report that many people are conscious in their astral bodies during sleep when the astral separates from the physical and that they have the ability to travel rapidly and easily for great distances by simply desiring to be somewhere. For most, all memory of such experiences is lost when waking into physical consciousness. When a person dies, both the etheric and astral vehicles remove themselves from the physical, whereas in sleep only the astral is removed. After death, the individual eventually becomes conscious in the astral body and remains in astral consciousness for intervals that vary with the individual, until finally shedding the astral body and passing on to consciousness in the mental body.

The Mental Body

As we can see from Figure 3, the mental body is composed of matter of the four lower subplanes of the mental plane and is the vehicle of concrete thought. Sections of the mental body are said to be related to sections of the physical brain. As in the case of the astral body, the mental body is said to take on different colors depending on the nature of the thoughts the person is engaged in. The mental body is subject to development and strengthening as a result of use. Thus, as a person exercises his mind along a certain line of thought, he strengthens its ability along that line and causes growth in the mental body.

The Causal Body

The causal body, termed the *Temple of the Soul*, is ovoid in shape, surrounding the physical body, and is described as ranging from the appearance of a colorless bubble in primitive man to a sphere of "the most lovely and delicate hues—an object beautiful beyond all conception"[13] in an individual who is unselfish and capable of abstract thought. The causal body is said to be developed by that which is good in life. Since it is composed of matter of the mental plane's higher subdivisions, it is incapable of responding to the baser thoughts, such as irritability, hate, pride, etc., which cause vibrations too low on the scale to affect the causal body. Thus a person can build into the causal body only good qualities. The New Testament of the Bible refers to the causal body as "That body not made with hands, eternal in the heavens."

The Soul

What is generally referred to as the soul* or Ego in man (which should not be confused with the ego as defined by most psychologists) forms the mental-plane link between spirit and matter. It has been termed by esotericists "the son of the father-spirit and the mother-matter," and it is referred to by St. Paul as "Christ within, the hope of glory." According to esoteric teachings, as a person advances spiritually, the personality nature begins to come gradually under greater control of the soul. The soul functioning in its personality vehicles acts as a redeemer of the lower nature where redemption is defined as raising the vibration of the lesser lives that make up the personality vehicles. This manifests outwardly as a nobler and more productive life. It is recognized scientifically, but not too often thought about in daily life, that the physical body is made up of lesser lives in the form of cells. A similar situation exists for the other personality vehicles.

As the soul proceeds in its work of redemption, it is in return offered a means of contacting the lower planes through the personality vehicles and is thus afforded an opportunity for experience and growth.

Further Comments on Invisible Bodies

The view posed by the esotericists of a supersensory structure behind man appears to answer the question, otherwise unanswered by science, as to the nature of the organizing intelligence and force that holds the cells of a human body together in a particular formation and causes the body to replenish itself in that given form.

A similar structure is said to be behind animal and plant life, but with the higher vehicles less developed or missing entirely. According to the esotericists, plants and animals are not individualized as in the case of humans, but are controlled by group souls related to the different species.

The description St. Augustine makes in his *Confessions* of personal mystical experience provides a testimony to the existence of the hidden nature of man that has been reconfirmed by saints and mystics in many lands down the ages.

> Thus step by step I was led upwards from bodies to the soul which perceives by means of bodily senses, and thence to the soul's inward faculty, to which bodily sense reports external facts.[14]

Books by Max Freedom Long[15] show that the early Hawaiian Kahunas, who exhibited remarkable powers of clairvoyance and control over natural forces, also held that man possesses an invisible structure, and that they were skilled in functioning at other than physical levels of consciousness.

---

*The word *soul* in general refers to the seat of consciousness and the principle of sensitive response in all forms. It is that which gives each form its particular quality and forces the body nature into activity. In this sense it can be considered the force of evolution.

The Egyptian Book of the Dead reveals that a similar view was held by Egyptian priests. The totem poles carved by the Indians of Alaska and Canada appear to symbolize the various bodies of man topped by the Soul, which is shown with wings. (The esotericists sometimes refer to the Soul as the Solar Angel.)

4. ANGELS

The existence of angels forms a part of the teaching of many religions as well as being a part of the esoteric tradition. According to the esotericists, angels—or *devas*,* as they are sometimes called—form a structured evolution parallel to the human. The basic function of the deva evolution is to build and sustain the form side of life. These entities do not possess dense physical bodies and so are invisible to most humans. They range from relatively simple creatures termed *nature spirits, sylphs, fairies, gnomes,* and *salamanders* to the more highly developed beings the Bible terms *cherubim, seraphim, principalities, powers, dominions* and *thrones.*

Some of these beings are said to be visible to clairvoyant sight, and photographs have even been made that appear to show them. Geoffrey Hodson, an accomplished clairvoyant, working with an artist, has produced a book[16] with color illustrations of entities of the deva evolution he has observed. Devas as depicted by Hodson do not have wings with feathers as shown in old paintings, but some have bodily extensions that might be considered winglike to the observer.

It is claimed that members of the deva evolution sometimes cooperate directly with humans. One example is the transmission of inspiration, relative to certain types of music, to the minds of composers who are sensitive to devic impression. Hodson says that angels sometimes cooperate in human religious services and ceremonies and describes[17] the participation of members of the deva evolution on their subtle planes of existence in a Mass conducted by humans. He indicates that angels are also attracted by the inspirational music associated with some religious observances.

5. THE SPIRITUAL HIERARCHY

The esotericists teach that man is not alone and not without guidance in his struggles in the world. There is said to be a group of advanced individuals, called the *Spiritual Hierarchy* by the esotericists, who work in support of the evolution of man and the rest of our planetary life. This group is referred to as "the Communion of Saints" in the creed used by Christians. They work in cooperation with what the esotericists term "the Plan of God," which provides the originating intelligence as to the desired

*A Hindu term.

direction of planetary evolution. They work also with the direction of energy in cooperation with the Plan and are much more active on the mental plane than on the physical as regards mankind, working most often with the souls of men and women.

The head of this Hierarchy, according to esotericists, is the Christ of the Christian New Testament, who they claim is the same individual identified in the Eastern tradition as Maitreya.

The Hierarchy are also known as the *Great White Brotherhood*, and the members are called *Masters of the Wisdom*. The term *adept* is used to describe one who is a Master of the Wisdom, and these highly evolved members of the human family are capable of utilizing powers that go far beyond those developed by the average person.

One of the activities said to be engaged in by some of these Masters is aiding the evolution of humanity by work on mental levels, providing inspiration for those of mankind capable of responding unconsciously or, in rare cases, consciously in fields such as science, healing, government, and the like. Examples of more direct work are cited in connection with three esoteric writers mentioned earlier: H. P. Blavatsky, Alice Bailey, and Helena Roerich.

All three of these writers state that much of their writing is not totally their own and indicate that they have acted consciously and cooperatively as vehicles for receiving information from very advanced teachers through telepathic means—not automatic writing, but conscious telepathic communication. Specifically, eighteen of Mrs. Bailey's twenty-four books indicate that they are fundamentally the work of an individual referred to as *the Tibetan* who lived on the borders of Tibet and at times presided over a large group of Tibetan lamas. Her later writings reveal that this individual also goes by the name Djwhal Khul, earlier identified in some of the Theosophical Society writings as one of the Masters. It is indicated that he also cooperated with Blavatsky in the writing of *The Secret Doctrine*.

As remarkable as this may seem, it is difficult to comprehend how the material in those books could have been set down by the authors with the resources available to them and without some form of extenal help. It is reported that Carl Jung attributed Mrs. Bailey's work to her "higher self," but Mrs. Bailey questions in her *Unfinished Autobiography* how her higher self could have sent her parcels all the way from India, which she says she received on occasion from the Tibetan. Mrs. Bailey also tells of a meeting between an acquaintance of hers, a Mr. Henry Carpenter, and the Tibetan which took place after Carpenter's third attempt to locate him in Tibet. Actually, the Tibetan is reported to have located Carpenter and to have discussed with him the work he was doing with Mrs. Bailey.

The Hierarchy are said to be organized into three major divisions corresponding to the three aspects of the Trinity as shown in Table 2.

TABLE 2. THE THREE MAJOR DIVISIONS OF THE HIERARCHY

ASPECT OF TRINITY	CHARACTERISTIC	FUNCTION RELATED TO HUMANITY
Father	Will	Government, World Political Progress
Son	Love and Wisdom	Religion, Education, Healing
Holy Spirit	Active Intelligence	Science, Economics and Finance, Industry, Capital and Labor, Intellectual Culture, the Arts

Christ heads the second major division as well as the entire Hierarchy and is termed the World Teacher. Although the Hierarchy provide inspiration and guidance for mankind in important fields of human activity, they do not interfere with the free will of man. They work through disciples, some of whom are conscious of the fact and work in active cooperation, as well as through many others who are simply receptive to inspiration but are not personally aware of the existence of the Hierarchy.

According to esotericists, the work of the Hierarchy over the last 500 years has resulted in raising the general level of human intelligence and increasing public awareness of world problems. Improvement in living conditions, economic security, and widespread education have helped make this possible. The Hierarchy have fostered and continue to emphasize those attitudes and activities that will lead to right relations between nations, races, and groups. The esotericists say that the concept of brotherhood that has gained in prominence in our modern civilization is an outgrowth of Hierarchical action that has resulted in the well-established and widespread practice of philanthropy that we see today. This was nonexistent in anything like its present form before A.D. 1500.

Improved communication and travel made possible by inspired men of vision in the scientific fields have brought the means for increased cooperation between communities and nations, which continues to be a major Hierarchical thrust.

6. VARIOUS PRESENTATIONS OF TRUTH

The following words by Alice Bailey are worthy of consideration with respect to the conflicts that arise between exponents of different religious or scientific presentations.

> All formulations of truth and of belief are only partial in time and space, and are temporarily suited to the temperaments and conditions of the age and race. Those who favor some particular approach to the truth will neverthe- less achieve the realization that other approaches and other modes of expres- sion and terminologies, and other ways of defining deity can be equally correct and in themselves constitute aspects of a truth which is greater and vaster than man's present equipment can grasp and express.[18]

> Forget not that all right ideas are temporary in nature and must eventually take their place as partial rights and give place to greater truth. The fact of the day is seen later as part of a greater fact.[19]

7. THE ESOTERICISTS' VIEW OF MASONRY

While acknowledging that the organization of modern Freemasonry had its start on June 24, 1717, in the Apple Tree Tavern on Charles Street, Covent Garden, London, when the four lodges in the south of England elected the first Grand Master of Masons, esotericists maintain that the masonic rituals and symbols have a much earlier origin. H. P. Blavatsky cites Elias Ashmole, whom she calls "the last of the Rosicrucians and al- chemists," as the first Operative Mason of any consequence. She indicates that he was admitted to the freedom of the Operative Masons Company in London in 1646 and died in 1692. At that time, she states, "Masonry was a true secret organization."[20] In her book *Isis Unveiled* she demon- strates the common thread between Masonry and the esoteric mystery teachings of antiquity and quotes the following from John Yarker, whose volume she says corroborates in many particulars what she writes in *Isis*:

> We think we have sufficiently established the fact of the connection of Free- masonry with other speculative rites of antiquity, as well as the antiquity and purity of the old English Templar Rite of seven degrees, and the spurious derivation of many of the other rites therefrom.[21]

Manly P. Hall makes the same point concerning the ties of Masonry to the Mystery Schools and specifically notes that "the school of the Druids was divided into three distinct parts, and the secret teachings embodied therein are practically the same as the mysteries concealed under the al- legories of Blue Lodge Masonry."[22]

Foster Bailey, in a book called *The Spirit of Masonry*, compiled from information set down by his wife, Alice Bailey, before her death, advances the hypothesis that "Masonry is the descendant of, or is founded on, a divinely imparted religion . . . and its allegorical rituals, and its symbols and numbers, is all that remains to us of the first world religion which flourished in an antiquity so old that it is impossible to affix a date."[23] Acknowledging that there is a Jewish coloring in modern Masonic rituals which was imparted at a relatively late date, Bailey states that the rituals preserve the basic "drama of a blindness which was transmuted into light, of an ignorance which was changed into wisdom, and of a death which was overcome by resurrection." He further notes that "The Jewish Mysteries (preserved now in the Masonic tradition) . . . wove into the story the . . . idea of BUILDING. The idea of God as T. G. A. O. T. U. [The Great Architect of the Universe] and the Builder of the temple of the world was emphasized. The symbolism of the construction of earthly expressions of an inner spiritual building, eternal and everlasting, which passes not away, began to be understood and thus they triumphantly proclaimed their belief in the unseen and immortal."[24] The immortality of the soul was symbolized as well as the theme of service in the building of the Temple.

While recognizing that much Masonic activity today is superficial, the esotericists predict a more deeply spiritual role for Masonry in the future as the spiritual significance of the teachings of the ancient Mystery Schools, partly preserved in Masonry, becomes more widely understood. Masonry is then expected to emerge as a more important vehicle for spiritual training.

It is significant to note also that the Catholic Church has removed the restriction that formerly prevented Catholics from becoming Masons.

8. SPIRITUAL ACTIVITY

The esotericists' view of spiritual work goes far beyond that which pertains to religion. It includes any work that fosters right human relations and good will and anything that tends to positively influence the evolution of life on our planet. As such, spiritual work is any activity that furthers the plan of God.

It is clear, then, that from the esoteric point of view spiritual work can be accomplished in almost any field of human endeavor. Government and politics, business, finance, education, science, technology, the arts, architecture, religion, philosophy, communications, healing arts—all of these and many others represent important fields for spiritual work.

6. Immortality

Immortality, or existence after physical death, is a belief common to all the major religions. It is also being explored with significant results by the scientific community, as we shall see in this chapter.

The Society for Psychical Research has been investigating phenomena related to continued existence for many years and has gathered data in a number of areas. The eminent psychologist William James was an important supporter in the early days of psychical research and has done some writing of his own on the subject.[1]

SURVIVAL AFTER DEATH

Three cases studied by the Society for Psychical Research that provide evidence of continued after-death existence are related in the book *Scientific Evidence of the Existence of the Soul* by Dr. Benito F. Reyes, a professor of philosophy and former Fulbright scholar.

The first of these concerns an apparition of a girl to her brother nine years after her death. The brother reported seeing a conspicuous scratch on her cheek. Their mother after being told of this revealed that she had accidentally made the scratch herself while preparing the body for burial. She covered the scratch with powder and it was never mentioned by her.

In another case, a father appeared after death to one of his sons, revealing the existence and location of a second will benefiting the son. The will was found where indicated.

The third was reported by a British general who saw an apparition of a lieutenant he knew but had not seen for two or three years. He was much more bloated in appearance than when the general had last seen him and he wore a beard that was also new. He was seen on a brown pony with black mane and tail. When inquiry was made, it was found that the lieutenant had died, that he had become bloated before his death, had grown a beard of the type the general described, and had bought and ridden to death a pony like the one he appeared on.

The common element that makes these three cases particularly interesting from the point of view of scientific investigation is the imparting of information (to those who saw the apparitions) that could not otherwise be known by them.

Persons who "died" and were later resuscitated were the subjects of research done by Drs. Kübler-Ross and Moody. This was discussed in the section on the etheric body in chapter 5 and it affords very significant evidence of life after death. Dr. Moody's Book *Life After Life* contains a model description by persons revived after clinical "death" or near-death that was partially quoted earlier. The description goes on to indicate that when a man collects himself after leaving his physical body,

> others come to meet and help him. He glimpses the spirits of relatives and friends who have already died, and a loving warm spirit of a kind he has never encountered before—a being of light—appears before him. This being asks him a question nonverbally, to make him evaluate his life and helps him along by showing him a panoramic, instantaneous playback of the major events of his life.

It is interesting that those who go through accidental or natural death report intense feelings of love, joy, and peace in the afterlife, but in the cases of attempted suicides, Dr. Moody says, "These experiences are uniformly characterized as being unpleasant." One revived suicide commented, "I didn't go where [my wife] was. I went to an awful place. . . . I immediately saw the mistake I had made. . . . I thought, "I wish I hadn't done it."

REINCARNATION

The subject of reincarnation, or the soul taking on a series of physical bodies with interspersed periods of withdrawal from physical life, is a key factor in comparing various religious teachings. This concept is universally accepted by the Eastern religions but is not customarily taught in Christianity or Islam. As we shall see, however, it is alluded to in the scriptures of both these religions. In pursuing this discussion it is important to distinguish between the reincarnation of the human soul in another human body and the transmigration to other life forms such as animals. The leading spiritual thinkers of both East and West do not accept that under normal circumstances a soul that has incarnated as a human will then incarnate in lower forms of life.

1. HINDUISM

The scriptures of Hinduism clearly support reincarnation, as indicated by the following from the Katha Upanishad:

> If a man fails to attain Brahman before he casts off his body, he must again put on a body in the world of created things.

In the Bhagavad Gita we find:

Just as the dweller in this body passes through childhood, youth and old age, so at death he merely passes into another kind of body. . . .
Bodies are said to die but that which possesses the body is eternal . . .

> Worn-out garments
> Are shed by the body:
> Worn-out bodies
> Are shed by the dweller
> Within the body.
> New bodies are donned
> By the dweller, like garments.

The Gita also comments on the manner by which the cycle of rebirths can be ended.

Devote yourself . . . to reaching union with Brahman. To unite the heart with Brahman and then to act: that is the secret of non-attached work. In the calm of self-surrender, the seers renounce the fruits of their actions, and so reach enlightenment. Then they are free from the bondage of rebirth, and pass to that state which is beyond all evil.

The Bhagavad Gita also refers to "the law of Karma, that chains men to rebirth." This law is well described by the words of St. Paul: "Whatsoever a man soweth that shall he also reap" (Gal. 6:7). It is the law of cause and effect and requires that a man make payment for transgressions, if not in the present life, then in another. As indicated in the above from the Bhagavad Gita, karma is avoided by nonattached action.

The following passage from the Gita states that the universe itself is subject to periodic manifestation and dissolution, a concept referred to in the East as the Days and Nights of Brahma.

All the worlds and even the heavenly realms of Brahma are subject to the laws of rebirth . . .

> There is day, also, and night in the universe;
> The wise know this, declaring the day of Brahma
> A thousand ages in span
> And the night a thousand ages.
>
> Day dawns and all those lives that lay hidden asleep
> Come forth and show themselves, mortally manifest:
> Night falls, and all are dissolved
> Into the sleeping germ of life.
> . . . .

But behind the manifest and unmanifest there is another Existence, which is eternal and changeless. This is not dissolved in the general cosmic dissolution. It has been called the unmanifest, the imperishable.[2]

2. BUDDHISM

In the Dhammapada,[3] the Buddha comments as follows on rebirth:

Him I called a Brahmana who knows the mystery of death and rebirth of all beings, who is free from attachment, who is happy within himself and enlightened. . . . Him I call a Brahmana who knows his former lives, who knows heaven and hell, who has reached the end of births, who is a sage of perfect knowledge and who has accomplished all that has to be accomplished.

3. TAOISM

Chuang-tzu, who has been referred to as the St. Paul of Taoism, writes as follows:

There was a beginning. There was a beginning before that beginning. There was a beginning previous to that beginning. Death and life are not far apart. When I look for their origin, it goes back into infinity; when I look for their end, it proceeds without termination. Life is the follower of death, and death is the predecessor of life. What we can point to are the faggots that have been consumed, but the fire is transmitted elsewhere.[4]

4. CHRISTIANITY

There are a number of passages in the New Testament of the Bible that have been cited as supporting reincarnation. Several of these are statements by Jesus to the effect that John the Baptist was a reincarnation of the Old Testament prophet Elijah or Elias (the Greek form).

Among them that are born of women there hath not risen a greater than John the Baptist. . . . For all the prophets and the law prophesied until John. And if ye will receive it, this is Elias, which was for to come. He that hath ears to hear, let him hear. (Matt. 11:11-15)

This last sentence, which is used elsewhere in the Bible, is said by esotericists to be the traditional indication of a hidden meaning in that which precedes it.

Later in Matthew (17:10-13), we find the following:

His disciples asked him, saying, "Why then say the scribes that Elias must first come?" And Jesus answered and said unto them, "Elias truly shall first come, and restore all things. But I say unto you, that Elias is come already, and they knew him not, but have done unto him whatsoever they listed. Likewise shall also the Son of man suffer of them."*

Then the disciples understood that he spake unto them of John the Baptist.

In John 9:1-3 is found an incident that has often been cited as an indication of belief in reincarnation and karma by Jesus and his disciples. The text reads:

---

*The prediction of the return of Elijah is found in Malachi 4:15 in the Old Testament.

And as Jesus passed by, he saw a man which was blind from his birth. And his disciples asked him, saying, "Master, who did sin, this man or his parents, that he was born blind?" Jesus answered, "Neither hath this man sinned, nor his parents: but that the works of God should be made manifest in him."

The logical question here, of course, is, how could the man have sinned prior to being born blind unless he had lived before?

In John 3:13 Jesus states: "No man hath ascended up to heaven, but he that came down from heaven," thereby clearly declaring preexistence before physical birth.

A statement in the New Testament that relates to the Eastern view on the end of the cycle of rebirth is found in Revelation 3:12–13:

> Him that overcometh will I make a pillar in the temple of my God, and he shall go no more out. . . . He that hath an ear, let him hear.

Researchers have concluded that although reincarnation is not generally taught in the Christian churches today, it was much more widespread in the early Church. The early Church fathers Origen (A.D. 185?–?254) and St. Clement of Alexandria (A.D. ca150–213) are cited as supporting reincarnation. Origen writes:

> Is it not rational that souls should be introduced into bodies in accordance with their merits and previous deeds, and that those who have used their bodies in doing the utmost possible good should have a right to bodies endowed with qualities superior to the bodies of others?
>
> The soul . . . at one time puts off one body, which was necessary before, but which is no longer adequate in its changed state, and it exchanges it for a second.[5]

St. Gregory (A.D. ca 335–ca 394), Bishop of Nyssa, wrote, "It is absolutely necessary that the soul should be healed and purified, and if this does not take place during its life on earth it must be accomplished in future lives."

In his book *Reincarnation, the Cycle of Necessity* Manly P. Hall indicates that "Arnobius, a Numidian apologist of Christianity . . . has left a record that Clement of Alexandria had written a most important account of metempsychosis [reincarnation]. Clement of Alexandria declared that reincarnation was a truth transmitted by St. Paul himself." He also references St. Jerome[6] as declaring "that the doctrine of transmigration was taught as an esoteric mystery in the early Church, being communicated only to a few specially selected members of the congregation." Mr. Hall also provides a reference citing advocates of reincarnation in the Middle Ages to include St. Francis of Assisi (1182–1276); Johannes Scotus Erigena (ca 810–ca 877), the learned Irish monk; St. Bonaventura (1221–1274), cardinal and general of the Franciscan order; and Thomas Campanella (1568–1639), a Dominican monk who was exiled for this belief.

Regarding the question of the doctrinal compatability of reincarnation with modern Christianity, Manly P. Hall quotes William R. Inge, late Dean of St. Paul's Cathedral, London, as a Protestant authority who finds no conflict between this, "the oldest creed," and modern Anglicanism. For the Catholic faith Hall cites Cardinal Mercier, the Belgian prelate and scholastic philosopher, who stated that the doctrine does not in any way conflict with Catholic dogma.

A factor that seems to have prevented dialogue concerning reincarnation in orthodox Christianity for many centuries was the generally held belief that the Second Council of Constantinople, opened in 553 (the Fifth Ecumenical Council), anathematized (cursed) the doctrine of the pre-existence of the soul before physical birth. (This despite the references to pre-existence in Jeremiah 1:5, Proverbs 8:22–31, Wisdom* 8:19–20, Ephesians 1:4, and John 17:5.) A denial of pre-existence, of course, precludes reincarnation.

Recent research by Catholic scholars who now have access to original Council records shows that this anathema was not approved by the Council (which was called for another purpose) or by the pope (who refused to attend the Council), but was issued at the direction of Emperor Justinian for political reasons in an attempt to condemn a sect of which he disapproved. Justinian not only convened the Council over the pope's objection but actually held the pope captive for a time. The facts concerning this episode are very thoroughly reviewed by Head and Cranston in their comprehensive book on the subject of reincarnation.[7]

In his recent book *Reincarnation in Christianity*, Dr. Geddes MacGregor, Emeritus Distinguished Professor of Philosophy at the University of Southern California, provides a detailed study of the subject of his title, including the proceedings of the Fifth Ecumenical Council, and concludes his book with the following paragraph:

> We can conclude that there is nothing in biblical thought or Christian tradition that necessarily excludes all forms of reincarnationism. We have seen many historical reasons why it has been suppressed both officially and at the popular level, in the history of the Christian Church. We have seen no reason why it must be in conflict with the historic teachings that have come to us through the Bible and the Church. We have seen, above all, that some form of reincarnationism could much enhance the spirituality of the West, not least at the present time when it stands so much in need of fresh avenues of development and new means of illumination.[8]

*The Book of Wisdom appears only in the Catholic version of the Old Testament.

Assuming, as was attributed to St. Jerome, that reincarnation was an esoteric or secret teaching of the Christian Church,* why the secret? Why would it not be openly taught as in the Eastern religions? Max Heindel in his book *The Rosicrucian Cosmo-Conception* offers an answer to this question. He states that in the process of evolution it was necessary that man

> . . . become thoroughly awake to the great importance of this concrete exis-
> tence, so that he might learn from it all that might be learned. So long as
> he knew for a certainty that physical life is a small part of real existence he
> did not take it seriously enough. He dallied his time away without develop-
> ing the resources of the world, as do the people of India today, for the same
> reason.

For the Western races, "this one single life was to be made paramount" and therefore, temporarily, the Law of Rebirth was not publicly taught. As a consequence of this, "the conquest of the world of matter is being made by the Anglo-Saxon and Teutonic races."

The book by Heindel quoted above was first copyrighted in 1909. It is interesting to note that now that the West has indeed progressed far in accomplishing the conquest of matter and has spread the knowledge gained throughout the world, the ideas of reincarnation and karma have recently begun to gain popular recognition in books, motion pictures, and even television in the West. This, together with a widespread interest in metaphysical subjects, is occurring in a civilization that earlier was moving toward a more materialistic outlook.

5. JUDAISM

In his book *Basic Judaism* (p. 161), Rabbi Milton Steinberg states that "the transmigration of the soul and its reincarnation have been affirmed by some and denied by others. Here as elsewhere, and here more than any-where else, the Tradition has allowed for latitude."

An Old Testament scriptural reference that appears to imply reincarna-tion is found in Psalm 90:1, 3-6.

> Lord, thou hast been our dwelling place in all generations. . . . Thou tur-
> nest man to destruction; and sayest, Return, ye children of men. For a thou-
> sand years in thy sight are but as yesterday when it is past, and as a watch
> in the night. Thou carriest them away as with a flood; they are as a sleep:
> in the morning they are like grass which groweth up. In the morning it
> flourisheth, and groweth up; in the evening it is cut down, and withereth.

---

*The concept of a hidden teaching in Christianity is suggested by Christ in Matt. 13:10-11: "And the disciples came, and said unto him, 'Why speakest thou unto them in parables?' And he answered and said unto them, 'Because it is given unto you to know the mysteries of the kingdom of heaven, but to them it is not given.' "

A first-century commentary on reincarnation is found in the writings of Jewish military commander and historian Flavius Josephus.[9] In attempting to dissuade some Jewish soldiers who were about to commit suicide rather than face capture by the Romans, he says, "The bodies of all men are, indeed, mortal, and are created out of corruptible matter; but the soul is ever immortal, and is a portion of the divinity that inhabits our bodies. . . . Do not you know that those who depart out of this life according to the law of nature . . . obtain a most holy place in heaven, from whence, in the revolution of ages, they are again sent into pure bodies, while the souls of those whose hands have acted madly against themselves are received by the darkest place in Hades?

The law of Rebirth and Consequence (or cause and effect) has always been a part of the teaching of the Kabbala, which is said to represent the hidden wisdom behind the Old Testament. The *Zohar*, the classic Kabbalistic *Book of Splendor* traditionally attributed to Rabbi Simeon ben Jochai, contains the following passage:

> All souls are subject to the trials of transmigration: . . . The souls must re-enter the absolute substance whence they have emerged. But to accomplish this end they must develop all the perfections the germ of which is planted in them; and if they have not fulfilled this condition during one life, they must commence another, a third, and so forth, until they have acquired the condition which fits them for reunion with God.[10]

The highly revered Rabbi Manasseh Ben Israel (1604–1651), whose efforts led to the removal of the 350-year legal prohibition of Jews from England, writes in his book *Nishmath Hayem*:

> The belief or the doctrine of the Transmigration of souls is a firm and infallible dogma accepted by the whole assemblage of our church with one accord, so that there is none to be found who would dare to deny it. . . . Indeed, there are a great number of sages in Israel who hold firm to this doctrine, so that they made it a dogma, a fundamental point of our religion. We are therefore duty bound to obey and to accept this dogma with acclamation . . . as the truth of it has been incontestably demonstrated by the Zohar, and all books of the Kabbalists.[11]

It should also be noted that reincarnation is a universal belief in the influential Jewish movement known as *Hasidism*, to which Martin Buber devoted much of his life.

6. ISLAM

In Sura III 27 of the Koran it is written:

> Thou causest the night to pass into day, and Thou causest the day to pass into the night. And Thou bringest forth the living from the dead, and Thou bringest forth the dead from the living.

This seems to suggest the preexistence of the soul and the cycle of death and reincarnation.

The Lebanese mystic Mikhail Naimy provides[12] the following translation of Sura II 28, which he interprets as referring to reincarnation:

> And you were dead, and He brought you back to life. And He shall cause you to die, and shall bring you back to life, and in the end shall gather you unto Himself.

The Koran makes the following statement of the law of cause and effect:

> Allah tasketh not a soul beyond its scope. For it [is only] that which it hath earned, and against it [only] that which it hath deserved. (Sura II 286)

Head and Cranston quote the following additional passages from the Koran (translated by Muslim scholar Dr. M. H. Abdi), which may be interpreted to refer to reincarnation:

> As the rains turn the dry earth into green, thereby yielding fruit, similarly God brings the dead into life so that thou mayest learn. (Chapter 8, Sura Iraf—Meccan Verses 6-6-13)
>
> And He sent down rains from above in proper quantity and He brings back to life the dead earth; similarly ye shall be reborn. (Chapter 25, Sura Zakhraf—Meccan Verses 5-10-6)

Dr. Abdi made the following comments in a series of articles, "Reincarnation: Islamic Conceptions":

> The position adopted by successive luminaries who followed [Muhammad] was to affirm the belief in reincarnation but not to propagate it as a teaching for the masses. This attitude was due to psychological reasons. The emphasis in Islamic teachings has throughout been on the purity of action. . . . Like so many other teachings, reincarnation was confined to the study and attention of the outer and inner students of Sufism. . . . [However,] there is no danger for a Muslim being called a heretic if he believes and expresses himself in favor of reincarnation.

The Sufis are the universally respected mystical cult who claim to carry forward the esoteric philosophy of Islam. Their influence appears to have been most significant on both the Christian and Arab worlds, especially in maintaining learning through the Dark Ages.

7. THE ESOTERICISTS

The doctrines of rebirth and cause-and-effect (karma) have always been a part of the esoteric teaching, and all the writers mentioned in the chapter on the esotericists support these views. The following from H. P. Blavatsky (quoted by Manly P. Hall)[13] provides an indication of the philosophical answers provided by these doctrines:

It is only the knowledge of constant rebirths of one and the same individuality throughout the life cycle . . . that can explain to us the mysterious problem of Good and Evil, and reconcile man to the terrible and apparent injustice of life. Nothing but such certainty can quiet our revolted sense of justice. For, when one unacquainted with the noble doctrine looks around him, and observes the inequalities of birth and fortune, of intellect and capacities; when one sees honor paid fools and profligates, on whom fortune has heaped her favors by mere privilege of birth, while their nearest neighbor with all his intellect and noble virtues—far more deserving in every way—is perishing for want and for lack of sympathy; when one sees all this and has to turn away, helpless to relieve the undeserved suffering, one's ears ringing and heart aching with the cries of pain around him—that blessed knowledge of Karma alone prevents him from cursing life.

To the esotericist, reincarnation and karma are the means by which evolution proceeds for humanity. The multiple births provide the opportunities for varied experiences, and the law of cause and effect provides the corrective action by which the teaching of the right path is imparted. Thus the soul grows through experience and trial and error, evolving toward a more perfect state incarnation after incarnation.

The esotericists maintain that, following physical death, the individual continues to occupy the astral body which is separated from the physical, thereby continuing his identity and consciousness in the astral world for a period of time. Following this, the astral body is abandoned and consciousness is transferred to the mental vehicle. Eventually, the mental body is also left behind, and the soul must eventually create new vehicles for the next incarnation. The time spent in various stages after physical death varies depending in part on the evolutionary status of the individual and the events of the preceding life. It is said that hundreds of years—and, in some cases, more than a thousand—may be spent in the higher worlds between incarnations.

In successive incarnations we are said to meet and interact with many of the same people, working out relationships or continuing cooperative efforts. People of long-standing association are drawn together by karmic ties to the same family. Individuals can, of course, build up good karma as well as debts to be paid, and particular good fortune may be the result of some positive action in an earlier incarnation.

A book by Alice Bailey makes the following interesting comments on the subject of reincarnation and current religious views:[14]

The spirit in man is undying; it forever endures, progressing from point to point and stage to stage upon the Path of Evolution, unfolding steadily and sequentially the divine attributes and aspects. This truth involves necessarily the recognition of two great natural laws—the Law of Rebirth and the Law of Cause and Effect. The churches in the West have refused officially to recognize the Law of Rebirth and have thereby wandered into a theological impasse and into a cul-de-sac from which there is no possible exit. The churches in the East have over-emphasized these laws so that a negative, acquiescent attitude to life and its processes, based on continuously renewed opportunity, controls the people.

8. LEADING THINKERS

The truth or falsity of reincarnation is difficult to prove directly. Tangible evidence cannot be offered by which one can draw an irrefutable conclusion. Perhaps the best evidence in favor of reincarnation are those cases where remembrance appears to have come through from former lives and where the facts presented have been checked for validity. Such cases will be considered in the next section.

Another interesting consideration is the view held by leading thinkers on the subject. While this does not constitute concrete evidence, it is clearly true that many of the important discoveries of mankind began as the logical deduction or intuitive insight of one or more great thinkers.

The concept of reincarnation dates back to antiquity, having been a part of myths and symbols from the earliest recorded times. Hermes Trismegistus, the great Egyptian sage, taught as follows: "The Soul passes from form to form; and the mansions of her pilgrimage are manifold. Thou puttest off thy bodies as raiment; and as vesture dost thou fold them up. Thou art from old, O Soul of man, yea, thou art from everlasting."[15]

Other early philosophers who taught reincarnation include the greatest of the Greeks: Orpheus, Pythagoras, Socrates, Plato, and Apollonius of Tyana. The Neoplatonists from Plotinus through Proclus also taught this doctrine.

Leonardo Da Vinci's notebooks clearly indicate that he accepted the pre-existence of the soul, and in one entry he writes, "Read me, O Reader, if you find delight in me, because very seldom shall I come back into this world." That someone as advanced as Leonardo would require few additional earth lives is, of course, consistent with the reincarnationists' view of evolutionary human development.

In the 1500s Paracelsus, who was quoted in an earlier chapter, and Giordano Bruno, the Italian philosopher (who was far ahead of his time and who suffered torture and death as a result), both taught reincarnation.

One of the earliest Americans to gain worldwide prominence for his intellect was Benjamin Franklin. Franklin's views on immortality are expressed in the following:

> When I see nothing annihilated in the works of God and not a drop of water wasted, I cannot suspect the annihilation of souls. . . . I believe, in some shape or other, I shall always exist and with all the inconveniences human life is

liable to, I shall not object to a new edition of mine, hoping, however, that the errata of the last may be corrected.

In his essay "Immortality," Ralph Waldo Emerson wrote: "We are driven by instinct to [store] innumerable experiences which are of no visible value and we may revolve through many lives before we shall assimilate or exhaust them." Entries in Emerson's journals also indicate his acceptance of reincarnation, and in a letter written following a visit to New York he makes the comment "In my next transmigration, I think I should choose New York."

Emerson's contemporary Henry David Thoreau not only expressed a belief in reincarnation, but, judging from his letters, he also had—or believed he had—recollection of past lives. Thoreau's writings display his deep insight and mystical tendencies. The sages of India claim that the ability to know past-life experience can be acquired through spiritual development. In a letter to Emerson, Thoreau wrote: "And Hawthorne, too, I remember as one with whom I sauntered in old heroic times along the banks of the Scamander amid the ruins of chariots and heroes."

Many of the world's great poets are among those who accepted reincarnation. Robert Browning wrote as follows in the third and fourth verses of his poem "Evelyn Hope," for a girl who died at 16 years of age:

> Is it too late, then, Evelyn Hope?
>   What, your soul was pure and true,
> The good stars met in your horoscope,
>   Made you of spirit, fire and dew—
> And, just because I was thrice as old,
>   And our paths in the world diverged so wide,
> Each was nought to each, must I be told?
>   We were fellow mortals, naught beside?
>
> No, indeed! for God above
>   Is great to grant, as mighty to make,
> And creates the love to reward the love,—
>   I claim you still, for my own love's sake!
> Delayed it may be for more lives yet,
>   Through worlds I shall traverse, not a few,
> Much is to learn, much to forget
>   Ere the time be come for taking you.

In "Song of Myself" from *Leaves of Grass*, Walt Whitman wrote:

> I do not despise you priests, all time, the world over,
> My faith is the greatest of faiths and the least of faiths,
> Enclosing worship ancient and modern and all between ancient and modern,
> Believing I shall come again upon earth after five thousand years. . . .

Births have brought us richness and variety,
And other births will bring us richness and variety.
. . . .

And as to you Life I reckon you are the leavings of many deaths,
(No doubt I have died myself ten thousand times before.)

In Henry Wadsworth Longfellow's poem "Rain in Summer" we find:

Thus the seer,
With vision clear,
Sees forms appear and disappear,
In the perpetual round of strange,
Mysterious change
From birth to death, from death to birth;
From earth to heaven, from heaven to earth;
Till glimpses more sublime,
Of things, unseen before,
Unto his wondering eyes reveal
The Universe, as an immeasurable wheel
Turning forevermore
In the rapid and rushing river of Time.

Among the other well-known poets who can be considered reincarnationists are Goethe, Tennyson, Yeats, Wordsworth, Shelley, Whittier, George W. Russell, and T. S. Eliot.

Through the work of Head and Cranston[16] we have a comprehensive cataloging of the views of prominent individuals on the subject of reincarnation through the ages. It might be useful here to list some who are favorable to the idea of reincarnation to show how widespread thinking on this subject has been.

Among philosophers not already mentioned are Hegel, Voltaire, Schopenhauer, and Nietzsche. Other prominent individuals include Thomas Carlyle, David Lloyd George, Mohandas Gandhi, Napoleon Bonaparte, Charles Fourier, Henry Ford, Thomas Edison, Thomas H. Huxley, Charles A. Lindbergh, Paul Gauguin, and General George S. Patton, as well as composers Richard Wagner, Gustav Mahler, and Jean Sibelius.

The list of authors is long, perhaps because their views are more often put in writing than is the case with others. Some of the most widely known are: Honoré de Balzac, Victor Hugo, George Sand, Sir Edward Bulwer-Lytton, Oliver Wendell Holmes, Edna Ferber, Herman Melville, Leo Tolstoy, Louisa May Alcott, Samuel Butler, Edward Schuré, Edward Carpenter, George Bernard Shaw, Arthur Conan Doyle, Rudyard Kipling, James Joyce, Jack London, Hermann Hesse, Kahlil Gibran, D. H. Lawrence, Eugene O'Neill, Henry Miller, Pearl S. Buck, Aldous Huxley, Thomas Wolfe,

Rumer Godden, J. D. Salinger, James Jones, Norman Mailer, and Richard Bach.

These lists show that many prominent individuals have come to believe in reincarnation despite their Western cultural background. As noted earlier, such belief does not constitute proof of anything in the usual scientific sense. Further, perhaps if the right questions had been asked and the data taken, a formidable list of prominent people who did not believe in reincarnation could have been developed. In the West, at least until very recently, belief in reincarnation has generally been the exception rather than the rule.

We now move on to some investigations of reincarnation that are more scientific in nature.

9. REMEMBRANCES OF PAST LIVES

One of the most widely published and best documented stories of past-life remembrances is that of Shanti Devi, a Hindu girl who at the age of four began to describe incidents of her previous life in the town of Muttra, 500 miles from Delhi, which was her home. She described many details and ultimately named the man she had been married to and the address where they had lived. A letter was sent to Kedar Nath Chaubey, the name she gave for her former husband, at the address she provided, and Chaubey replied by mail stating that the information given by the girl was true. Chaubey, who had since remarried, came to Delhi and was immediately recognized by Shanti Devi, who provided information to him that could not be known to anyone but his former wife.

The girl correctly described the town of Muttra and her former home in great detail. On a subsequent visit (accompanied by a party of fifteen) the girl, who was eleven at the time, led the group directly to her former home. She even identified on her own a place where money had been hidden in the house.

Shanti Devi then went to the house of her claimed previous parents, who were still living, correctly identified them out of a group of more than 50 people, and called them by name. She also used the dialect familiar to Muttra (which differed from that used in Delhi) even before she visited Muttra.

It is significant that Shanti Devi's case was thoroughly investigated in 1936 by a commission of the Indian government that participated in bringing her to her former relatives and issued a well-documented report in which they conclude that the story of Shanti Devi is entirely genuine.

Perhaps the leading scientific investigator of stories of past lives is Dr. Ian Stevenson, Carlson Professor of Psychiatry at the University of Virginia Medical School, where he was formerly chairman of the department of neurology and psychiatry.

Dr. Stevenson has thousands of cases on file and has written a carefully documented book, *Twenty Cases Suggestive of Reincarnation.*[17] The cases in the book are very convincing and his methods of investigation as well as the painstaking checks made to preclude fraud or error are most impressive.

It has been suggested that the reason why memory of the immediate past life is sometimes present with children who claim to have lived relatively recently is that in these cases the astral and mental bodies are not discarded to dissipate after death as would be the case if there were a long interval between births. Apparently in rare cases the individual retains these vehicles and uses them in the next incarnation rather than creating new ones. Possibly this occurs occasionally in the case of one who dies young because insufficient experience has been gained to justify a long time between births. With the mental body retained, memory of the immediate past life is also retained and is spontaneously present.

An area of investigation that is building up a substantial body of information on alleged past lives is the use of hypnotism to regress an individual to a past-life experience. The case of Bridey Murphy was well publicized through the success of the best-selling book *The Search for Bridey Murphy*[18] by Morey Bernstein. Jess Stearn wrote a popular book called *The Search for a Soul: Taylor Caldwell's Psychic Lives*[19] based on tape recordings of past-life descriptions given by Mrs. Caldwell under hypnotic regression.

An early investigator of regression recall is Dr. Alexander Cannon of England. Dr. Cannon, who has degrees from nine universities and who was knighted for his scientific achievements, wrote a book published in 1953 called *The Power Within*, in which he stated: "For years the theory of reincarnation was a nightmare to me and I did my best to disprove it and even argued with my trance subjects to the effect that they were talking nonsense. . . . Now well over a thousand cases have been so investigated and I have to admit that there is such a thing as reincarnation."

There are many reported cases of hypnotic regression where detailed facts such as names, places, and events have been described by the regressed person which have later been verified after research into old records not available to the person being hypnotized. People under hypnotic regression often display familiarity with the languages of the personality they claim to be, although the language is unknown to them in their present life.

In a book titled *Reliving Past Lives*[20] psychologist Dr. Helen Wambach reports on about 1000 hypnotic regressions into past lives in which data was collected from all the participants concerning their sex, appearance, clothing, landscapes, buildings, food, utensils they used, etc. The data gathered is plotted against a time period in the book and shows the expected changes relating to advancing civilizations. An interesting statistic given is that the subjects reported 49.4 percent of their lives as women and 50.6 percent as men, which is in "accord with biological fact." Many subjects gave details demonstrating an accuracy that would seem to preclude fantasy. Generally, those who reported on their moment of death in previous lives described leaving their physical bodies, with a pleasant conscious existence continuing after death.

Similar regression studies on a large number of subjects have been performed by psychologist Dr. Edith Fiore and reported in her book *Have You Been Here Before?*

Psychologist Dr. Kenneth Lyons has done a great deal of work with hypnotic regression, originally in an effort to rebut the Bridey Murphy story. However, as he regressed a great number of people, he began to see convincing patterns develop. In his book *Yoga, Youth and Reincarnation* Jess Stearn discusses a number of Dr. Lyons's regressions and one in particular that is well researched and that Dr. Lyons believes is clearly indicative of reincarnation. Working with other scientists, Lyons regressed a Wilmington, Massachusetts, electrician who had no interest in reincarnation and who had volunteered for hypnosis without knowing he was to be taken back in time and asked about previous lives.

While in a trance he stated that he had been a farmer in Andover, Massachusetts; about 1850 he had moved to Wilmington, which he described as it was in that period. The fact that the time was fairly recent (about 100 years) and the locale not remote made it possible to pursue the investigation on site. The man was hypnotized, regressed, and taken out to the Wilmington graveyard, which went back to colonial times. On the way to the graveyard he pointed out houses and named the people who had lived there a hundred years earlier. At the cemetery he correctly pointed out the graves of his period and named the dead. He pointed to a spot and said, "There is a red stone there." There was no stone, but later investigation revealed that there *had* been a red stone, which was later moved to another part of the cemetery. He also pointed to a nonexistent mound and named a couple who were to be buried there. Investigation revealed that there had been a mound over a vault intended as the burial place for the people he mentioned, but before their death the couple replaced the mound with a couple of urns.

Another method by which reincarnation investigation is pursued is through persons with psychic ability. Perhaps the best known of these is the late Edgar Cayce, who while in a trance not only described past lives of individuals whose names were given to him but was also well known for remarkable diagnoses and methods for cure that he was able to provide for people who were ill. In his past-life readings there was usually emphasis on the significance of the information given to the person's present life and that which should be accomplished or worked out. Cayce's record is astounding in correctly describing, discussing, and diagnosing people he had never met and who were often in some distant location. The correlation between present talents or problems and past-life activities is also very convincing. Records of Cayce's readings are maintained by the Association for Research and Enlightenment in Virginia Beach, Virginia. Two popular and interesting books on Edgar Cayce are his biography *There Is a River*, by Thomas Sugrue, and *Many Mansions*, by psychologist Gina Cerminara.[21]

Jess Stearn writes[22] about a past-life reading given by a clairvoyant named Betty McCain for a man named Gordon Meyers, a concert singer and composer in New York. Working from a trance condition as did Edgar Cayce, she not only told him many details of his present life that she could not have known, along with advice for dealing with problems, but also described a past life. She said he had been a Methodist minister, a follower of Wesley, in the late 1700s or early 1800s. She indicated that he had been in England and Ireland and had gone to Canada and the United States to teach Methodism. She gave his name as Philip Embury.

This reading led Meyers to an investigation described in detail by Stearn, which spanned several years and confirmed the existence of a Methodist minister named Philip Embury at that time, who had lived in England and Ireland and then traveled to New York and later Canada. Embury, who had been converted to Methodism by John Wesley, actually conducted the first Methodist service on the mainland of America. Meyers's investigation also revealed that Embury had been a carpenter as well as a minister, and carpentry had long been an avocation of Meyers's. Furthermore, Meyers was a Methodist and had considered entering the ministry. Meyers's investigations finally led to the discovery of an old portrait of Philip Embury and to the further discovery that there was a strong facial resemblance between himself and Embury.

Although this episode falls short of uncovering what might be considered scientific proof of reincarnation, it was for Gordon Meyers a profound experience that changed his outlook from one of frustration over lack of accomplishment to a new sense of purpose, direction, and contentment in his life.

Another category of alleged knowledge of past life through psychic means is the rare individual who claims to have knowledge of his or her own past lives. It is said that some of those advanced in Raja Yoga (the yoga of the mind) may develop the ability.

Two well-known military leaders who claimed to remember previous lives were Napoleon Bonaparte and World War II General George S. Patton. Napoleon, who is reported to have been a psychic in other ways also, insisted on a number of occasions that he was the reincarnation of the emperer Charlemagne.

General Patton's[23] case is especially interesting because he not only claimed to recall past lives but was able while in France for the first time at the ancient Roman town of Langres to correctly direct his driver to, and identify, the old Roman amphitheater, the drill ground, the forum, and the temples of Mars and Apollo. He accomplished this even though some of the structures had been torn down or built over. He also correctly identified the site where Caesar had pitched his tent. Patton was convinced that he had been in Langres in a past life. In response to his nephew Fred Ayer, who asked if he really believed in reincarnation, he replied, "I don't know about other people, but for myself there has never been any question. I just don't think it, I damn well know."

CONCLUSIONS

As a result of the efforts of researchers such as those mentioned in this chapter and the increasing body of documented data being gathered, the doctrine of immortality, which in the past had to be taken on faith, is now beginning to come much closer to being scientifcally demonstrable. It further appears that the idea of reincarnation, which has in the past been cited as a basic difference between Eastern and Western religious teachings, is becoming far more widely understood and accepted in the West. This is a result of the body of information published on hypnotic-regression experiments and on investigations of claimed spontaneous recall of past lives. This Western interest in the subject of reincarnation is part of a widespread interest in Eastern philosophies that has only recently developed.

One of the reasons that the theory of reincarnation, which initially may seem very foreign to someone with a Western religious background, gains acceptance after deeper investigation is that it provides answers to some otherwise very puzzling questions. Rebirth, for example, gives an explanation for a child prodigy, such as a musical genius. The reincarnationist will explain that the individual has worked with music many times before. Cause and effect, or karma, explains the apparent injustice of one who is born crippled or with some other affliction. Rebirth also accounts for the difference between the ignorant savage and the cultured highly intelligent individual, the latter being an "older, more developed soul."

In general, then, there seems to be a closing of the gap between East and West taking place in this area of apparent difference.

7. Creation and the Creator

In the Katha Upanishad we read

> The Lord is One without a second. Within man He dwells and within all other beings. He projects the universe, maintains it, and withdraws it into Himself.

The unity of God is also affirmed by Judaism, Christianity, and Islam. Moses preached: "Hear, O Israel: the Lord our God is One" (Deut. 6:4). And Muhammad stated: "Your God is One God, there is no God save Him" (Koran 2:109). This view was also held by Zoroastrianism, which preceded these religions.

Buddhism affirms that "There is . . . an unborn, not become, not made, *uncompounded*" and thus concurs in the unity of the transcendent God.

The concept that God is immanent (as well as transcendent) as stated above in the Katha Upanishad and repeated throughout the Hindu scriptures is supported also by Christian scripture, where we read: "There is one God and Father of all, who is above all and through all, and in you all" (Eph. 4:6). The concepts of immanence and transcendence are suggested also by the following from the Tao Te Ching.

> From What-is all the world of things was born
> But What-is sprang from What-is-not.

In his book *Basic Judaism*, Rabbi Milton Steinberg comments as follows on the Judaic view of the subject:

> Affirming God, Judaism permits considerable latitude as to conception of Him. It allows the individual to decide whether He is to be envisaged as transcendent or immanent, whether as an abstract principle of being as with Maimonides* and the Kabbalistic mystics, or, what is more common, as supremely personal.

---

*Moses Maimonides—the undisputed master of all medieval Jewish theologians.

The idea of ultimate return to God contained in the quotation that opens this chapter is echoed in the continuation of the last-quoted Buddhist passage: ". . . and were it not, monks, for this unborn not become, not made, uncompounded, no escape could be shown here for what is born, has become, is made, is compounded."* The Koran states the concept as follows: "Unto Allah belongeth whatsoever is in the earth; and unto Allah all things are returned" (3:109). In the mystical language of the Tao Te Ching we read, "The movement of the Way is a return."

Scriptures declare that God is eternal. In the Bhagavad Gita we read: "That Brahman is beginningless, transcendent, eternal." The Bible refers to "him that liveth for ever and ever, who created heaven . . . and the earth." (Rev. 10:6)

LIGHT, ENERGY, AND LIFE

"God is light and in him is no darkness at all" (1 John 1:15). "He is the one light that gives light to all" (Katha Upanishad). In these passages and others in Hindu scripture and the Bible we come across the concept of God as light. In another Hindu scripture we read, "Primal energy is Brahman." If we couple this with the assertion of our modern scientists that light is energy and that indeed matter and energy are fundamentally the same, we can reconcile all of the above with the following passage, said to come from an ancient esoteric archive: "Energy is all there is . . . but is not known."[1]

The Bible also tells us that God is Spirit. The Chandogya Upanishad states: "Truly has this Universe come forth from Brahman. In Brahman it lives and has its being." In almost the same words the Bible declares: "God that made the world and all things. . . . He is not far from every one of us: for in him we live, and move and have our being" (Acts 17: 24–28).

What, then, is the relationship of Spirit to Life? Paracelsus (1493–1541), philosopher, esotericist, and credited with being the founder of modern medicine equates Life with Spirit and states that the two of these produce all things, and that they are essentially a Unity. He further explains that there is nothing dead in Nature.

It is clear from the discoveries of modern science relative to the nature of molecules and atoms that everything, whether it is what we term animate or inanimate, is in motion and also seems to exhibit some form of organizing intelligence. The most dense elements of the mineral kingdom can from this point of view be said to have life, although they do not fit the customary definition of organic life forms.

*Samyutta Nikaya.

THE WORD

> By the word of the Lord were the heavens made; and all the host of them
> by the breath of this mouth. (Psalm 33:6)

> In the beginning was the Word, and the Word was with God, and the Word
> was God . . . All things were made by him; and without him was not any
> thing made that was made. (John 1:1–3)
> Saith the Lord . . . so shall my word be that goeth forth out of my mouth:
> it shall not return unto me void, but it shall accomplish that which I please,
> and it shall prosper in the thing whereto I sent it. (Isaiah 55:11)
> The word is Brahman. (Brihadaranyaka Upanishad)

The Eastern religions and many esoteric writings hold that the process
of creation involves God meditating deeply on the creation that is to be
manifested and then, when a thought image has been formed, sounding
forth out of himself the "Word," which causes the creative process to occur. This Word is also referred to as the *Great Breath*. As we see in the
quotations above, the Bible also refers to the Word and the Breath of God.

The Sounding of the Word is described elsewhere as being a sevenfold
process that must continue uninterrupted as long as manifested creation
exists. The Sacred Word is described in terms of human language in Hindu
scripture as having the sound OM. The following passages from the Upanishads mention the roll of thought and the Word in the creative process:

> Desiring that he should become many, that he should make of himself many
> forms, Brahman meditated. Meditating, he created all things. (Taittiriya
> Upanishad)
> The Syllable OM which is the imperishable Brahman, is the universe. What-
> soever has existed, whatsoever exists, and whatsoever shall exist hereafter,
> is OM. And whatsoever transcends past, present and future, that also is OM.
> All that we see without is Brahman. This Self that is within is Brahman.
> This Self, which is one with OM, has three aspects, and beyond these three,
> different from them and indefinable—the Fourth.
> This self beyond all words, is the syllable OM. This syllable, though indivis-
> ible, consists of three letters—A.U.M. (Mandukya Upanishad)

The Self mentioned above refers to the inner spiritual man. The text
in the Mandukya Upanishad goes on to say that the letters A-U-M cor-

respond to the three aspects mentioned above; *A* relating to physical nature, *U* to mental nature, and *M* to dreamless sleep. It then adds that

> The Fourth, the Self, is OM, the indivisible syllable. This syllable is unutterable, and beyond mind. In it the manifold universe disappears. It is the supreme good—One without a second. Whosoever knows OM, the Self, becomes the Self.

This is certainly a bit obscure, but some element of explanation may be inferred from the writings of Alice Bailey.[3] It is pointed out there that as far as man is concerned, the OM is the Sound of the Soul. It is also stated that:

> The A.U.M. and the Amen* are both of them an expression of . . . active intelligent substance in the divine manifestation, and have served human need in that phase of material and form development [including] the development of mind or of mental form. The personality as a whole, when perfected and brought under control of the soul, is the "Word made flesh." . . . the OM . . . is not the Word made flesh, but the Word released from form, and expressing itself as soul-spirit and not as body-soul-spirit. It might therefore be said that: The A.U.M. . . . brings the soul-spirit aspect down on to the physical plane and anchors it there by the force of its ongoing vibration. . . . The OM, rightly sounded, releases the soul from the realm of glamour and enchantment. It is the sound of liberation, the great note of resurrection and of the raising of humanity to the Secret Place of the Most High.

The OM is said to be the "Lost Word" of Masonry.

It is also predicted in this writing that "the use of the Amen in the ritual of the Christian Church will eventually be discouraged because it is basically a materialistic affirmation being usually regarded by the average churchgoer as setting the seal of divine approval upon his demand to the Almighty for protection, or for the supply of his physical necessities."[4]

THREE, FOUR, AND SEVEN

The concept of God manifesting in three aspects is found in many religions. Table 3 shows the corresponding identifications for the three persons of the trinity from several of these. The characteristics of the three persons listed in the table are from esoteric writings.

In the Tao Te Ching the trinity is described as follows:

> The Way begot one,
> And the one, two;
> Then the two begot three,
> And three, all else.

*The Amen of Judaic and Christian religion is said to be the A.U.M. distorted by distance, time, and language.

TABLE 3. THE TRINITY: CORRESPONDENCES AND CHARACTERISTICS

Christian	Hindu	Hebrew[a]	Egyptian	Characteristic
Father	Shiva	Kepher	Osiris	Will or Power
Son	Vishnu	Binah	Horus	Love-Wisdom
Holy Spirit	Brahma	Chochmah	Isis	Active Intelligence

[a]From the Kabbala.

The trinity, of course, is well known in Christianity, but in Revelation 4:5 the following less familiar symbolic concept is found:

> From the throne came flashes of lightning and peals of thunder; before it burned seven flaming torches,* the seven spirits of God. . . . At the very center around the throne itself stood four living creatures covered with eyes front and back.

In the Bhagavad Gita is found the following similar passage: "Forth from my thought came the Seven Sages, The Ancient Four." In Buddhist writings there is reference to "The gods of the heaven of the four Great Kings"[5] and to "seven precious things, infinite in number."[6]

James Churchward, who has made extensive studies of ancient civilizations, indicates that what he terms the Sacred Four appears on tablets and in records of many ancient civilizations.[7] Through the symbology on a particular stone tablet uncovered in Mexico he concludes that the Sacred Four refer to the Four Great Primary Forces emanating from the Creator. He also states that the ancient Naga sages used a seven-headed serpent to symbolically depict the seven commands in Creation.

In *A Treatise on Cosmic Fire*, by Alice Bailey, it is stated (p. 41) that the Sacred Four are:

Unity
a. Father——Mahadeva (Shiva)——1st Logos——Will——Spirit

Duality
b. Son——Vishnu——2nd Logos——Love-Wisdom

Trinity
c. Mother (Holy Spirit)——Brahma——3rd Logos——Intelligent Activity

Sacred Four
d. The united manifestation of the three——Macrocosm

*In every synagogue is found the menorah with seven flames from the seven candlesticks.

The Seven Spirits, also called the Seven Rays, emanate from the above and are defined in the same work (p. 827) as follows:

1. The Lord of Cosmic Will——First Ray
2. The Lord of Cosmic Love——Second Ray
3. The Lord of Cosmic Intelligence——Third Ray
4. The Lord of Cosmic Harmony——Fourth Ray
5. The Lord of Cosmic Knowledge——Fifth Ray
6. The Lord of Cosmic Devotion——Sixth Ray
7. The Lord of Cosmic Ceremonial——Seventh Ray

All of the above are said to be "the subjective consciousness, the cause of manifestation." The same work quotes T. Subba Rao, who says on page 20 of his *Esoteric Writings*,

> As a general rule, whenever seven entities are mentioned in the ancient occult science of India in any connection whatsoever, you must suppose that those seven entities came into existance from three primary entities and that these three entities again are evolved out of a single entity or monad.

A great deal is written in Mrs. Bailey's books* about the significance of the Seven Rays to the life forms of our planet and especially to man. Geoffrey Hodson has also written a small volume called *Seven Human Temperaments*, which indicates, as does Mrs. Bailey's writings, that different individuals reflect different ray characteristics, and he discusses some of the effects of these on human personality.

An "archaic manuscript" containing what is termed the "Stanzas of Dzyan" is quoted by H. P. Blavatsky and deals with the creation of the cosmos and of man. The language is symbolic and requires interpretation, but the following passages show a correspondence with the earlier quotations:

> . . . Thus stands the eternal cause of existence—the parent of the gods, which is: "Darkness," the boundless, or the no-number, primeval cause of existence, root-substance, the boundless circle:
>
> I. The primeval ancient, the number, for he is one.
> II. The voice of the word . . .
> III. The "formless square."
>
> And these three, enclosed within the boundless circle, are the sacred four. . . . Then come the "sons," the seven fighters.[8]

A book by Leinani Melville, called *Children of the Rainbow*, shows that the ancient Hawaiians in their legends, symbols, and religion depicted concepts very similar to those contained in other scriptures. Figures 6 and 7

---

*She has written a five-volume work titled *A Treatise on the Seven Rays*.

Fig. 6. Tau Toru—the Triple Cross of the Holy Trinity:
Ancient Hawaiian Design

From Leinani Melville, *Children of the Rainbow* (Wheaton, Ill.: Theosophical Publishing House, 1969). Used by permission of the publisher.

are ancient Hawaiian designs illustrated in the book.[9] The description of
the first, titled "Tau Toru—the Triple Cross of the Holy Trinity," states
that "the lines which form the diamond reveal that this is the Cross of
the Supreme Triune Godhead." For Figure 7, titled "The Seven Who Surround the Throne of God," the text states that "the Absolute Ruler of
heaven is portrayed in the center of this design. . . . Spread out around
Him are the Seven who surround His Sacred Shrine."

Those familiar with the Kabbala of the Hebrew mystics and the diagram
of the ten Sefiroth (see Fig. 10, p. 166), which represent God in manifestation, will recognize the correspondence with the three persons of God
and the seven spirits. At the top of the diagram is the Kether, or Crown,
and issuing from this are the two that are translated Wisdom and Intelligence. Below these three and proceeding from them are the seven others.

The *Zohar*, which is the best-known Kabbalistic text, has the following
view of the threefold nature of the Godhead:

Fig. 7. The Seven Who Surround the Throne of God:
Ancient Hawaiian Design

From Leinani Melville, *Children of the Rainbow* (Wheaton, Ill.: Theosophical Publishing House, 1969). Used by permission of the publisher.

These three persons contain and unite all that was, is and will be; but they in turn are reunited in the white head, in the Ancient of Ancients, for all is He, and He is all in all.[10]

Beyond this the Kabbalists consider the Intelligence aspect to be feminine, or the Mother aspect, which is said to be "in keeping with the verse 'Thou shalt call understanding mother.'"[11]

THE FEMININE ASPECT OF DEITY: THE MOTHER

It is not only in the Kabbala where this feminine aspect is brought out. In the Tao Te Ching (v. 52) Lao-tzu writes:

> It began with a matrix:
> The world had a mother.

And in verse 40:

> Alone I am and different
> Because I prize and seek
> My sustenance from the Mother!

In Hinduism there are sects that emphasize worship of Durga, the Divine Mother. In Northern Buddhism there is Kwan-yin, the Mother of Mercy and Knowledge.

The Great Mother is the title of a book by Eric Newman published in the Princeton Bollingen Series which shows that the concept of the feminine creative deity abounds in legend and myth. Heinrich Zimmer writes that the "old pre-Aryan concept of the Universal Mother . . . goes back to the Neolithic Age, when it was distributed throughout western Asia and the lands surrounding the Mediterranean . . . and to this day her worship survives in modern Hinduism."[12]

Sri Ramakrishna was described by Jawaharlal Nehru[13] as "completely beyond the average run of man. He appears rather to belong to the tradition of the great rishis [Holy sages] of India." Swami Prabhavananda, a disciple of Ramakrishna, writes:

> In the life of Sri Ramakrishna we find how, many times during the day he would become absorbed in God. . . . In that state, where the universe disappeared, and the sense of ego was lost, there would remain the undifferentiated Brahman;* again, as he remembered himself in normal consciousness, he would have the vision of the benign form of the blissful Divine Mother.

In the biblical book of Revelation St. John describes the following vision: "And there appeared a great wonder in heaven; a woman clothed with the sun, and the moon under her feet, and upon her head a crown of twelve stars." (Rev. 12:1)

There are two books that provide similar interpretations of this symbology contained in the book of Revelation (The Apocalypse). The first of these is derived from the trance statements of Edgar Cayce, termed the *Sleeping Prophet*, who was able to affect remarkable cures of people he had never met through directions for applications of medications and other treatments that he provided while in a trance. Many books have resulted from his trance readings. One such compilation is titled *Revelation: A Commentary on the Book.* When asked for an explanation of the woman clothed with the sun, Cayce responded: "The woman—or the mother—earth; the source from which all materiality is to become a conscious thing—and these are brought forth."[14]

The second book, *The Apocalypse Unsealed*, by James M. Pryse, is a well-researched analysis of St. John's symbology. He comments as follows on the woman:

> Thereupon appears the Woman clothed with the Sun, star-crowned and standing on the moon; . . . She symbolizes the Light of the Logos, the World-Mother, that is the pristine force-substance from which is moulded the solar body.

*Brahman in the Hindu religion refers to the one Universal Spirit that manifests as a Three-in-One God. The three aspects of Brahman are Shiva, Vishnu, and Brahma.

A small compilation from the writings of Helena Roerich entitled *Mother of the World* brings together the many references on the subject in her works. The foreword to this compilation reads (in part) as follows:

> In the Hermetic Writings of old are found references to "the Woman clothed with the Sun." Is this a symbol or a sublime Reality of the Higher World?
>
> Ancient religions, inspired by Messengers of the Planetary Hierarchy, accorded great reverence to the Feminine Principle in Creation, the Mother aspect of Deity.
>
> The highest manifestation of this Feminine Principle has been called by many names, among them: Mother of the Universe, World Mother, Isis, Ishtar, and Sophia. To the Gnostic Christians She was known as the Holy Spirit, one of the Divine Triad.

The World Mother is also discussed in Theosophical literature. C. W. Leadbeater authored a small volume entitled *The World Mother as Symbol and Fact*. Geoffrey Hodson has included a chapter on the World Mother in his book *Kingdom of the Gods*. These works similarly relate the World Mother to the feminine aspect of Deity, and Leadbeater discusses at length the symbolic relationship between Mary the mother of Jesus and the World Mother.

THE ESOTERICISTS' VIEW OF CREATION

The esotericists acknowledge that the absolute, infinite, all-embracing source is beyond our present knowledge. They do state, however, that within this absolute there are many universes and in each a vast number of solar systems, and that each solar system is the outward expression of a great Being to which they give the name *Solar Logos*. This Solar Logos permeates and animates the entire solar system and transcends it, existing also in invisible worlds beyond the seven planes of the solar system described in chapter 5. These seven planes in total are referred to as the "Cosmic Physical Plane." The Solar Logos is what most scriptures describe as God. The esotericists agree with the various scriptures which indicate that God manifests as a trinity. Below our Solar Logos, yet somehow also a part thereof, are the earlier-mentioned seven great Entities referred to in the Bible as the Seven Spirits before the Throne and corresponding to what esotericists call the *Seven Rays*. These are also said to be regents of seven of the planets (not including earth), which are termed *sacred planets*. Below them are many orders of beings concerned with the evolution of life, some identified in biblical terms as cherubim, seraphim, thrones, dominions, principalities, and powers.[15]

Our planet is said to be the outward manifestation of a Being referred to in the Bible as "The Ancient of Days"[16] and in Hindu scripture as Sanat Kumara, who controls the evolution of life on this planet. Esotericists call Him the *Planetary Logos*.

The following quotations from the writings of Alice Bailey are a good summary of the esoteric view of God:

> What the scientist calls energy, the religious man calls God, and yet the two are one, being but the manifested purpose, in physical matter, of a great extra-systemic Identity. Nature is the appearance of the physical body of the Logos. . . . The life of God, His energy and vitality, are found in every manifested atom; His essence indwells all forms. This we call Spirit, yet He Himself is other than those forms, just as man knows himself to be other than his bodies. He knows himself to be a will, and a purpose. . . . So with the planetary Logos and solar Logos. They dwell within, yet are found without, the planetary scheme or solar system.[17]

> We have spoken of God in terms of Person, and we have used therefore the pronouns, He and His. . . . The Buddhist teaching recognizes no God or Person. Is it therefore wrong from our point of view and approach or is it right? . . .

> Both schools of thought are right, and in no way contradict each other. In their synthesis and in their blending, the truth as it really is can begin—aye, dimly—to appear. There is a God Transcendent Who "having pervaded the whole universe with a fragment of Himself" can still say: "I remain." There is a God Immanent, Whose life is the source of the activity, intelligence, growth and attractiveness, of every form in all the kingdoms of nature. . . .

> Behind the manifested universe . . . stands the formless One. That which is not an individual, being free from the limitations of individualized existence. Therefore the Buddhist is right when he emphasizes the non-individualized nature of Deity. . . . The Father, Son and Holy Spirit of Christian theology, embodying as they do the triplicities of all theologies, disappear also into the One when the period of manifestation is over. . . . An analogy to this appears when a man dies. His three aspects, mind or will, emotion or love, and physical appearance—vanish. . . . Yet, if one accepts the fact of immortality, the conscious being remains . . . united with his undying soul.[18]

It is interesting to compare the view of the esotericists just described with the view held by Benjamin Franklin, whose biographer Carl Van Doren called him "the most eminent mind that has ever existed in America." In his *Articles of Belief and Acts of Religion*, written in 1728, Franklin stated:

> I believe there is one supreme most perfect Being, Author and Father of the Gods themselves. For I believe that Man is not the most perfect Being but one, rather that as there are many Degrees of Beings his inferior, so there are many Degrees of Beings superior to him.

> Also, when I stretch my Imagination thro' and beyond our System of Planets, beyond the visible fix'd Stars themselves, into that space that is every way infinite, and conceive it filled with Suns like ours, each with a Chorus of Worlds forever moving around him, then this little Ball on which we move, seems even in my narrow imagination, to be almost Nothing.

> I conceive, then, that the Infinite has created many beings or Gods, vastly superior to Man . . . that each of these is exceeding wise and good and very

powerful; and that Each has made for himself one glorious Sun, attended with a beautiful and admirable System of Planets.

It is that particular wise and good God, who is the author and owner of our system, that I propose for the object of my praise and adoration.

The cosmic view of deity expressed above fits with the definition given by Dane Rudhyar in *New Mansions for New Men* (p. 74): "God who is always, at any stage of development, the next 'greater Whole,' 'in whom we live and move and have our being.' "

There is a statement in the Bible on the nature of God to which esotericists ascribe a significance not clear to one unfamiliar with esoteric concepts. This is "God is love," which is said to refer to the inherent nature of the Logos of our solar system in whom the Second Ray of love-wisdom is dominant.

Another significant aspect of the esoteric teachings is mankind's potential for development. Given a great deal of time, effort, and the workings of the evolutionary process, humans, it is claimed, are capable of advancing to the stage where they can become a planetary logos or a solar logos. This concept brings another dimension to the scriptural statement, "God created man in his own image" (Gen 1:27) and Christ's reiteration of the Old Testament declaration "thou art gods."

Considering the esotericists' view of man's potential, along with the familiar assessment by astronomers that there are more stars in the heavens than all the grains of sand on all the beaches in the world, we come to recognize simultaneously our great insignificance from one point of view and our possible greatness from another.

8. Christ, Krishna, and the Buddha

Considering the great importance of these three individuals to the religious views of today's world, we will review a bit more deeply their teachings and lives pointing out certain remarkable parallels. Views as to the special significance of these great identities will also be explored. We noted earlier that while the Koran attributes a special status to Jesus, it does not accept the orthodox Christian view of Jesus as God. This question will also be commented on later in the chapter.

First, in order to further explore religious links between East and West, let us consider Sri Krishna and Jesus Christ to see if in their lives and teachings common elements can be found.

CHRIST AND KRISHNA

The Bhagavad Gita (which can be translated "The Lord's Song") is the most popular Hindu religious work and can be considered to be the Gospel of India. It has for centuries had a profound effect on the thinking of India's leaders in all fields of endeavor. The Bhagavad Gita is the record of a conversation between Sri Krishna (*Sri* is a title of reverence) and the warrior Arjuna, who questions him prior to a great battle. The Gita is believed by scholars to have been written between 200 B.C. and 500 B.C.

In the introduction to the translation of the Bhagavad Gita by Swami Prabhavananda and Christopher Isherwood[1] it is stated that "Sri Krishna has been called the Christ of India. There are in fact some striking parallels between the life of Krishna, as related in the Bhagavatam and elsewhere, and the life of Jesus of Nazareth."

William Kingsland comments as follows on some of these parallels:

> He [Krishna] has also a legendary history which is almost an exact parallel of the Gospel story. His mother was Devaki, who was overshadowed by Vishnu, and thus gave birth to Krishna as that god's Avatara. Kansa, the Indian King Herod, sought to slay him, and in doing so slew thousands of newly born babes. His birth was announced by a star in heaven. He was also said

144

to have been put to death on a tree, and to have risen again. The tree symbol seems to have been interchangeable with that of the cross. In Acts 5:30, Jesus is said by Peter to have been hanged on a tree.[2]

It has also been pointed out that the names Christ and Krishna, the first derived from Greek and the other from Sanskrit, come from a root word that means "to be rubbed on" or "to rub over." Hence both names signify "the anointed one."[3]

Alice Bailey's writings claim* that Krishna is an earlier appearance of Christ, and the following words of Krishna in the Bhagavad Gita are of interest in this connection:

> When goodness grows weak,
> When evil increases,
> I make myself a body.
>
> In every age I come back
> To deliver the holy,
> To destroy the sin of the sinner,
> To establish righteousness.

In John 10:16 Christ says:

> I have other sheep
> that do not belong to this fold.
> I must lead them, too,
> and they shall hear my voice.

The Hindus consider Krishna to be an incarnation of Vishnu, the second aspect of the threefold Godhead,† which is indeed how Christ is viewed by Christians. This Hindu viewpoint is supported by chapter 11 of the Bhagavad Gita, where at Arjuna's request Krishna provides him a view of his "transcendent, divine Form." Commenting at length on what he observes, Arjuna concludes, "I see you, Vishnu omnipresent."

Considering the view that these two great figures are one and the same, it is of special interest to compare some of the teachings attributed to each of them. The words of Krishna in the passages from the Bhagavad Gita that follow are placed side by side with passages from the New Testament, which show a remarkable similarity in teaching.

---

*Discipleship in the New Age II, p. 270, states, "The goal for thousands everywhere is the demonstration of the Christ spirit, and the exemplification of a life conditioned by love and modeled upon that of Christ or Shri Krishna, His earlier incarnation."
†The Hindu Trinity is Shiva, Vishnu, and Brahma, corresponding to the Father, the Son, and the Holy Spirit in the Christian trinity.

Krishna *Bhagavad Gita**	Christ *New Testament*
CH. 12 Be absorbed in me, Lodge your mind in me: Thus you shall dwell in me, Do not doubt it, Here and hereafter.	Abide in me, and I in you. As the branch cannot bear fruit of itself, except it abide in the vine; no more can ye, except ye abide in me. (John 15:4)
CH. 9 My devotees dwell Within me always: I also show forth And am seen within them.	On that day you will know that I am in my Father, and you in me and I in you. (John 14:20)
CH. 7 Knowing me, they understand the nature of the relative world and the individual man, and of God who presides over all action.	He that hath seen me hath seen the Father. . . . I am in the Father and the Father in me. (John 14:9–10)
CH. 18 Lay down all your duties In me, your refuge.	Come to me all ye that labor and are heavy laden, and I will give you rest. (Matt. 11:28)
CH. 4 Flying from fear, From lust and anger, He hides in me His refuge, his safety; Burnt clean in the blaze of my being, In me many find home.	
CH. 4 Whatever wish men bring me in worship, That wish I grant them. Whatever path men travel Is my path: No matter where they walk, It leads to me.	Ask and you will receive, Seek, and you will find. Knock and it will be opened to you. For the one who asks, receives. The one who seeks, finds. The one who knocks enters. (Matt. 7:7–8)

Song of God, Bhagavad Gita, trans. Swami Prabhavananda and Christopher Isherwood (Mentor Books).

Krishna *Bhagavad Gita*	Christ *New Testament*
CH. 9 You find yourself in this transient, joyless world. Turn from it, and take your delight in me. Fill your heart and mind with me.	Jesus looked at him with love and told him ". . . Go and sell what you have and give to the poor. . . . After that come and follow me." (Mark 10:21)
CH. 3 Shake off the fever of ignorance; Stop hoping for worldly reward. **CH. 6** When a man loses attachment to sense objects and to action, when he renounces lustful anxiety and anxious lust, then he is said to have climbed to the height of union with Brahman.	Lay not up for yourself treasures on earth . . . but lay up for yourselves treasures in heaven . . . for where your treasure is there will your heart be also. (Matt. 6:19–21)
CH. 9 Whatever your action, Food or worship; Whatever the gift That you give another; Whatever you vow To the work of the spirit: O son of Kunti, Lay these also As offerings before me. . . . offer up everything to me.	Then shall the righteous answer him, saying "Lord, when did we see thee hungry and fed thee? or thirsty and gave thee drink?". . . Verily I say unto you: Inasmuch as you have done it unto one of the least of these my brethren, ye have done it unto me. (Matt. 25:37–40)
CH. 2 Those who lack discrimination may quote the letter of the scripture, but they are really denying its inner truth. They are full of worldly desires, and hungry for the rewards of heaven.	Ye hypocrites, Well did Esaias prophesy of you, saying, "This people draweth nigh unto me with their mouth and honoureth me with their lips; but their heart is far from me. But in vain they do worship me, teaching for doctrines the commandments of men." (Matt. 15:7–9)

Krishna *Bhagavad Gita*	Christ *New Testament*
CH. 12 Concentration which is practiced with discernment is certainly better than mechanical repetition of a ritual or prayer. Absorption in God—to live with Him and be one with Him always—is even better than concentration. But renunciation brings instant peace to the spirit.	Whenever you pray, go to your room, close your door, and pray to your Father in private. . . . In your prayer do not rattle on like the pagans, they think they will win a hearing by a sheer multiplication of words. (Matt. 6:6–7)
CH. 9 Worshipping me With the rites appointed, Drinking the wine Of the gods' communion, Cleansed from their sinning: These men pray For passage to heaven.	Then, taking the bread and giving thanks, he broke it and gave it to them saying "This is my body to be given for you. Do this as a remembrance of me." He did the same with the cup after eating, saying as he did so: "This cup is the new covenant in my blood, which will be shed for you." (Luke 22:19–20)
CH. 14 He who worships me with unfaltering love transcends those gunas.* He becomes fit to reach union with Brahman. For I am Brahman within this body, Life immortal That shall not perish: I am the Truth and the Joy for ever.	Jesus told him: "I am the way and the truth and the life; no one comes to the father but through me. If you really know me you would know my Father also. From this point on you know him; you have seen him." (John 14:6–7)
CH. 15 He who is free from delusion, and knows me as the supreme Reality, knows all that can be known. Therefore he adores me with his whole heart. This is the most sacred of all the truths I have taught you.	Thou shalt love the Lord thy God with all thy heart, and with all thy soul, and with all thy mind. This is the first and greatest Commandment. (Matt. 21:27–28)
CH. 18 United with me, you shall overcome all difficulties by my grace.	The law was given by Moses, but grace and truth came by Jesus Christ. (John 1:17)

*Gunas: "Bonds that bind the undying dweller imprisoned in the body." (Bhagavad Gita, 14)

Krishna *Bhagavad Gita*	Christ *New Testament*
CH. 5 When thus he knows me . . . Lord of the worlds . . . Shall he not enter The peace of my presence?	Peace I leave with you, my peace I give unto you. (John 14:27) These things I have spoken unto you, that in me ye might have peace. (John 16:33)
CH. 15 Part of myself is the God within every creature.	Christ in you, the hope of glory. (Col. 1:27)
CH. 8 In this way you will come finally to the Lord who is the light giver.	I am the light of the world; he that followeth me shall not walk in darkness, but shall have the light of life. (John 8:12)
CH. 10 I am the beginning, the middle and the end in creation:	I say to you, before Abraham was, I am. (John 8:58)
CH. 7 I am the . . . OM in all the Vedas, the word that is God.	In the beginning was the Word and the Word was with God and the Word was God. (John 1:1)
CH. 9 The man that loves me, he shall not perish.	. . . whosoever believeth in him [Christ] shall not perish but have eternal life. (John 3:16)
CH. 18 Learn from me now . . . how a man made perfect is one with Brahman.	Be ye therefore perfect, even as your Father which is in heaven is perfect. (Matt. 5:48)

The preceding excerpts serve to show many virtually identical elements in the teachings of Krishna and Christ, but because of their brevity, they do not adequately portray the profound and vital message of the complete works.

The Bhagavad Gita and the Gospels both provide important guidance for mankind, and they should be read in their entirety to be appreciated fully.

Some aspects of the message of Krishna are well summarized for us in the following quotation:

Krishna laid down in the Gita the simple rules whereby depression and doubt can be overcome.

a. Know thyself to be the undying One.
b. Control thy mind, for through that mind the undying One can be known.
c. Learn that the form is but the veil which hides the splendor of Divinity.
d. Realize that the One Life pervades all forms so that there is no death, no distress, no separation.
e. Detach thyself therefore from the form side and come to Me, so dwelling in the place where Light and Life are found. Thus illusion ends.[4]

THE BUDDHA

H. P. Blavatsky makes the following observation concerning the three individuals discussed in this chapter.

Kapila, Orpheus, Pythagoras, Plato, Basilides, Marcian, Ammonius, and Plotinus, founded schools and sowed the germs of many a noble thought, and disappearing, left behind them the refulgence of demigods. But the three personalities of Krishna, Gautama [the Buddha], and Jesus appeared like true gods, each in his epoch, and bequeathed to humanity three religions built on the imperishable rock of ages. . . . Purify the three systems of the dross of human dogmas, and the pure essence remaining will be found to be identical.[5]

The Buddha appeared about 500 years before Christ and his significance is attested to by the many people who have called themselves Buddhists and by the spread of culture and learning that has been accomplished by Buddhists in the East. Beyond that, however, his importance is highlighted for us through the power and timelessness of his teachings.

We have seen in chapter 1 that the basic teachings of the Buddha as to how man should conduct himself with regard to his fellow men are essentially the same as those of other great religions. The Buddha was a Hindu who showed the need for reform but did not deny the basic concepts of Hinduism, just as Christ did not deny the basic concepts of Judaism. In the East, incidentally, it is not uncommon for religious people to acknowledge the validity of several religions. The sense of exclusivity is not as prevalent as in the West.

A concept especially stressed by the Buddha is that one should not look to dogmas or the pronouncements of others to understand what is right and true, but rather to rely on one's own observation, reason, logic, and intuition. In his farewell address to his disciples, he said:

Be ye lamps unto yourselves. Rely on yourselves, and do not rely on external help.
Hold fast to the truth as a lamp. Seek salvation alone in the truth. Look not for assistance to anyone besides yourselves.[6]

He also clearly points out the great importance of the human mind and the process of thought.

The other key elements of the Buddha's teachings are that extremes should be avoided and one should not place great importance on desire for material possessions, earthly existence, pleasure, and power. Buddhism further teaches the importance of right human relations, along with compassion for and service to each other; and that the ability to render effective service requires the control of emotions and desire.

Some of these principles are expounded in the Four Noble Truths and the Eightfold Path, which are fundamental elements of the teaching of the Buddha. These he revealed shortly after his illumination in the Sermon at Benares. They have been translated as follows:

THE FOUR NOBLE TRUTHS

The First Noble Truth is that old age is suffering; illness is suffering; death is suffering; being exposed to what one dislikes is suffering; being separated from what one likes is suffering; failure to realize one's ambitions and desires is suffering.

The Second Noble Truth is that suffering comes from the desire for being, which leads from birth to rebirth, together with lust and desire, which find gratification here and there. The desire for being, the desire for pleasure, and the desire for power—these are the sources of suffering.

The Third Noble Truth is that suffering can be dissolved with the complete annihilation of desire, separating oneself from it and completely expelling it.

The Fourth Noble Truth is that the cessation of all desire can be gained by following the Eightfold Path. (*Vinaya-Pitaka; Maha-Vagga*)[7]

THE EIGHTFOLD PATH

Right Belief—that Truth is the guide of man.

Right Resolve—to be calm at all times and not to harm any living creature.

Right Speech—never to lie, never to slander anyone, and never to use coarse or harsh language.

Right Behavior—never to steal, never to kill, and never to do anything one may later regret or be ashamed of.

Right Occupation—never to choose an occupation that is considered bad.

Right Effort—always to strive for that which is good and avoid that which is evil.

Right Contemplation—of the Noble Truths, in calmness and detachment.

Right Concentration will then follow and lead to the path of perfect peace.   (*Vinaya-Pitaka; Maha-Vagga*)[7]

The Buddhist is guided in life by the ten perfections, which are: Giving, Duty, Renunciation, Insight, Courage, Patience, Truth, Resolution, Loving-Kindness, and Serenity. Many of these are expanded on in the comparisons in chapter 1.

An interesting parallel appears in the lives of Jesus Christ and Gautama Buddha. The Buddha meditated for forty days and forty nights under the Bodhi tree before receiving enlightenment. At the end of this time he was tempted by Mara the temptress but successfully resisted. Many statues of the Buddha show this episode, depicting him sitting cross-legged, with one hand touching the ground to signify that since he was alone when he achieved his victory over temptation, he called upon the earth as a witness. Jesus, of course, underwent a similar experience when after forty days and forty nights in the wilderness he was tempted by Satan but did not yield.

Alice Bailey comments as follows on the message of the Buddha and Christ:

> The Buddha came embodying in Himself the divine quality of wisdom; He was the manifestation of Light, and the Teacher of the way of enlightenment. He demonstrated in Himself the process of illumination and became "the Illumined One." Light, wisdom, reason as divine yet human attributes were focused in the Buddha. He challenged the people to tread the Path of Illumination, of which wisdom, mental perception, and intuition are aspects.
>
> Then came the next great Teacher, the Christ. He embodied in Himself a still greater divine principle—greater than the Mind, that of Love; yet at the same time He embraced within Himself all that the Buddha had of Light. Christ was the expression of both Light and Love. Christ also brought to human attention three deeply necessary concepts:
>
> 1. The extreme value of the individual son of God and the necessity for intense spiritual effort.
> 2. The opportunity, presented to humanity, to take a great step forward and undergo the new birth.
> 3. The method whereby man could enter into the kingdom of God, voiced for us in his words, "Love your neighbor as yourself." Individual effort, group opportunity and identification with each other—such is the message of the Christ.[8]

Mrs. Bailey maintains that although the Buddha has stated that he will not again appear in human form, he still works subjectively in cooperation with Christ for the benefit of humanity.

PREDICTIONS OF CHRIST'S APPEARANCE

Alice Bailey's books do, however, assert that Christ will appear again in the not-too-distant future (probably in the first half of the twenty-first century) with his senior disciples to set the stage for the New Age we are in the process of entering. (It is interesting that Edgar Cayce also predicted that Christ would appear again around the year 2000.) Mrs. Bailey comments that Christ symbolically predicted his return at the beginning of the astrological Aquarian Age when he ordered his disciples to follow a man carrying a pitcher of water (Luke 22:10) and that the frequent use of fish in the gospel story symbolizes the Piscean Age, which started around the time of the birth of Christ and has continued for the last 2000 years. The water carrier is, of course, the symbolic representation of the zodiacal sign Aquarius. The symbology of this incident is discussed further in chapter 17 on Astrology.

This coming of the Christ, the Messiah, or an avatar is anticipated in all the major religions. Roman Catholics recently emphasized this by adding the words "Christ will come again" as an affirmation by the entire congregation in their liturgy. Buddhists await Maitreya, the great one who is to come; Islam looks for the appearance of the Imam Mahdi; and the words of Krishna quoted earlier, "When goodness grows weak . . . I make myself a body," assure Hindus that they will not be left without spiritual guidance.

Jews, of course, still await the coming of the Messiah. Along this line, it may be revealing for those not familiar with them to review some of the messianic predictions of the Old Testament in comparison with the life of Christ as related in the New Testament. Such a comparison is contained in the Appendix, and it serves to emphasize the link between Christianity and Judaism.

The Old Testament Book of Isaiah is one of the important sources of predictions of the life of Christ. A recent discovery from an early Essene community of a complete text of the Book of Isaiah that predates the birth of Jesus and contains the prophesies of his life as they appear in the modern texts proves that the modern texts were not altered after the fact to conform to what is recorded in the Gospels.

In connection with the predicted reappearance of Christ, Mrs. Bailey's writings are careful to caution that Christ predicted that there would be false claims. Those who simply claim to be Christ or those who claim to know who or where he is should not be believed. Rather, one should look for an effective world work with a message to benefit all mankind. Christ's own caution, "By their fruits shall ye know them," is the proper criterion.

CHRIST AND JESUS

Esoteric writings,[9] including the Rosicrucian writings of Max Heindel, Theosophical works, and the books by Alice Bailey, hold that in the life and person of Jesus Christ two distinct and different individuals are involved. One of these is Jesus, an initiate of high spiritual development who was born in Bethlehem and grew to manhood. Then, it is stated, beginning at the time of Jesus' baptism by John, Jesus allowed his body to be used by the Christ, the Teacher of Angels and Men, who carried out his mission on earth in the relatively short time of the ministry of the central figure of the Gospels. It is interesting to note that the Virginia Beach "sleeping prophet" Edgar Cayce used the phrase "Jesus who became the Christ" in some of the trance readings where he referred to the events of the New Testament.

Mrs. Bailey's writings state that five events in the life of Jesus Christ— the Birth, Baptism, Transfiguration, Crucifixion, and Resurrection/Ascension—are symbolic of and bear the same names as five key events in the lives of a reincarnating human being. These events are major expansions of consciousness termed *initiations* that an individual earns and achieves as he progresses toward perfection. She claims that Christ referred to the first of these initiations when he spoke to Nicodemus of the need to be born again. A person who has successfully progressed through all five of these initiations is termed an *adept* or a *Master of the Wisdom*.

Geoffrey Hodson in his book *The Christ Life from Nativity to Ascension*[10] agrees that these events in the life of Jesus Christ depict the major initiations. These five major initiations were also a part the teachings of the Buddha and the great Hindu reformer Sri Shankaracharya.

Mrs. Bailey's writings also contend that Jesus achieved his fourth initiation during his incarnation in Palestine, his fifth in a later incarnation as Appolonius of Tyana, and that he now is a Master of the Wisdom working with other such individuals under the direction of the Christ for the benefit of mankind. Her books credit the Master Jesus with "overshadowing" the prophet Muhammad in the founding of the Islamic religion.

THE RELATIONSHIP OF JESUS TO GOD

We have seen earlier that while some Christians equate Jesus with God,* Muslims state that He is not identical with God,† but the Koran acknowledges that he is "the Messiah . . . illustrious in the world and . . . brought near unto Allah."[11] The view held by esotericists seems to provide some reconciliation of these two apparently conflicting beliefs. First, as we have just noted, from the esoteric viewpoint we should talk in terms

---

*This doctrine was first promulgated as a result of the Council of Nicaea in A.D. 325, where the emperor Constantine settled a major disagreement on this issue, there being bishops but no pope as such at the time. The bishop of Rome did not attend the Council.

†Mary Baker Eddy, the founder of Christian Science, also made a similar point when she wrote, "Jesus Christ is not God, as Jesus himself declared, but is the Son of God. This declaration of Jesus, understood, conflicts not at all with another of his sayings: 'I and my Father are one,'—that is, one in quality, not in quantity. As a drop of water is one with the ocean, a ray of light one with the sun, even so God and man, Father and son, are one in being. The Scripture reads: 'For in Him we live, and move, and have our being' " (*Science and Health with Key to the Scriptures*, p. 238).

of Christ and not Jesus in this connection. The esotericists further maintain that we are all a part of God, but more specifically that Christ is today the highest representation of the second aspect of God involved with taking incarnation in human form and directly guiding human evolution. He is, they claim, the head of the spiritual Hierarchy of our planet. As such, Christ has evolved to the point where his consciousness is absorbed in what we term God to the extent that He is able to faithfully represent and reflect God on earth. Considering mankind's point in evolution and ability to comprehend, and considering Christ's assigned role, then for all practical purposes, if we hear the words of Christ, we hear the words of God—or more specifically of the Son, the second aspect of God, or Vishnu in Hindu terms.

Literally, however, the esotericist would acknowledge that the Koran is correct in its assertion and in its comment that Jesus never himself made the claim to be God.

9. Symbolic Writing and Allegory

It is important for those who read and study the scriptures of the great world religions to know that many passages are believed to be subject to various levels of interpretation as knowledge and intuitive insight are expanded. In this way a richer and deeper message may be veiled by the outer and more obvious interpretation of the written words. In the *Hadith*, Muhammad states that "the Koran was sent down in seven dialects, and in every one of its sentences there is an outer and an inner meaning." In the Koran itself we read, "He it is who hath revealed unto thee [Muhammad] the scripture wherein are clear revelations—they are the substance of the Book—and others [which are] allegorical."

Saint Paul indicates the use of allegory in the books attributed to Moses (the Torah) when he writes:

> It is written that Abraham had two sons, the one by a bondmaid, the other by a freewoman. But he who was of the bondwoman was born after the flesh; but he of the freewoman was by promise. Which things are an allegory. (Gal. 4:22–24)

The Book of Daniel in the Bible gives examples of the interpretation of symbols, and the Book of Revelation is full of symbols, some of which will be discussed later in this chapter.

What is factual, literal history and what is allegory in scripture is a point that has been discussed and argued by theologians and thinkers over the years. In some cases it may not be unreasonable to assume that certain scriptures can be both factual events and at the same time have a symbolic meaning, for "with God all things are possible." In the preceding chapter the story of the man carrying a jar of water and the possible hidden meaning behind five key events in the life of Christ (birth, baptism, transfiguration, crucifixion, and resurrection/ascension) present cases where historical events might also have a symbolic meaning.

Mahatma Gandhi held that the battle of Kurukshetra mentioned in the Bhagavad Gita is an allegory. Others similarly believe that this battle and

156

the Armageddon in the Bible are symbolic of the battle that must take place in the evolution of man between the higher and lower natures. Geoffrey Hodson[1] quotes Rabbi Moses Maimonides, the great Jewish theologian, who wrote:

> Every time you find in our books a tale the reality of which is repugnant to both reason and common sense, then be sure that the tale contains a profound allegory veiling a deeply mysterious truth; and the greater the absurdity of the letter, the deeper the wisdom of the spirit.

Christ states that some knowledge is purposely not openly revealed. Completing a parable with the injunction, "He that hath ears to hear, let him hear," he goes on to say privately to his disciples:

> Unto you it is given to know the mysteries of the kingdom of God: but to others in parables; that seeing they might not see, and hearing they might not understand. (Luke 8:8–10)

Elsewhere Christ comments on the reason for this secrecy:

> Give not that which is holy unto the dogs, neither cast ye your pearls before swine, lest they trample them under their feet and turn again and rend you. (Matt. 7:6)

Certain knowledge can be destructive in the hands of those who are morally unprepared—destructive to self as well as to others, as we shall see later in the discussion of the Book of Revelation.

In *The Secret Doctrine*, H. P. Blavatsky claims that there are indeed seven keys that must be used to fully understand certain important passages of scripture, thus shedding light on the statement by Muhammad quoted earlier in this chapter. Geoffrey Hodson in his multivolume *Hidden Wisdom in the Holy Bible* provides his view of some of these keys. One of these, which relates to the universal symbolic meaning of certain objects and words to those who hold the key, is also discussed by Max Freedom Long in his books *The Huna Code in Religions* and *What Jesus Taught in Secret*. Long came upon his symbolic interpretation through study of the Kahunas, who were seers and magicians among the Hawaiian people. He interprets certain Bible passages using symbolic meanings for objects mentioned.

In *The Cipher of Genesis*[2] Carlos Suares interprets certain passages in Genesis through the Kabbalistic letter/number code of the Hebrew alphabet, providing a cosmic view of the Creation story which fits far better with some of today's scientific theories than the story as interpreted literally.

Hodson believes that the seven keys are allegorically referred to in the Bible story of the fiery furnace (Dan. 3:19), which had to be heated "seven times more than it was wont to be heated" before Shadrach, Meshach, and Abednego were joined by a fourth "like the Son of God," and in the story of the walls of Jericho (Josh. 6), which had to be walked around seven times on the seventh day before they fell down.

It is interesting to note in view of the hidden significance of the number seven, indicated by the esotericists (e.g. seven planes of the solar system, seven rays, seven sacred planets), that this is the most prominent number in the Bible, appearing in almost 600 passages.

In the remainder of this chapter some of the symbolism said to be contained in sacred writing is overviewed so that the significance of this factor in fully understanding scripture may be evaluated. The area of symbology is one in which we again discover more underlying unity between the teachings of different faiths as we begin to probe deeper.

THE PRODIGAL SON

The story of the Prodigal Son as told by Jesus Christ (Luke 15:11–32) appears in slightly altered form in the Old Testament, in other religions, and in the mythology of many lands.

The parable concerns a man who had two sons. The younger asked for his portion of the family's goods and took them into a "far country" where he "wasted his substance with riotous living." Then a famine came over the land and he, being in want, went and "joined himself to a citizen of that country" who "sent him into his fields to feed swine. And he would fain have filled his belly with the husks that the swine did eat: and no man gave unto him."

Being hungry, he comes "to himself" and decides to "arise," return home, and throw himself on his father's mercy.

> When he was yet a great way off, his father saw him, and had compassion, and ran and fell on his neck and kissed him.
> And his son said unto him, Father, I have sinned against heaven, and in thy sight, and am no more worthy to be called thy son.
> But the father said to his servants, Bring forth the best robe, and put it on him, and put a ring on his hand, and shoes on his feet;
> And bring hither the fatted calf, and kill it; and let us eat and be merry:
> For this my son was dead, and is alive again, he was lost and is found.

In addition to the obvious outward lesson of life taught by this parable, the esotericists claim that the basic story can be interpreted with several levels of hidden meaning relating to the cycles of forthgoing and return (involution and evolution) associated with the universe, the solar system, and man in his various aspects. The correspondence between universal and human characteristics was stated by Lao-tzu, who wrote, "The universe is man on a large scale," and by Moses, who stated that man is created in the image of God.

From the point of view of the human being, the story can be related to each cycle of incarnation as the man descends from the superphysical worlds to the "far country" of physical-plane existence and back again. More useful from a teaching point of view, however, is its application to the longer cycle of a series of lifetimes wherein man has descended deeper and deeper into matter on the involutionary cycle. It is then necessary for him to come "to himself" (face reality) and realize that his place is not among the husks of the material world. He "hungers" for the things of the spirit and "arises" to go to his father's house. The father can be viewed as the man's spiritual nature, which, according to esoteric teaching, literally does move out to help close the gap between the lower and higher natures as the "son" approaches the "father's house."

Commenting on the status of humanity in general today, "the Tibetan," through the writings of Alice Bailey, states that "The race is at a point where the prodigal son is conscious of the husks and of the futility of earthly life."[3] In another place,[4] with further reference to the story of the prodigal son, he says:

> When Christ was relating this story, He made it abundantly clear that there was no impulse to return until the pilgrim in the far country had come to himself or to his senses, as a result of satisfied desire, through riotous living. This was followed by consequent satiety and loss of contentment, and then by a period of intense suffering, which broke his will to wander or to desire. A study of this story will be found revealing. In no scripture is the sequence of events (as they deal with the pilgrim's existence and life in a far country and his return) so concisely or so beautifully treated. Seek out your Bibles, and study this tale, and read for yourselves the pilgrim's way.

One who has read this story and gleaned much from it is Geoffrey Hodson. He writes very extensively on its symbology and its significance, right down to the ring, the robe, and the fattened calf. He devotes more than forty pages in *Hidden Wisdom in the Holy Bible*, vol. 1, to this analysis and discusses it from the cosmic as well as the individual viewpoint.

Hodson also points out that the Bible story of Joseph being lowered into a pit in the earth (the densest matter) and sold into bondage conveys a similar, symbolic message. He also states that the story from Greek mythology of Persephone, who must descend to the underworld periodically, can be related to the periodically reincarnating human being who must continue this cyclic activity until the means of liberation is found. In the story of Persephone the rescuer and redeemer is Hermes, who enables her to escape. The symbolgy of the staff of Hermes, the caduceus, and its relation to this theme will be discussed shortly.

In Mahayana Buddhism we also find a parable of "The Prodigal Son and the Seeking Father." This story, to be found in *Teachings of the Compassionate Buddha*, by E. A. Burtt, begins as follows:

It is like a youth who, on attaining manhood, leaves his father and runs away. For long he dwells in some other country, ten, twenty, or fifty years. The older he grows, the more needy he becomes. Roaming about in all directions to seek clothing and food, he gradually wanders along till he unexpectedly approaches his native country.

The story is longer and somewhat more involved than the New Testament story, but the final outcome is the same.

Another story from Greek mythology that is particularly appropriate to this theme is that of Theseus, who is sent out by the king into the labyrinth of Crete. Ariadne gave Theseus a ball of golden thread, which he unwound as he moved into the dark maze. After slaying the Minotaur at the center of the maze, Theseus is able to find his way out by following the golden thread.

Natalie N. Banks[5] gives the following symbolic correspondence:

The King	Spirit
Ariadne	Soul
Thesus	Personality
The Minotaur	Ignorance, Greed, and Selfishness
Labyrinth (its center)	The darkest stage of the descent
The Golden Thread	The Teachings of the Ageless Wisdom

A second level of interpretation seems susceptible of application to the symbol of the golden thread in this story. According to esoteric teaching, there exists a "golden thread" connecting the personality with the higher spiritual nature. This thread or stream of energy is presumably visible to those with sight at the higher levels and is in a sense a path that must be followed as a man progresses toward spiritual awakening. This brings us to another symbolic term commonly used in world scriptures.

THE PATH OR THE WAY

Scripture references to the Path or Way from four religions are found in chapter 2. The Hindus refer to it as "Like the sharp edge of a razor, narrow and difficult to tread." Similarly, Christ speaks of the wide gate and broad way that leads to destruction, contrasted with the narrow gate and close way that leads to life. The Buddha speaks of the "Noble Middle Path," which "produces insight and knowledge, and tends to calm, to higher knowledge, enlightenment, Nirvana." Lao-tzu similarly speaks of avoiding excess and walking carefully along the middle road.

Lao-tzu also likens the way to a river: "Those who are on the Way might be compared to rivulets flowing into the sea." Similarly, in the Mundaka Upanishad we read: "As rivers flow into the sea and in so doing lose name and form, even so the wise man, freed from name and form, attains the Supreme Being, the Self-Luminous, the Infinite." These quotations bring to mind a verse from the Psalms: "There is a river, the streams whereof shall make glad the city of God, the holy place of the tabernacle of the most high" (Ps. 46:4).*

In the thirty-fifth chapter of Isaiah the following verses are found:

> And an highway shall be there, and a way, and it shall be called The Way of Holiness; the unclean shall not pass over it; but it shall be for those: the *way*faring men, though fools, shall not err therein. No lion shall be there, nor any ravenous beast shall go up thereon, it shall not be found there; but the redeemed shall walk there. (vv. 8, 9)

The esotericists refer to an ancient aphorism that "Before a man can tread the Path he must become that Path himself." This statement, as well as those quoted above from scripture, are said to have outer and inner significance. Outwardly a man (or woman) lives a life dedicated to serving his fellow man and working toward world betterment. He maintains a pure motive, a spiritual outlook, and strives toward the heights, avoiding fanatical and unreasoned extremes, and he can be said to be treading the Path. Inwardly he works to create a path that enables a flow of energy from his spiritual nature to his personality—a Path that provides him consciousness of higher knowlege. This inner path he builds out of himself, and thus he becomes the path. Success in this endeavor results in the true intuitive thinker, who brings down the ideas that change the world and an attitude of goodwill that encourages their proper application. Treading the path has been defined as "self-conscious participation by man in the fulfillment of nature's plan."[6]

THE STRAIGHT OR MIDDLE PATH AND THE SPINAL CHANNELS

In the fortieth chapter of Isaiah there appear the well-known words:

> The voice of him that crieth in the wilderness, Prepare ye the way of the Lord, make straight in the desert a highway for our God. Every valley shall be exalted, and every mountain and hill shall be made low: and the crooked shall be made straight, and the rough places plain. And the glory of the Lord shall be revealed. (vv. 3–5)

Similar words are found in the Tao Te Ching:

> The sayings of old men is not in vain
> "The crooked shall be made straight"
> To be perfect return to it. (22)

The beginning of the quotation from Isaiah was, of course, used by John the Baptist in describing his mission. However, the similarity of the rest of the passage to the words of Lao-tzu suggests that there might be some other veiled meaning.

---

*As pointed out later in this chapter, the city of God in Hindu scripture and in symbolic interpretation refers to man.

It has been stated that wilderness and deserts symbolically "refer to those states of spiritual aridity to which all mystics bear testimony" as contrasted to the "Promised Land" of spiritual fruitfulness.[7]

With this as background, let us consider the possible correspondence between the passage in Isaiah and a description of a stage of spiritual advancement given by Alice Bailey,[8] in which she discusses "the period wherein the aspirant struggles to achieve that inner quiet and directed attentiveness which will enable him to hear the Voice of the Silence. That voice expresses to him through symbol and interpreted life experience the purposes and plans with which he may cooperate." This is followed by a "period wherein he habituates himself to the clear hearing and correct interpretation of the inner voice of the soul." During this period there is a constant flow of force between the soul and the human form along the thread of energy called the *sutratma*, which sets up a vibratory response between the brain and the soul.

> The reflection of the sutratma in the human organism is called the spinal cord and expresses itself in three nerve channels. These three are called the ida, pingala, and the central channel, the sushumna. When the negative and positive forces of the body, which express themselves via the ida and pingala nerve routes, are equilibrized, the forces can ascend and descend by the central channel to and from the brain, passing through the centers up the spine without hindrance. When this is the case we have perfected soul expression in the physical man. . . . Let him find the "noble middle path" between the pairs of opposites, and incidentally he will find that the forces he uses on the physical plane will employ the central nerve channel up the spine.

These nerve channels up the spine along with the force centers are shown in the picture of a person in meditation as found in many books (Fig. 8). As can be seen, the ida and pingala are crooked and twisting, while the sushumna is straight. A comparison of Figure 8 with the caduceus, the staff of Hermes (or Mercury) used as an emblem by the medical profession (Fig. 9), shows a clear symbolical resemblance.

Mrs. Bailey comments further that:

> Those ideas and concepts (speaking in symbol) which come via the sutratmic negative channel are well meaning, but lack force and peter out into insignificance. They are emotionally coloured, and lack the organized form which pure mind can give. Those which come via the opposite channel (speaking figuratively) produce too rapid concretion, and are motivated by the personal ambition of a ruling mentality. The mind is ever egoistic, self-seeking, and expresses that personal ambition which carries within it the germ of its own destruction.
>
> When, however, the sutratmic sushumna, the central nerve channel and its energy is employed, the soul, as a magnetic intelligent creator, transmits its energies. The plans can then mature according to divine purpose.

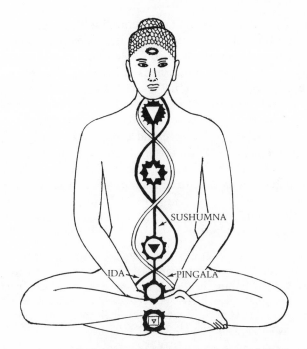

Fig. 8. Symbolic Representation of Spinal Force
Centers and Nerve Channels

Fig. 9. The Caduceus

Acknowledging that there can be several levels of meaning to the symbolic words of Isaiah, one possible interpretation is obvious from the foregoing. The still small voice of the soul is detected by the aspirant in the midst of the spiritually arid wilderness or desert. The term *wilderness* is perhaps as appropriate to modern life as it was in the time of Isaiah. As the aspirant balances the negative and positive forces in the body (which may be viewed in Isaiah's terms as exalting the valleys and making low the mountains) and responds more and more to his soul urge, an energy flow is set up along the straight path (or highway), the central sushumna, contrasted with the crooked ida and pingala. Eventually "the glory of the Lord" is revealed, as the man functions under control of his soul on the physical plane.

The symbology of the previously mentioned caduceus is commented on as follows by Geoffrey Hodson:

> The Caduceus has another meaning [beyond the "serpentine triple creative power in man"]. The two serpents represent also the pairs of opposites, such as success and failure, heat and cold, pleasure and pain, happiness and despair. . . . Before the soul can be perfected and fully liberated it must have become equipoised in consciousness between all the pairs, being equally indifferent to either of their components.

This comment perhaps sheds light on a further meaning of the Noble Middle Path of the Buddha.

The appropriateness of the serpent figures in the caduceus is made clear in the following by Manly P. Hall:

> All symbols having serpentine form symbolize solar energy in one of its many forms . . . the divine energy coursing through the body of man . . . until transmuted . . . manifests itself as a writhing, twisting monster—man's greeds, passions and lusts.[9]

Esotericists have also interpreted the caduceus as symbolically describing the involutionary descent of man from the spiritual realms into matter and the subsequent evolutionary ascent out of matter with the knowledge and development gained therefrom. The paths traced by the two serpents represent the involutionary and evolutionary spirals. The man who is spiritually oriented can choose to step off the evolutionary spiral and follow the straight and narrow way up the center shaft, thus taking his evolution in hand.

In the case of most symbols and symbolic writing, that which applies to man the microcosm also has macrocosmic significance. The Hermetic axiom "As above so below" applies. Thus it is with the caduceus, which is discussed as follows in *The Secret Doctrine*,[10] which quotes a "commentary in the esoteric doctrine":

The trunk of the Asvattha (the tree of Life and Being, the rod of the caduceus) grows from and descends at every Beginning (every new manvantara) from the two dark wings of the Swan (Hansa) of Life. The two Serpents, the ever-living and its illusion (Spirit and matter) whose two heads grow from the one head between the wings, descend along the trunk, interlaced in close embrace. The two tails join on earth (the manifested Universe) into one, and this is the great illusion.

Madame Blavatsky goes on to explain that the original symbol, modified by the Greeks, had three serpent heads.

The word *manvantara* is the Hindu term for a cycle of manifestation or creation. The Asvattha tree is described in the Bhagavad Gita and also as follows in the Katha Upanishad:

> This universe is a tree eternally existing, its root aloft, its branches spread below. The pure root of the tree is Brahman, the immortal, in whom the three worlds have their being, whom none can transcend, who is verily the Self.

The Bible also makes reference to the Tree of Life in Genesis 3:22 and the twenty-second chapter of Revelation, while in Zoroastrianism Ahura Mazda is said to have planted the sacred Tree of Life called Haoma.

In the Kabbalah of Jewish mysticism the Tree of Life is associated with the Sefiroth, which emanate from the root cause of creation, En-Sof, and can be considered to be the basis of manifestation. As noted earlier, the ten Sefiroth can be related to the three persons of God together with the seven spirits before the throne in Christianity. Charles Poncé[11] suggests a correspondence between the Sefiroth on a macrocosmic level and the microcosmic ida, pingala, and sushumna along with the force centers up the spine.

Referring to Figure 10 showing the Sefirothic Tree of the Kabbalists, Poncé relates the three Sefiroth on the right side to the pingala channel, noting that the Kabbalists relate Hokhmah (or Cochma) to the sun, which is the same relationship drawn for pingala. The left channel headed by Binah is related to the moon* along with the ida channel. The central channel, of course, corresponds to the sushumna; the crown chakra at the top of the head relates to the Kether (Crown) Sephirah, and the Malkuth Sephirah corresponds to the center at the base of the spine.

THE BOOK OF REVELATION—THE APOCALYPSE

This last book of the New Testament leaves most readers of the Bible aware that they are looking at a work with profound symbolic significance that they are unable to fully comprehend. Manly P. Hall comments that

---

*Thus the right and left channels are opposites, e.g. light and dark, spirit and matter, etc.

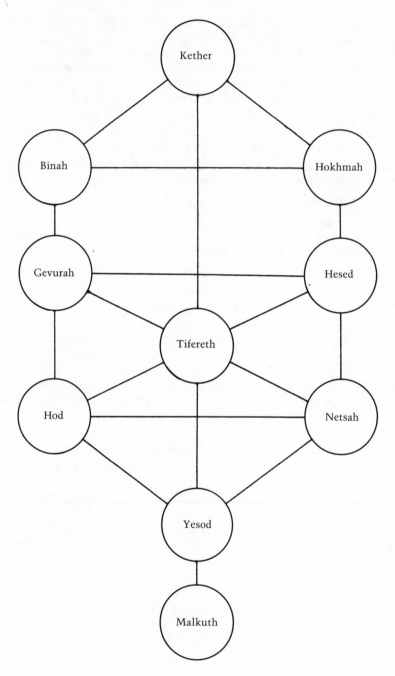

Fig. 10. The Sefiroth

"the intrinsic value of the book lies in its magnificent epitome of the Universal Mystery—an observation which led St. Jerome to declare that it is susceptible of seven entirely different interpretations."[12] James M. Pryse, who has investigated this book in depth and has written a well-studied and logical interpretation, calls it " one of the most stupendous allegories ever penned by the hand of man."

As mentioned earlier, Pryse's analysis of the symbolic writing in the Apocalypse is recorded in his remarkable book completed in 1910 and entitled, *The Apocalypse Unsealed*.[13] As we shall see, his interpretations correlate very well with those obtained during trance readings by Edgar Cayce, the "Sleeping Prophet" of Virginia Beach, whose readings on this subject are brought together in the previously referenced compilation entitled *Revelation: A Commentary on the Book*.

Pryse summarizes the hidden theme of the Apocalypse as the "process of transcendental self-conquest, the giving birth to oneself as a spiritual being, evolving from the concealed essence of one's own embryonic nature or self-luminous immortal body." Similarly, Cayce comments that "the visions, the experiences, the names, the churches, the places, the dragons, the cities, all are but emblems of those forces that may war within the individual in its journey through the material, or from the entering into the material manifestation to the entering into the glory, or the awakening in the spirit."[14]

H. P. Blavatsky comments as follows on the Book of Revelation: "The fact is, that no less than the book of Job, the whole of Revelation is simply an allegorical narrative of the Mysteries and initiation therein of a candidate, who is John himself. . . . Paracelsus maintained the same some centuries ago."[15]

Pryse agrees that the Apocalypse is an account of the initiation of John himself and adds:

> Many actors apparently play their parts in the drama of the Apocalypse; yet in reality there is but one performer—the neophyte himself . . . who awakens all the slumbering forces of his inner nature, passes through the terrible ordeals of the purificatory discipline and the telestic labors, and finally emerges as the Conqueror, the self-perfected Man who has regained his standing among the deathless Gods.[16]

John addresses his "Revelation" to the "seven churches which are in Asia" and directs a message received when he was "in the Spirit" to each church, closing each message with the familiar sign of a hidden meaning: "He that hath an ear, let him hear."

Both Pryse and Cayce agree that these churches represent the seven major ductless glands or the seven major nerve centers (ganglia) in the sympathetic nervous system of man. These glands and ganglia are associated in turn with seven major force centers in man's subtle bodies as discussed earlier in the chapter on the esotericists. These force centers, whose approximate positions are shown in Figure 8, are mentioned in the Upanishads, where they are called *chakras* (wheels) because they appear to those with clairvoyant sight as wheel-like vortices.

Pryse provides explanations too detailed to be repeated here for his identification of each of the seven Asian cities (mentioned by John as the site of the "churches") with its respective chakra. The matching up is based on statements made in the Bible verses, the known characteristics of the chakra, and major features known to be located in the cities named.

Manly P. Hall concurs in the symbolic significance of the churches, writing as follows:

> When related to the Eastern system of metaphysics, these churches represent the chakras or nerve ganglia, along the human spine, the "door in heaven" being the brahmarandra, or point in the crown of the skull (Golgotha) through which the spinal spirit fire passes to liberation. The church of Ephesus corresponds to the muladhara, or sacral ganglion, and the other churches to the higher ganglia according to the order given in Revelation.[17]

John writes later of a book written "within and on the backside" and sealed with seven seals. Both Pryse and Cayce again agree that these seals also refer to the seven cerebro-spinal force centers, the phrase *within and on the backside* referring to the location of the spine. The symbology of seals in Revelation 5 through 8 is quite appropriate beause the subject matter is the opening or energizing of these force centers.

This perhaps requires a bit of explanation. In the undeveloped person these force centers are relatively inactive. As a man or woman evolves, various of these centers become active or they are "opened," and in the perfected, spiritually evolved individual the centers come into full functioning activity. The centers are said to be formed of streams of force from the soul, which in turn responds to higher levels. Their main functions are:

> First, to vitalize the physical body.
> Second, to bring about the development of self-consciousness in man.
> Third, to transmit spiritual energy and sweep the entire man into a state of spiritual being.[18]

Mentioned in the Upanishads and in many esoteric books is a force that is said to lie coiled up at the base of the spine in man. This force is termed Kundalini, the "Serpent Fire." Toward the end of man's cycle of development it is raised up by an act of the spiritual will (consciously or unconsciously as far as the brain is concerned) through the three spinal channels pictured in Figure 8. The portion ascending via the sushumna passes through each of the spinal centers in turn and ultimately exits through the top of the head. When all this is accomplished, a state of high spiritual consciousness is possible.

One of the reasons for the symbolic writing used in the Book of Revelation is brought out in the following comment on energizing the force centers:

> The whole subject of the centers is dangerous if misunderstood; the centers constitute a menace when prematurely awakened, or unduly energized, and this entire subject can prove most dangerous to the curiosity-impelled man and to the ignorant experimenter.[19]

What then, is the safe method of unfolding these centers? The following, from the writings of Alice Bailey, provides an answer:

> Let a man apply himself to a life of high altruism, to a discipline that will refine and bring his lower vehicles into subjection, and to a strenuous endeavour to purify and control his sheaths. When he has done this and has both raised and stabilized his vibration, he will find that the development and functioning of the centers has pursued a parallel course, and that . . . the work has proceeded along the desired lines. Much danger and dire calamity attends the man who arouses these centers by unlawful methods, and who experiments with the fires of the body without the needed technical knowledge. He may, by his efforts, succeed in raising the fires and in intensifying the action of the centers, but he will pay the price of ignorance in the destruction of matter, in the burning of bodily or brain tissue, in the development of insanity, and in opening the door to currents and forces undesirable and destructive.[20]

Mrs. Bailey comments further:[21]

> If the aspirant but seeks spiritual development, if he but aims at sincerity of purpose, and at compassionate altruism, if he with serene application concentrates on the subjugation of the emotional body, and the enlargement of the mental, and cultivates the habit of abstract thinking, the desired results upon the centers will be produced from necessity, and danger will be eliminated.

These warnings relative to the centers and the premature arousing of Kundalini are also put forth by other esoteric writers and by Cayce and Pryse. Cayce says, "Do not attempt to open any of the centers of the book until self has been tried in the balance of self's own conscious relationship to the Creative Forces and not found wanting by the spiritual answer in self."

The Apocalypse states that only the "Lamb that was slain" is worthy to open the seals. Pryse interprets this as follows: "The sacrificial Lamb, the neophyte who has attained to the intuitive, noetic consciousness—which is symbolized by his having seven horns and seven eyes, that is, mental powers of action and perception—opens the seals (arouses the chakras) successively."[22]

Pryse points out that in Sanskrit works correspondences between the chakras and the planets of the solar system are given, beginning with muladhara at the base of the spine, which corresponds to Saturn, and progressing in order through Jupiter, Mars, Venus, Mercury, and the Sun. Each of these planets has a corresponding zodiacal sign, beginning with Capricorn, which corresponds to (or in astrological terms is "ruled by") Saturn, and then in the same order: Sagittarius, Scorpio, Libra, Virgo, Cancer, and Leo.

The first seal that is opened by the Lamb reveals "a white horse: and he that sat on him had a bow" (Rev. 6:2). This is the familiar symbol for the astrological sign Sagittarius. Pryse points out that John avoids calling this the first seal but uses the phrase "one of the seals," and that the Kundalini current is rightly started at the second chakra, corresponding to Sagittarius, this being the origin of the ida and pingala channels. The sushumna channel, which starts at the first center, does not energize until ida and pingala reach the forehead.

The second seal to be opened reveals "another horse that was red: and power was given to him that sat thereon to take peace from the earth, and that they should kill one another: and there was given unto him a great sword" (Rev. 6:4). This is Mars the War-God, and the planet Mars is associated with the sign Scorpio. With the opening of the third seal John beheld "a black horse; and he that sat on him had a pair of balances in his hand" (Rev. 6:5). This, of course, represents the astrological sign Libra, the Balance.

Pryse goes on to associate each of the seals with a sign of the Zodiac and its corresponding chakra. He also relates some of the occurrences given in Revelation as the seals are opened to the effects of energizing various of the centers. For example, when the sixth seal is opened, "there was a great earthquake; and the sun became black . . . and the moon became as blood; and the stars of heaven fell unto the earth" (Rev. 6:12–13). Pryse relates the sixth seal to the muladhara chakra at the base of the spinal chord and says:

> When this chakra is awakened, the sushumna passes along the spinal cord and impinges on the brain. Words cannot adequately describe the sensations of the neophyte upon the first experience of the effect produced by this mighty power: it is as if the earth crumbled instantly to nothingness, and sun, moon and stars were swept from the sky, so that he suddenly found himself to be an unbodied soul above in the black abyss of empty space.

As the seventh seal is opened, "there was silence in heaven about the space of half an hour" (Rev. 8:1). Commenting on this last chakra to be opened (the head center), Pryse says, "Here reigns the mystic Silence."

As further concurrence in the idea that one theme of the Book of Revelation is the human force centers and their awakening, Alice Bailey provides an interpretation of the one hundred forty-four thousand from the seventh and fourteenth chapters of Revelation.

The force centers when energized display what have been termed *petals*, because the circular chakras appear divided to the sight of the clairvoyant, similar to the petals in a flower.[23] The table below lists the number of petals in each center.

1.	Base of the spine	4 petals
2.	Sacral center	6 petals
3.	Solar plexus center	10 petals
4.	Heart center	12 petals
5.	Throat center	16 petals
6.	Center between the eyebrows	96 petals divided into 2 major petals
7.	Head center	1000 petals

Mrs. Bailey points out that if the number of petals in the first six centers are added together, "the number one hundred and forty-four appears. . . . To these figures, one hundred and forty-four, add that of the number one thousand (the number of petals in the lotus of the head center) and you have the number of the saved in the Book of Revelation, the one hundred forty-four thousand who can stand before God. . . . When man has completed within himself the great work, when the number one hundred forty-four thousand is seen as symbolizing his point of attainment, then he can stand before God."[24]

The Apocalypse has many more symbols than we are able to discuss here. Pryse in his book provides an interpretation of most of them, which weaves a coherent picture of some of the steps in the development of a highly evolved individual.

Many Christians have attributed a prophetic character to the Book of Revelation. The question arises in the light of the interpretations given by Pryse (which do not mention prophecy), is there anything prophetic about the book relative to world events? In considering this, the comment of Saint Jerome concerning many levels of interpretation must be taken into account.

The Tibetan who wrote through Alice Bailey made the statement in his writings that the Beast of the Apocalypse has already appeared on earth, thus indicating that he views the book as prophetic. The fact that he also views it symbolically is clear from his interpretation of the one hundred forty-four thousand mentioned earlier and his indication that "the city that lieth four-square" in chapter 21 of Revelation refers to man.[25] (This is similar to the Upanishads, which refer to the body as the city of Brahman.)

The Tibetan states that the beast of the Apocalypse was none other than

Adolph Hitler. He states further that Hitler and some of his close associates were controlled, through possession, by representatives of the Dark Forces, or Forces of Evil associated with our planet. These black adepts are a materialistic correspondence to the planetary Hierarchy mentioned in the chapter on the esotericists. Hitler and his group (including Tojo of Japan) opened themselves to this control through their already existing ambitions and sadistic inclinations.

This view is independently expressed by Trevor Ravenscroft, the author of *The Spear of Destiny*.[26] This book, the author indicates, should have been written by Dr. Walter Johannes Stein, who gathered much of the material. Dr. Stein was a Vienna-born scientist and esotericist who acted as a confidential advisor to Sir Winston Churchill on Hitler and the leading Nazis during World War II. Stein knew Hitler even before he rose to power and was aware of the influence of practices that might be termed "black magic" involved in his development. Dr. Stein fled Germany when Heinrich Himmler ordered his arrest in 1933.

Ravenscroft refers to "the Apocalyptic Beast possessing the demented ex-corporal"[27] and unfolds a story which shows that Hitler knowingly and willingly used illicit means to prematurely energize certain of the force centers mentioned earlier. He was aided in this by certain individuals who were knowledgeable in these areas and were motivated by evil intent. One of these, Dietrich Eckart, one of the seven founders of the Nazi Party and also a dedicated satanist, commented on his deathbed in 1923: "Follow Hitler! He will dance, but it is I who have called the tune! I have . . . opened his centers in vision and given him the means to communicate with the Powers. Do not mourn for me: I shall have influenced history more than any other German."[28]

Ravenscroft also states that Hitler and other Nazis were possessed by evil forces. He further indicates that "in both public and private lectures"[29] the esotericist Dr. Rudolph Steiner (who is mentioned in ch. 6) had indicated the nature of the demonic spirit inhabiting Adolf Hitler and inspiring the Nazi party. Dietrich Eckart felt that Dr. Steiner was a threat to the party, believing their hidden activities could not be kept from his clairvoyant powers. Steiner was also openly engaged in warning Germany of the secret aims of the Nazi party. Therefore Eckart organized an attempt on Steiner's life in Munich. Steiner, however, escaped to Switzerland, having been warned by Walter Johannes Stein, who had learned of the plot by infiltrating a group behind the Nazi party.

THE BELOVED

A symbolic term used to describe the inner spiritual self by mystics through the ages is "the Beloved." It has appeared in prose and poetry, veiling the true meaning with this romantic term. The term is also found in scripture, and in this passage from the Upanishads the symbolic meaning becomes quite clear:

> Do we wish for our beloved, among the living or among the dead, or is there aught else for which we long, yet for all our longing do not obtain? Lo, all shall be ours if we but dive deep within, even to the lotus of the heart, where dwells the Lord. Yea, the object of every right desire is within our reach, though unseen, concealed by a veil of illusion.
>
> As one not knowing that a golden treasure lies buried beneath his feet, may walk over it again and again, yet never find it, so all beings live every moment in the city of Brahman, yet never find him, because of the veil of illusion by which he is concealed.[30]

We find a similar sense expressed in a passage from Buddhism:

> Passion is overcome only by him who has won through stillness of spirit the perfect vision. Knowing this, I must first seek for stillness; it comes through the contentment that is regardless of the world. What creature of a day should cling to other frail beings, when he can never again through thousands of births behold his beloved?[31]

In the Song of Solomon (Song of Songs) from the Old Testament, however, the meaning is more obscure:

> My beloved is like a roe or a young hart; behold, he standeth behind our wall, he looketh forth at the windows, showing himself through the lattice. . . .
>
> O my dove that is in the clefts of the rock, in the secret places of the stairs, let me see thy countenance, let me hear thy voice. (2:9, 14)

The Song of Solomon has always appeared to be something of an enigma as a book of scripture. Gershom Scholem provides a view that may help explain the book:

> According to the testimony of Origen (third century), it was not permitted to study the Song of Songs in Jewish circles before the age of full maturity, obviously because of esoteric teachings like the Shi'ur Komah which were connected with it. The Midrashim on the Song of Songs reflect such esoteric understanding in many passages.[32]

In this chapter we have only scratched the surface of this vast subject of symbology and allegory. The intent is simply to provide an appreciation for the possibilities of greater depths of significance than that those disclosed by a casual reading of the scriptures of the world.

PART II

SCIENCE AND RELIGION

10. Differences and Their Resolution

The centuries leading up to our modern era have brought increased focusing of attention on the secrets of the physical world, culminating in a remarkable expansion of scientific and technical knowledge during the last 200 years. The increase of scientific knowledge has often resulted in science and religion appearing to be at odds, with the fixed dogmatic ideas of some religious spokesman being challenged by the hypotheses and discoveries of science, and with some scientists refusing seriously to consider anything beyond what could be seen, touched, or measured.

Early encounters in this battle were hard on scientists, as in the well-known case of Galileo. He was tried by the Church and sentenced to indefinite imprisonment (which was modified to house arrest) for upholding the theory of Copernicus—that the earth moves around the sun. Copernicus' work was placed on the Index of Prohibited Books and remained there for 200 years.

Perhaps Copernicus would have fared better if he had lived in India. Copernicus was challenging the theory of a nonrotating earth that was fixed in space. Everything else—sun, planets, and stars—was believed to rotate around the central earth. Long before Copernicus' time, Sri Krishna recognized the rotation of the earth. In the Bhagavad Gita are the words "thus the revolutions of the world go round."

Giordano Bruno, another follower of the theories of Copernicus, was dealt with even more severely. He went beyond Copernicus, stating his belief that space was boundless and that there were other systems similar to the sun and its planets, speculating also that there might be other inhabited worlds. Bruno was tried by the Inquisition and burned at the stake in 1600.

Even in fairly recent times the work of scientists has sometimes brought comments of concern from churchmen. Following Einstein's disclosure of his theory of relativity, Boston's Cardinal O'Connell stated that relativity was "cloaked in the ghastly apparition of atheism." Einstein, for his part, like many of the greatest contributors to science, was not an atheist but held a belief based on understanding, which he expressed as follows: "Everyone who is seriously involved in the pursuit of science becomes convinced that a spirit is manifest in the laws of the Universe—a spirit vastly superior to that of man, and one in the face of which we with our modest powers must feel humble."[1]

Taking a broad look at events in the nineteenth and twentieth centuries, it may be concluded that religion is losing ground in the debate with science as more and more scientific views are accepted, at least in part, by a large segment of the public. Religious fundamentalists have great difficulty logically maintaining that the letter of the scriptures is correct when Carbon 14 and other dating techniques show the age of man and the world to be much greater than a literal interpretation of the Bible would claim.

The dilemma faced by some Christians and Jews in relating biblical accounts to the discoveries of science may be resolved when the possibility that some scriptural writing is symbolic or allegorical is taken into account. Blavatsky, for example, states that "Those who based history on Jewish chronology . . . would lose themselves, for the Jewish account could only be followed through Kabbalistic computation, and with a key to it in the hand."[2] She also claims that "It was a 'day of Brahma' that the Kabbalistic author of Genesis had in mind each time when he said: 'And the evening and the morning were the first [or fifth or sixth, or any other] day.' "[3] A day of Brahma is said to be 4,320,000,000 earth years.[4]

An interesting contribution toward the challenge of correlating scientific and religious views comes from the director of NASA's Goddard Institute for Space Studies, Dr. Robert Jastrow, who has written a book entitled *God and the Astronomer*.[5] Dr. Jastrow states that "The astronomical evidence leads us to a biblical view of the origin of the world . . . the details differ, but the essential elements in the astronomical and biblical accounts of Genesis are the same."[6]

Physicist Fritjof Capra states that in a similar way the Hindu scriptures show close agreement with modern theories on the creation and dynamics of the universe. He writes:

> This idea of a periodically expanding and contracting universe, which involves a scale of time and space of vast proportions, has arisen not only in modern cosmology, but also in ancient Indian mythology. Experiencing the universe as a organic and rhythmically moving cosmos, the Hindus were able to develop evolutionary cosmologies which come very close to our modern scientific models. . . .
>
> The Hindu sages . . . gave the name kalpa to the unimaginable time span between the beginning and end of one creation. The scale of this ancient myth is indeed staggering; it has taken the human mind more than two thousand years to come up again with a similar concept.[7]

Astronomer Dr. Carl Sagan in the television series "Cosmos"[8] went to India to film a sequence where he points out the correlation between the cosmology of the Hindu scriptures and modern science's "Big Bang" theory of the beginning of the universe.

As we shall see later, relatively recent scientific discoveries have moved us significantly along the path of reconciling scientific and religious views and have placed us at the threshold of even deeper understanding. The opportunities presented for scientists to expand human knowledge in areas formerly considered the realm of the mystic have increased dramatically.

The words of physicist Max Planck set a theme for working toward enlightened understanding for the benefit of mankind:

> Religion and natural science are fighting a joint battle in a second never-ending crusade against skepticism and dogmatism, and against superstition. The rallying cry for their crusade has always been and always will be "on to God!"[9]

11. Modern Physics

This highly complex branch of science, which involves man's deepest penetration into the understanding of the physical world, is surpisingly an area where the ideas of scientific and religious thinkers seem to converge. This point has been effectively brought out in two separate studies. One was conducted by Austrian-born high-energy research physicist Fritjof Capra and documented in his book *The Tao of Physics.* The second was accomplished by psychologist Lawrence LeShan and is contained in his book *The Medium, the Mystic and the Physicist.*

Dr. Capra's book provides an excellent overview of some of the major theories and experimental determinations of modern physics, including relativity theory, quantum mechanics, and subatomic particle phenomena. He reviews the basic findings about the nature of existence uncovered by the leading members of his branch of science and goes on to show that many of these had been revealed much earlier by men of religion. Capra states it as follows:

> Eastern thought and, more generally, mystical thought provide a consistent and relevant philosophical background to the theories of contemporary science—a conception of the world in which man's scientific discoveries can be in perfect harmony with his spiritual aims and religious beliefs.[1]

Dr. Capra further makes clear that some of the pioneers of modern physics were not unaware of this common view. He quotes three of the most renowned modern physicists to illustrate their recognition of the similarity of views they developed in the pursuit of the secrets of nature, and the philosophical views of the great Eastern sages:

> The general notions about human understanding . . . which are illustrated by discoveries in atomic physics are not in the nature of things wholly unfamiliar, wholly unheard of, or new. Even in our own culture they have a history, and in Buddhist and Hindu thought a more considerable and central place. What we shall find is an exemplification, an encouragement, and a refinement of old wisdom.

> —J. Robert Oppenheimer

For a parallel to the lesson of atomic theory . . . [we must turn] to those kinds of epistemological problems with which already thinkers like the Buddha and Lao Tzu have been confronted, when trying to harmonize our position as spectators and actors in the great drama of existence.

—Niels Bohr

The great scientific contribution in theoretical physics that has come from Japan since the last war may be an indication of a certain relationship between philosophical ideas in the tradition of the Far East and the philosophical substance of quantum theory.

—Werner Heisenberg

In *The Medium, the Mystic and the Physicist,* LeShan reviews an extensive investigation he conducted in an attempt to better understand the mechanism of paranormal events such as telepathy, clairvoyance, and precognition. He worked with what he terms "serious sensitives who had a high frequency of paranormal events in their lives" and determined that at the point when these events were occurring, the sensitives "used a different metaphysical structure of the world than our ordinary everyday metaphysical structure."*

After analyzing their different picture of the world he realized that:

Two other groups of searchers into the meaning of things had reached identical conclusions: That there are two ways of being-in-the-world, our usual one and another, and what this other way is. These two other groups are the great Eastern and Western Mystics and the Einsteinian physicists.

Among the great Eastern and Western mystics LeShan lists Plotinus, Meister Eckhart, Richard Rolle, Isaac Luria, St. Richard of Victor, St. John of the Cross, St. Teresa of Avila, the Baal Shem Tov, George Fox, Evelyn Underhill; and from the East, the Lord Buddha, Shankara, Kabir, Dogen, Rumi, Vivekananda, and Ramakrishna.

LeShan also goes through a theoretical investigation of what happens to the "personality" at biological death in an appendix to his book and concludes—much to his surprise—"that conscious, personal survival was unquestionable if one applied to the problem the methods and standards of field theory in modern physics."

From his study of sensitives and mystics LeShan lists among the central aspects of what he terms the *Clairvoyant Reality*:

1. There is a central unity to all things. The most important aspect of a "thing" is its relationships, its part in the whole. Its individuality and separateness are secondary and/or illusory.
2. Pastness, presentness, and futurity are illusions we project onto the "seamless garment" of time. There is another valid view of time in which these separations do not exist.[2]

*From *The Medium, the Mystic and the Physicist.* Copyright © 1966, 1973, 1974 by Lawrence LeShan. This and other excerpts reprinted by permission of Viking Penguin, Inc.

Capra's studies as well as LeShan's show that both of these ideas are also included in the theories of modern physics.

Capra also states: "As we study the relativistic models and theories of modern physics, we shall see that all of them are impressive illustrations of the two basic elements of the Eastern world view—the basic oneness of the universe and its intrinsically dynamic character."

The above concepts and related themes will be reviewed in the following pages by comparing the statements of scientists and religious thinkers.

THE FUNDAMENTAL UNITY OF ALL THINGS

The idea that all things are interrelated and that there is a fundamental unity behind the different forms in the world of the senses is a recurrent theme in the Eastern religions. This concept is also expressed by serious mystics and esotericists and is suggested in the Bible description of God as "He in whom we live and move and have our being" and in the Kabbalistic concept of En-Sof, out of whom all creation is projected.

The modern physicist, exploring deeply into the world of matter, appears to have come to the same conclusion. Physicist Capra writes:

> The basic oneness of the universe is not only the central characteristic of the mystical experience, but is also one of the most important revelations of modern physics. It becomes apparent at the atomic level and manifests itself more and more as one penetrates deeper into matter, down into the realm of subatomic particles.[3]

It is interesting that esotericist Alice Bailey predicted that science would eventually come to this conclusion, stating "The unity of life will be a known and scientific fact."[4]

The concept of unity as stated by scientists and religious thinkers is illustrated by the following quotations:

FUNDAMENTAL UNITY

Science

In modern mechanics . . . it is impossible to obtain an adequate version of the laws for which we are looking, unless the physical system is regarded as a whole. According to modern mechanics, each individual particle of the system, in a certain sense, at any one time, exists simultaneously in every part of the space occupied by the system.[5]

—Max Planck

One is led to a new notion of unbroken wholeness which denies the classical idea of analyzability of the world into separately and independently existing parts . . . Rather we say that inseparable quantum interconnectedness of the whole universe is the fundamental reality, and that relatively independently behaving parts are merely particular and contingent forms within this whole.[6]

—D. Bohm and B. Hiley

In the hadron bootstrap,* all particles are dynamically composed of one another in a self-consistent way and in that sense can be said to "contain" one another.[7]

—Fritjof Capra

Religion

When is a man in mere understanding? I answer, When he sees one thing separate from another. And when is a man above mere understanding? That I can tell you: When a man sees All in all, then a man stands beyond mere understanding.[9]

—Meister Eckhart

Nothing to the supramental sense is really finite; it is founded on a feeling of all in each and of each in all. . . . The material object becomes . . . something different from what we now see, not a separate object on the background or in the evironment of the rest of nature but an indivisible part and even in a subtle way an expression of the unity of all that we see.[10]

—Sri Aurobindo

All objects are in origin like space, and multiplicity has no place in them in any sense.

—Mandyyuka Rarita Upanishad

He on whom the sky, the earth, and the atmosphere are woven, and the wind, together with all life-breath, Him alone know as the One Soul.

—Mundaka Upanishad

---

*Hadrons are subatomic particles that exhibit strong electromagnetic interactions. Protons and neutrons are examples, and their interaction holds the nucleus of atoms together. The bootstrap theory is a hypothesis as to the nature of such particles.

Science	Religion
A human being is a part of the whole, called by us the "Universe," a part limited in time and space. He experiences himself, his thoughts and feelings as something separated from the rest—a kind of optical delusion of his consciousness. This delusion is a kind of prison for us, restricting us to our personal desires and to affection for a few persons nearest to us. Our task must be to free ourselves from this prison by widening our circle of compassion to embrace all living creatures and the whole of nature in its beauty. Nobody is able to achieve this completely, but the striving for such achievement is in itself a part of the liberation and foundation for inner security.[8] —Albert Einstein	He in whom we live and move and have our being. —Holy Bible When the one is set against all the others, the one is seen as pervading them all and at the same time embracing them all in itself.[11] —D. T. Suzuki The core of the Avatamsaka Sutra, one of the main sciptures of Mahayana Buddhism, is the description of the world as a perfect network of mutual relations where all things and events interact with each other in an infinitely complicated way.[12] —Fritjof Capra

While the words in the above passages are quite comprehensible, the overall concepts expressed are not easily visualized in terms we are familiar with. Along this line Capra notes that:

> Buddhists insist that the concept of interpenetration is not comprehensible intellectually, but is to be experienced by an enlightened mind in the state of meditation . . . . In modern physics, the situation is quite similar. The idea of every particle containing all the others is inconceivable in ordinary space and time. It describes a reality which, like the one of the Buddha, has its own rules. In the case of the hadron bootstrap, they are the rules of quantum theory and relativity theory, the key concept being that the forces holding particles together are themselves particles exchanged in the cross channels.[13]

Although the idea of interrelationship is not something that would occur to the average individual, it is clear that some deeper thinkers have expressed it. Naturalist John Muir observed, "When we try to pick out anything by itself we find it hitched to everything else in the universe." Capra uses lines from a poem of William Blake to show that this well-known mystic grasped and beautifully expressed the concept:

To see a world in a grain of sand
And a heaven in a wild flower,
Hold infinity in the palm of your hand,
And eternity in an hour.

TIME

When Einstein pointed out that past, present, and future all exist continuously, he was expressing a point of view earlier stated by esotericists and mystics. Esotericists have consistently claimed that time is a phenomenon (or illusion) of the physical plane and does not exist on the higher planes.* This is not to say that time is not an important factor in the normal daily lives that we find ourselves bound to. Rather, it is the case that we need to work with this limitation as we seek to accomplish that which we set out to do.

As noted earlier, LeShan's studies of clairvoyants also indicate that to them time as we know it is limited to states and experiences of our normal waking consciousness.

In the Clairvoyant Reality, say the sensitives, time takes on quite a different structure. All events are, they do not happen. The past, the present, and the future are all equally in existence, even though we can ordinarily only observe those events located in the present.[14]

Capra makes the point that both Eastern mystics and modern physicists appear to have come to just about the same conclusion as the clairvoyants have:

The Eastern mystics link the notions of both space and time to particular states of consciousness. Being able to go beyond the ordinary state through meditation, they have realized that the conventional notions of space and time are not the ultimate truth. The refined notions of space and time resulting from their mystical experiences appear to be in many ways similar to the notions of modern physics, as exemplified by the theory of relativity.[15]

Examples of views and observations on the subject of time by prominent figures in the fields of science and religion are given in the following quotations:

---

*For example, H. P. Blavatsky states: "Time is only an illusion produced by the succession of our states of consciousness as we travel through eternal duration and it does not exist where no consciousness exists in which the illusion can be produced." *The Secret Doctrine*, vol. 1, p. 37.

TIME

SCIENCE

In space-time everything which for each of us constitutes the past, the present, and the future is given en bloc. . . . Each observer, as his time passes, discovers, so to speak, a new slice of space-time which appears to him as successive aspects of the material world, though in reality the ensemble of events constituting space-time exist prior to his knowledge of them.[16]

—Louis de Broglie

The real revolution that came with Einstein's theory . . . was the abandonment of the idea that the space-time coordinate system has objective significance as a separate physical entity. Instead of this idea, relativity theory implies that the space and time coordinates are only the elements of a language that is used by an observer to describe his environment.[17]

—Mendel Sachs

These two ways of thinking, the way of time and history and the way of eternity and timelessness, are both parts of man's efforts to comprehend the world in which he lives. Neither is comprehended in the other, neither telling the world the whole story.[18]

—J. Robert Oppenheimer

RELIGION

The intuitive higher knowledge is timeless and spaceless, without any here and now. . . . Perception here means seeing in the light that is in time, for anything I think of I think of in the light that is in time. . . . Yet take away this now of time and thou art everywhere and hast the whole of time.[21]

—Meister Eckhart

Time, space and causation are like the glass through which the absolute is seen, and when it is seen . . . it appears as the universe. Now we at once gather from this, that in the absolute, there is neither time, space nor causation.[22]

—Swami Vivekananda

In the spiritual world there are no time dimensions such as the past, present and future; for they have contracted themselves into a single moment of the present where life quivers in its true sense. . . . The past and the future are both rolled up in the present moment of illumination, and the present moment is not something standing still with all its contents, for it ceaselessly moves on.[23]

—D. T. Suzuki

Science	Religion
In man's brief tenancy on earth he egocentrically orders events in his mind according to his own feelings of past, present and future. But except on the reels of one's own consciousness, the universe, the objective world of reality, does not "Happen"—it simply exists. It can be encompassed in its entire majesty only by a cosmic intellect.[19] —Lincoln Barnett	It is believed by most that time passes; in actual fact it stays where it is. This idea of passing may be called time, but it is an incorrect idea, for since one sees it only as passing, one cannot understand that it stays just where it is.[24] —Dogen (Zen master)
Space-time is a concept of limited validity . . . the concepts of space-time and time itself are not primary but secondary ideas in the structure of physical theory.[20] —J. A. Wheeler	

THE FUNDAMENTAL NATURE OF MATTER

The theories of modern physics and the results of high-energy particle experiments have dramatically changed man's view of the constituents of matter. The interchangeability of energy and mass is vividly displayed in the high-energy accelerator where more and more particles are created as the energy level of interactions is increased. In commenting on high-energy scattering experiments Capra notes that:

> Matter has appeared in these experiments as completely mutable. All particles can be transmuted into other particles; they can be created from energy and can vanish into energy. In this world, classical concepts like 'elementary particle' material substance or 'isolated object,' have lost their meaning; the whole universe appears as a dynamic web of inseparable energy patterns.[25]

Let us now explore some key concepts relative to the nature of matter in the light of modern physics and religious or esoteric thinking.

1. ARE THERE ELEMENTARY PARTICLES?

The atoms that had been assumed to be the indivisible building blocks of matter in Newtonian physics have now been divided many times over, and physicists are questioning whether there is such a thing as an elementary particle. Werner Heisenberg, a member of the international team of eminent physicists who set down the basic theories of modern physics in the 1920s, comments as follows:

We had assumed that visible matter was composed of smaller units, and that, if we only divided these long enough, we should arrive at the smallest units, which Democritus had called "atoms" and which modern physicists called "elementary particles." But perhaps this entire approach had been mistaken. Perhaps there was no such thing as an indivisible particle. Perhaps matter could be divided ever further, until finally it was no longer a real division of a particle but a change of energy into matter, and the parts were no longer smaller than the whole from which they had been separated. But what was there in the beginning? A physical law, mathematics, symmetry? In the beginning was symmetry.[26]

The May 1973 *M.I.T. Reports on Research* comments on "the growing belief among physicists that the nuclear constituents are themselves composite particles." Capra notes similarly that "the constituents of the atomic nuclei . . . do not seem to be the ultimate elementary particles, but seem to be composed of other entities."[27] He further comments that "the notion of the elementary particles as the primary units of matter has to be abandoned. . . . As more and more particles were discovered over the years it became clear that not all of them could be called 'elementary' and today there is a widespread belief among physicists that none of them deserves this name."[28]

Physicist Allen D. Allen writes:

A number of physicists, including the author, have taken quite another approach to the problem of finding the basic unit of matter. We have decided that it doesn't exists. After all, every time we think we've found it, it turns out we haven't. We call this new idea the "bootstrap theory," because it almost creates something out of nothing and physicists think of this as pulling yourself up by your bootstraps.

The bootstrap theory says that rather than using objects—such as particles—for raw material, nature uses the fundamental laws of physics—such as the law of conservation of momentum. . . . This concept, that ultimately the world is constructed from principles rather than from units of matter, is almost theological in character. Yet it is now an established (if competing) theory in the mainstream of theoretical physics.[29]

This concept and the last three sentences in the earlier quotation from Heisenberg seem to be along the same line of thought and are consistent with the statement found in Blavatsky's *Secret Doctrine* that "Absolute intelligence thrills through every atom."[30]

Geoffrey Chew, one of the chief developers of the bootstrap theory, makes an interesting observation regarding an elementary particle:

A truly elementary particle—completely devoid of internal structure—could not be subject to any forces that would allow us to detect its existence. The mere knowledge of a particle's existence, that is to say, implies that the particle possesses internal structure![31]

Many years before the emergence of what we term modern physics, Madame Blavatsky stated without equivocation the esotericists' view of the subject: "It is on the doctrine of the illusive nature of matter, and the infinite divisibility of the atom, that the whole science of Occultism is built."[32]

2. The Field, the Void, Brahman, Tao, God

A theory called *quantum electrodynamics*, which merges electrodynamics and quantum theory and incorporates relativity theory, has been formulated by modern physics to describe all electromagnetic interactions between subatomic particles. This theory introduces the concept of a "quantum field" in which "the classical contrast between solid particles and the space surrounding them is completely overcome. The quantum field is seen as the fundamental physical entity: a continuous medium which is present everywhere in space. Particles are merely local condensations of the field, concentrations of energy which come and go."[33] Albert Einstein comments as follows on this: "We may therefore regard matter [as] constituted by the regions of space in which the field is extremely intense. . . . There is no place in this new kind of physics both for the field and matter, for the field is the only reality."[34]

Blavatsky in *The Secret Doctrine* makes the statement "Space is an entity,"[35] and Alice Bailey similarly writes "Space is an eternal Entity."[36]

Commenting along this same line in *The Tao of Physics*, Capra expands on what he observes to be a similarity in concept between the idea of the quantum field, where "physical things and phenomena" are seen as "transient manifestations of an underlying entity," and the view of Eastern mystics, who also "consider an underlying entity as the only reality" and all its phenomenal manifestations as transitory and illusory. Capra points out, however, that this reality of the Eastern mystic cannot be identified (at least directly) with the quantum field, because it is seen as the essence of all phenomena and consequently beyond all concepts and ideas, whereas the quantum field is a well-defined concept that accounts only for some phenomena.

He suggests, however, that "the Brahman of the Hindus, like the Dharmakaya of the Buddhists and the Tao of the Taoists, can be seen perhaps as the ultimate unified field from which spring not only the phenomena studied in physics but all other phenomena as well."[37]

Capra also notes that this underlying reality defies all description and therefore is said to be void, empty, or formless. It is not to be taken for nothingness but is the essence of all forms. Quoting the Upanishads, "Brahman is life, Brahman is joy, Brahman is the void."[38]

Buddhists, Capra notes, call the ultimate reality Śunyata—"Emptiness" or "the Void"—and Taoists call the Tao empty. Lao-tzu compares it to "a vessel which is forever empty, and thus has the potential of containing an infinity of things." But in each case this emptiness is a "living Void which gives birth to all forms."[39]

Blavatsky, in giving the esotericists' view of the same subject, states that:

> The One All is like Space—which is its only mental and physical representation on the Earth. . . . Space is neither a "limitless void," nor a "conditional fullness" but both: being on the plane of absolute abstraction, the ever-incognisable Deity, which is void only to finite minds, and on that of mayavic perception, the Plenum, the absolute Container of all that is, whether manifested or unmanifested, it is therefore that ABSOLUTE ALL. There is no difference between the Christian Apostle's "In Him we live and move and have our being," and the Hindu Rishi's "The Universe lives in, proceeds from, and will return to, Brahma." . . . the God of the Apostle-Initiate and of the Rishi being both the Unseen and the Visible SPACE.[40]

3. THE DYNAMICS OF MATTER

The new physics has made it clear that at the subatomic level there are no such things as fixed static objects, but rather we must think in terms of dynamic patterns in space as well as in time. Thus the modern physicist must take into account the four-dimensional space-time continuum, where the space aspect of subatomic particles "makes them appear, as objects with a certain mass, their time aspect as processes involving the equivalent energy."[41]

Capra summarizes the way in which the two key theories of modern physics have revealed the dynamic nature of matter:

> Quantum theory has shown that particles are not isolated grains of matter, but are probability patterns, interconnections in an inseparable cosmic web. Relativity theory, so to speak, has made these patterns come alive by revealing their intrinsically dynamic character. It has shown that the activity of matter is the very essence of its being. The particles of the subatomic world are not only active in the sense of moving around very fast; they themselves are processes! The existence of matter and its activity cannot be separated. They are but different aspects of the same space-time reality.[42]

The dynamic nature of the world of modern science is further amplified in the following two statements by Werner Heisenberg. "The world thus appears as a complicated tissue of events, in which connections of different kinds alternate or overlap or combine and thereby determine the texture of the whole."[43] "Modern Science has demonstrated that in the real world surrounding us, it is not the geometric forms, but the dynamic laws concerning movement (coming into being and passing away) which are permanent."[44]

As is the case with the principles reviewed earlier, this idea of the dynamic nature of matter is reflected also in religious thinking. Sarvepalli Radhakrishnan writes:

A wonderful philosophy of dynamism was formulated by Buddha 2,500 years ago. . . . Impressed with the transitoriness of objects, the ceaseless mutation and transformation of things, Buddha formulated a philosophy of change. He reduces substances, souls, monads, things, to forces, movements, sequences and processes, and adopts a dynamic conception of reality.[45]

Radhakrishnan goes on to question:

How do we come to think of things, rather than processes in the absolute flux? By shutting our eyes to the successive events. It is an artificial attitude that makes sections in the stream of change and calls them things. . . . Life is no thing or state of a thing, but a continuous movement or change.[46]

A. K. Coomaraswamy also states this concept in very similar words:

We are deceived if we allow ourselves to believe that there is ever a pause in the flow of becoming, a resting place where positive existence is attained for even the briefest duration of time. It is only by shutting our eyes to the succession of events that we come to speak of things rather than processes.[47]

D. T. Suzuki notes that "Buddhists have conceived an object as an event and not as a thing or substance."[48]

Perhaps even more specifically focused in terms familiar to physicists, H. P. Blavatsky states: "Atoms are called vibrations in Occultism."[49] On a broader scale, Blavatsky in describing "the one absolute Reality which antecedes all manifested, conditioned, being" refers to it as "Be-ness" as opposed to Being. She goes on to state:

This "Be-ness" in the Secret Doctrine is symbolized under two aspects. On the one hand, absolute abstract Space, representing bare subjectivity, . . . On the other, absolute Abstract Motion representing Unconditioned Consciousness. Even our Western thinkers have shown that Consciousness is inconceivable to us as apart from change, and motion best symbolizes change, its essential characteristic. This latter aspect of the one Reality, is also symbolized by the term, "The Great Breath." . . . Thus, then, the first fundamental axiom of the Secret Doctrine is this metaphysical ONE ABSOLUTE—BE-NESS—symbolized by finite intelligence as the theological Trinity.*

It is clear from all of the preceding that matter in manifestation, down to its smallest known constituents, is in constant motion. This movement brings up the logical question:

---

*The Secret Doctrine, vol. 1, p. 14. The concept of the Trinity in this context is further elaborated on page 11 of the same volume, which quotes the following questions and answers from the Occult Catechism: "What is it that ever is?" "Space." "What is it that ever was?" "The Germ in the Root." "What is it that is ever coming and going?" "The Great Breath." "Then there are three Eternals?" "No, the three are one. That which ever is, is one; that which ever was is one; that which is ever being and becoming is also one: and this is Space."

4. DOES MATTER HAVE LIFE?

Max Born has this to say on the subject:

> We distinguish between living and dead matter, between moving bodies and bodies at rest. This is a primitive point of view. What seems dead, a stone or the proverbial "door-nail," is actually forever in motion. We have merely become accustomed to judge by outward appearances, by the deceptive impressions we get through our senses. We shall have to learn to describe things in new and better ways.[50]

The question, then, of whether an atom of matter, for example, has life is bound up in our definition of life. Clearly the atom is in motion and is capable of taking orderly action in engaging in chemical processes. It is reasonable to assume, however, that an atom does not possess the level of consciousness of a human being or an animal. But that does not necessarily rule out some level of consciousness, not comprehensible to us. It is thus quite possible that as we presently speak of different forms of life from man down to the amoeba, our definition might be expanded as we begin to understand more about what we have termed inanimate matter.

The esotericists take the position that all matter is living matter. Alice Bailey follows up a series of observations concerning the nature of the atom with the statement: "We have found the atom is a living entity, a little vibrant world, and that within its sphere of influence other little lives are to be found."[51] Mrs. Bailey also makes a prediction concerning scientific acceptance of this idea, declaring "life in matter will no longer be a theory but a fundamental of science."[52]

Blavatsky points out that earlier thinkers have come to similar conclusions: "From Anaxagoras down to Epicurus, the Roman Lucretius, and finally even to Galileo, all those philosophers believed more or less in ANIMATED atoms, not in invisible specks of so-called 'brute' matter."[53]

THE RELATIONSHIP OF MIND AND THOUGHT TO MATTER

The fact that matter at the subatomic, atomic, and molecular levels behaves in an ordered, organized way brings into question the possibility of an underlying directing intelligence behind the substance of our world. We shall see that this idea has been expressed by many scientists and religious thinkers and that the work of the modern physicists seems to be leading more convincingly in this direction.

We will look at opinions on this subject expressed by scientists starting with physicist Sir James Jeans, who wrote:

> Today there is a wide measure of agreement which on the physical side of science approaches almost to unanimity, that the stream of knowledge is heading towards a nonmechanical reality; the universe begins to look more like a great thought than like a great machine. Mind no longer appears as an ac-

cidental intruder into the realm of matter; we are beginning to suspect that we ought rather to hail it as the creator and governor of the realm of matter.[54]

Physicist Sir Arthur Eddington states very simply: "The stuff of the world is mind stuff."[55]

Erwin Schrödinger, one of the international team who worked out the details of quantum theory, states: "The reason why our sentient, percipient and thinking ego is met nowhere in our world picture can be easily indicated in seven words: Because it is ITSELF that world picture. It is identical with the whole and therefore cannot be contained in it as part of it."[56]

Geoffrey Chew concludes from recent theories concerning interactions at the subatomic level: "Carried to its logical extreme, the bootstrap conjecture implies that the existence of consciousness, along with all other aspects of nature, is necessary for self-consistency of the whole."[57]

Thomas Edison in an interview reported in *Harper's Magazine* for February 1890 stated:

> I do not believe that matter is inert, acted on by an outside force. To me it seems that every atom is possessed by a certain amount of primitive intelligence. Look at the thousands of ways in which atoms of hydrogen combine with those of other elements, forming the most diverse substances. Do you mean to say they do this without intelligence?
>
> "But where does this intelligence come from originally?" [asked the interviewer.]
>
> "From some power greater than ourselves."
>
> "Do you believe then in an intelligent Creator, a personal God?"
>
> "Certainly; the existence of such a God can, to my mind, be proved from chemistry."[58]

Turning to religious thinkers, we find the concept of intelligence behind all manifestation clearly expressed in Buddhist writings. The Dhammapada states: "It is the mind which gives to things their quality, their foundation, and their being."[59]

From the Śurangama Sutra: "All things in the universe are all alike merely the excellently bright and primeval mind of Bodhi, and . . . this mind is universally diffused, and comprehends all things within itself." The Zen master Hsi Yun, who lived about A.D. 840, expresses a similar view: "All sentient beings are nothing but universal mind, besides which nothing exists. This mind which has always existed is unborn and indestructible. . . . It is the substance that you see before you."[60]

St. Thomas Aquinas wrote, "There is a certain Eternal Law, to wit, Reason, existing in the mind of God and governing the whole universe."[61]

Sri Aurobindo, the Indian mystic and philosopher of modern times, sums up his view on the matter most completely and concisely: "It is difficult to suppose that mind, life and matter will be found to be anything else than one energy, triply formulated."[62]

The esotericists' view of mind and matter is expressed as follows by Blavatsky in *The Secret Doctrine*:

> Spirit (or Consciousness) and Matter are . . . to be regarded not as independent realities, but as the two facets or aspects of the Absolute . . . which constitute the basis of conditioned Being, whether subjective or objective.
>
> Considering this metaphysical triad as the Root from which proceeds all manifestation, the Great Breath assumes the character of precosmic Ideation. It . . . supplies the guiding intelligence in the vast scheme of cosmic Evolution. On the other hand, precosmic root-substance . . . is that aspect of the Absolute which underlies all the objective planes of Nature.
>
> But just as the opposite poles of subject and object, spirit and matter, are but aspects of the One Unity in which they are synthesized, so, in the manifested Universe, there is "that" which links spirit to matter, subject to object.
>
> This something, at present unknown to Western speculation, is called by the occultists Fohat. It is the "bridge" by which the "Ideas" existing in the "Divine Thought" are impressed on Cosmic substance as the "laws of Nature." Fohat is thus the dynamic energy of Cosmic Ideation . . . the "Thought Divine" transmitted and made manifest through the Dhyan Chohans (called by the Christian theology: Archangels, Seraphs, etc.), the Architects of the visible World. . . . Fohat, in its various manifestations, is the mysterious link between Mind and Matter, the animating principle electrifying every atom into life.[63]

The influence of mind on matter is an area of psychic phenomena that has received recent widespread notoriety as a result of the feats performed by Uri Geller and others, which include bending metal objects with the power of the mind. Some of Mr. Geller's activities have apparently been verified by controlled experiments at Stanford Research Institute, Menlo Park, California, by Dr. Harold Puthoff and Mr. Russell Targ. These experiments included Mr. Geller's causing a laboratory balance to deflect as if a force had been applied, without physical contact with the balance. Spoon-bending was also recorded on film. It is most interesting that when Mr. Geller appeared on television in Japan and appeared to bend spoons with his mind, thousands of Japanese school children were able to duplicate the feat. This spoon-bending has been included in some mind-control training classes presented to children in the United States with great success. I have witnessed very stiff metal spoons bent in a very short time presumably by the thought power of young children. Adults seem to have a lower success rate than children with this, which is attributed by some to mental inhibition or lack of faith.

All of this brings us back to the premise quoted earlier by Sir James Jeans that he suspects we ought to hail mind "as the creator and governor of the realm of matter."

THE EXPANDING UNIVERSE, BLACK HOLES,
AND DAYS AND NIGHTS OF BRAHMA

There is now ample evidence to indicate that the universe is in the process of expanding, with celestial bodies moving away from each other as if they might all be moving away from some central point. Astrophysicists have proposed a theory of the creation of the universe called the "Big Bang" theory, which suggests that at the beginning of time for our system, there was a great explosion, which began the expansion of the universe.

Another theory, which astrophysicists have recently found physical evidence to support,* is that collapsed stars termed *black holes* exist in the universe. In a black hole the matter forming the remains of a burned-out star is compressed by immense gravitational forces, unopposed by the heat and radiation-induced forces in an active star. The star thus becomes extraordinarily diminished in volume and its density becomes so great that gravity forces do not even permit light to escape. Anything that comes in the vicinity of a black hole will, of course, be drawn in and crushed. Since the atoms of matter in a black hole are crushed by the forces involved, matter as we recognize it ceases to exist.

There is also an interesting conjecture by some astrophysicists that black holes form singularities in the universe through which other universes may be entered or which may form a passageway to another part of our universe.

It is predicted by relativity theory that when the expansion of the universe has run its course and the gravity forces of the various bodies in the universe balance the inertia of the moving bodies, the universe will begin to draw in on itself. This collapse of the universe will accelerate with time, and it is suggested that this will ultimately result in a black hole of the universe, at which point the unverse will be at, or very close to, complete immobility or rest.

An answer to the question, "What happens next?" is suggested by a statement by S. W. Hawking in an article in the January 1977 issue of *Scientific American* entitled "Quantum Mechanics of Black Holes." He comments: "The Big Bang resembles a black hole explosion, but on a vastly larger scale."

Princeton University professor John A. Wheeler, who originally coined the phrase "black hole" and who has been engaged in a detailed study of

*Astronomers have discovered an X-ray source in the constellation Cygnus, called Cygnus X-1, which many believe indicates the presence of a black hole, rotating with a visible star around a common center of gravity. The X-rays are believed to be caused by material from the glowing star being drawn into the black hole with such force that it is heated on its way to a high enough temperature to emit X-rays. Evidence has also been found of black holes at the center of the Milky Way Galaxy and two other galaxies.

black holes and the implications of the black hole of the universe, states: "We can well expect that when the universe collapses, there's a certain probability that it will start a new cycle."[64] In the late 1950s Wheeler came up with the concept of superspace, something out beyond the universe and not a part of it. With the concept of something beyond the universe, Wheeler puts forth "the idea that the dynamics goes on in superspace, that the universe makes many cycles."

This concept bears a great similarity to the Hindu scriptures, which describe the Days and Nights of Brahma. Hindus believe in an endless cycle of appearances and disappearances of the universe. In an earlier quoted passage from the Bhagavad Gita we read:

> There is a day, also, and a night in the universe:
> The wise know this, declaring the day of Brahma
> A thousand ages in span
> And the night a thousand ages.[65]

The Creation Hymn from the Rig-Veda contains the following words:

> Darkness there was, and all at first was veiled
> In gloom profound—an ocean without light.
> The germ that still lay covered in the husk
> Burst forth, one nature, from the fervent heat.[66]

With a little imagination this passage from the Rig-Veda could be interpreted to be describing first the condition in a black hole, followed by the Big Bang of astrophysics.

12. Esotericism: Common Ground

The esotericists have created, through the concepts they have put forth, a kind of common ground between science and religion. While the views of the esotericists are not necessarily accepted by the scientific or religious communities in general (although interest in these concepts is growing in both camps), an objective overview of esoteric writings shows that esotericism is inclusive of the fundamental ideas of both science and religion and further provides concepts that might prove useful for the deeper penetration of both fields.

Esotericism holds the leading thinkers of both science and religion in high regard, while chiding those with narrow views in both fields. Commenting on the importance of science, Alice Bailey writes:

> The way of science is as deeply needed by mankind, as is the way of religion, for "God" is found equally on both ways. The scientific way leads the aspirant into the world of energies and forces . . . revealing the Universal Mind and the workings of that great Intelligence which created the manifested universe.[1]

She further states:

> Much of the true revelation since the time of Christ has come to the world along the line of science. The presentation, for instance, of material substance (scientifically proven) as essentially only a form of energy was as great a revelation as any given by the Christ or the Buddha. . . . It related energy to force, form to life, and man to God and held the secret of transformation, transmutation and transfiguration. The revelations of science when basic and fundamental are as divine as those of religion, but both have been prostituted to meet human demand.[2]

Einstein, of course, stated that matter and energy were different forms of the same thing, and that one could be converted to the other, in an addendum to his special theory of relativity published in 1906. He set down the well-known equation $E = MC^2$ at that time as $M = L/C^2$, L being the symbol he then used for energy, and M and C representing mass and the speed of light respectively. The concept was dramatically demonstrated about forty years later with the first nuclear explosion at White Sands, New Mexico.

As we noted, H. P. Blavatsky links matter with what religion terms spirit, declaring: "Matter is spirit at its lowest point of manifestation and spirit is matter at its highest." In another place, she writes, "Spirit and Matter are the two States of the ONE which is neither Spirit nor Matter, both being the absolute life latent."[3] To which Mrs. Bailey adds, "Spirit and energy are synonymous terms and are interchangeable. Only in the realization of this can we arrive at the reconciliation of science and religion and a true understanding of the world of active phenomena by which we are surrounded and in which we move."[4]

One scientist who recognized the possibility of what the esotericists declare to be a fact was psychologist Carl Jung, who wrote, "When you say 'matter,' you are really creating a symbol for something unknown, which may just as well be 'spirit.' "[5]

That there is some close relationship between what religion calls God and what science calls energy is also suggested by scripture. The Bible asserts that God is spirit, and the Christian Nicene Creed, reflecting the New Testament, equates God with light, which is universally accepted as a form of energy. The Bhagavad Gita uses the phrase "the creative energy which is in Brahman."[6]

We shall see later that those persons we have classed as esotericists may have influenced some of our most important scientific contributors much more than is generally realized. It is further clear that the esotericists have had a remarkable record of predicting the discoveries of science. Joseph Head and S. L. Cranston note this in commenting on H. P. Blavatsky's book *The Secret Doctrine*:

> What has fascinated the scientists who have studied the work is that the author anticipated so many discoveries in their own fields. When the physicists and chemists of her day were convinced that the atom was the ultimate building block of the universe, she affirmed the infinite divisibility of the atom. When anthropologists were grudgingly allowing man an antiquity of only seven hundred thousand years, she spoke, as present researchers do, in terms of millions. She considered as fact such later scientific discoveries as the identity of substance and energy; the transmutation of elements; the illusory nature of matter—that matter is not what we see; that space is not empty, there being no vacuity anywhere; that life is possible on other planets and worlds; that the moon was not torn from the earth but was older than the earth. (Scientists were recently astounded to discover that the moon rocks brought back by the astronauts were older than any to be found on the earth!)[7]

The works of Mrs. Bailey are no less remarkable in this regard. Her writings predicted among other things the releasing of the energy of the atom and the discovery of Kirlian photography. She also stresses the future importance of "the mystery of electricity—the greatest spiritual science and area of divine knowledge in the world, the fringes of which have only just been touched."

As to the influence of esoteric thinking on leading contributors to science, the earlier quoted *Reincarnation: the Phoenix Fire Mystery* makes the statement that "Albert Einstein was said to have always had *The Secret Doctrine* on his desk,"[8] and goes on to explain:

> In checking the source of this information, we learned that a niece of Einstein, when in India during the 1960's, paid a special visit to the headquarters of the Theosophical Society at Adyar, Madras. She explained that she knew nothing of Theosophy or the society, but had to see the place because her uncle always had a copy of Madame Blavatsky's *Secret Doctrine* on his desk! The individual to whom the niece spoke was Eunice Layton, a world-traveled theosophical lecturer who happened to be at the reception desk when the visitor arrived.

Einstein was himself something of a mystic, making great use of imagination in pursuing answers to the mysteries of nature. He gives a description of imagining he was riding on a beam of light as he worked out his theory of relativity. He once puzzled a colleague by speaking about going to his laboratory, until he explained that his laboratory was subjective—a pleasant place where he imagined himself to be as he worked mentally on problems. Einstein used the path of imagination rather than the path of mathematics to create his theories, working up the needed mathematics around the idea. He once said, "Imagination is more important than knowledge."

Einstein's own words best describe his profound respect for the mystical outlook:

> The most beautiful and most profound emotion we can experience is the sensation of the mystical. It is the source of all true science. He to whom this emotion is a stranger, who can no longer wonder and stand rapt in awe, is as good as dead. To know that which is impenetrable to us really exists, manifesting itself as the highest wisdom and the most radiant beauty which our dull faculties can comprehend only in their primitive forms—this knowledge, this feeling is at the center of true religiousness.[9]

Physicist and biographer Jeremy Bernstein characterizes Einstein as "the only modern scientist one can begin to compare from the point of view of achievements, with Newton." It is then of interest to question whether Newton was in any way influenced by esoteric thinking. Apparently he was! We read that "Thomas Vaughn . . . was one of the mystical philosophers Sir Isaac Newton devotedly read. The Brittanica states that Sir Isaac 'spent much time in the study of the works of the alchemists'; also that he 'diligently studied the works of Jacob Boehme.' "*

It is interesting to note that Thomas Edison, the greatest inventor in recorded history, was also no stranger to esotericism. He became involved with H. P. Blavatsky and the Theosophical Society in New York in 1878 and was awarded a Diploma of Fellowship.[10] He was also quite interested in psychic phenomena and conducted some experiments along this line, working with psychics.

Considering the view held by esotericists that Sir Francis Bacon was an incarnation of a key member of the Spiritual Hierarchy of the planet, the following statement by Manly P. Hall is significant to the subject being considered: "The Baconian, or inductive, system of reasoning (whereby facts are arrived at by a process of observation and verified by experimentation) cleared the way for the schools of modern science."[11] This would seem to be a proper guiding role for a member of the Hierarchy, and it appears to establish a strong but little-recognized link between esotericism and modern science.

A modern scientist and philosopher, who was also a man of religion, was the Jesuit priest and anthropologist Pierre Teilhard de Chardin. He became embroiled in controversy as a result of his attempts to advance man's insight into the workings of the universe. His writings make it clear that he was a mystical visionary, and his world view is essentially the same as that of the esotericists. In *The Phenomenon of Man* he writes:

> Without the slightest doubt there is something through which material and spiritual energy hold together and are complementary. In the last analysis, somehow or other, there must be a single energy operating in the world. And the first idea that occurs to us is that the "soul" must be as it were a focal point of transformation at which, from all points of nature, the forces of bodies converge, to become interiorized and sublimated in beauty and truth.

Those familiar with the writings of esotericists will recognize that this statement and many others throughout Teilhard de Chardin's books correspond to the concepts expressed by the esotericists.

*Quoted from Head and Cranston, *Reincarnation: the Phoenix Fire Mystery*, p. 264. Thomas Vaughn was a 17th-century British Hermeticist, Neoplatonist, Kabbalist, and alchemist. Jacob Boehme (1575–1624) was a giant of Christian mysticism, whose extensive writings deal with man and the universe as well as God and the soul. He inspired Blake, William Law, and Saint-Martin. He himself studied the works of Paracelsus.

With regard to one of the greatest points of disagreement between religion and science, the origin and development of man and the universe, the esotericists take a middle ground. They hold that religion and science are both partially correct, indicating that creation and evolution are both part of the total scheme of things and that there is a directing agency behind manifested existence. They maintain that the scriptures are to some extent allegorical and can be interpreted to be consistent with what science has thus far revealed if the right keys are understood. Commenting on the Creation story from Hindu and Judaic/Christian scripture, H. P. Blavatsky writes:

> Let the impartial critic compare the two accounts—the Vishnu Purana and the Bible—and he will find that the "seven creations" of Brahma are at the foundation of the "week" of creation in Genesis 1. The two allegories are different, but the systems are all built on the same foundation stone. The Bible can be understood only by the light of the Kabbala [the esoteric teachings of the Hebrews].[12]

Blavatsky also discusses the nebular theory at some length in *The Secret Doctrine* (1888), indicating that esoteric teaching agrees with some of the concepts put forth in connection with this theory and pointing out some areas of disagreement. She goes on to comment that "with the theories of such men of learning as Kepler, Kent, Oersted, and Sir William Herschel, who believed in a Spiritual world . . . Occult Cosmogony might . . . attempt a satisfactory compromise. But the views of those physicists differed vastly from the latest modern speculations."

In *A Treatise on Cosmic Fire*, by Alice Bailey, are found the following statements that provide interesting food for thought:

"The solar system is a cosmic atom."

"Each Heavenly man is an atomic unit."

"Each human Monad is an atom in the body of one of the Heavenly Men" (p. 1041). However, in elaborating on these concepts, Mrs. Bailey notes that the analogy between a system, a planet, a man, and an atom is "never exact in detail but only in certain broad basic correspondences" (p. 245).

With regard to the development of man, Blavatsky's *The Secret Doctrine* agrees with a long evolutionary process but rejects the concept of man being evolved from the great apes, indicating that mankind represents a separate development that is not haphazard, as the early evolutionists claimed, but a planned and directed process. It is interesting that Louis and Mary Leakey's modern anthropological research also led to the conclusion that man and ape are both parallel evolutionary developments and man did not descend from the apes. The Leakeys and their anthropologist son, Richard, also consider man's appearance on earth to have taken place far earlier than had previously been believed, thus supporting Blavatsky's position on this.

We conclude this section with a statement from the writings set down by esotericist Helena Roerich: 'Not without reason is it said that *metaphysics* does not exist, only physics.''[3]

This expresses the view, held by esotericists, that what we from our persepctive term supernatural phenomena are in reality natural. It is only a matter of limitation of consciousness and lack of familiarity with certain laws of behavior interrelating the visible and (to us) invisible worlds that makes certain occurrences seem mysterious to us.

13. Psychology

This section will show through the writings of a number of well-known psychologists that the basic concepts expressed by the great religious thinkers are not only compatible with the science of psychology but, further, provide valuable insights that can be, and have been, employed in advancing psychological thought.

Psychologist Erich Fromm* points out that even Freud, who was critical of religion, nevertheless supports the same ideals as the founders of the world's great religions. Fromm writes:

> Freud holds that the aim of human development is the achievement of these ideals: knowledge (reason, truth, logos), brotherly love, reduction of suffering, independence and responsibility. These constitute the ethical core of all great religions on which Eastern and Western culture are based, the teachings of Confucius and Lao-tse, Buddha, the Prophets and Jesus.[1]

THE RELATIONSHIP OF PSYCHOLOGY TO RELIGION

This topic has been touched upon by many psychologists over the years. Perhaps the most widely known of these is Carl Jung, who did a great deal of study and writing on religion and related topics, especially in his later years. This emerges from volumes such as *Psychology and Religion West and East*, *Psychology and Alchemy*, and *Aion* from his Collected Works, and his book *Modern Man in Search of a Soul*. This, coupled with his pioneering work in the practice of psychotherapy, gave him a solid foundation of experience and knowledge on which to base his conclusions. Recognizing that science and religion in general are perceived to be in conflict, Jung comments as follows:

> The conflict between science and religion is in reality a misunderstanding of both. Scientific materialism has merely introduced a new hypothesis. . . . It

*Erich Fromm was a practicing psychoanalyst and author of many widely read books, and taught in Germany, Mexico, and at a number of universities in the United States.

has given another name to the supreme principle of reality. . . . Whether you call the principle of existence "God," "matter," "energy," or anything else you like, you have created nothing, you have simply changed a symbol. . . . Faith, on the other hand, tries to retain a primitive mental condition on merely sentimental grounds [and] . . . refuses to share in the spiritual adventure of our age.[2]

Drawing on his experience as a practicing psychotherapist, Jung summarized observations concerning the profound psychological effect that a religious outlook can have on a person's life:

During the past thirty years, people from all civilized countries on the earth have consulted me. . . . Among all my patients in the second half of life—that is to say, over thirty-five—there has not been one whose problem in the last resort was not that of finding a religious outlook on life. It is safe to say that every one of them fell ill because he had lost that which the living religions of every age have given to their followers, and none of them has been really healed who did not regain his religious outlook. This, of course, has nothing whatever to do with a particular creed or membership of a church.[3]

Another early leader in the field of psychotherapy, Alfred Adler, comments in a similar vein: "The best conception hitherto gained for the elevation of humanity is the idea of God."[4]

Jung's conviciton that there is a reality beyond that which is apparent to the senses is communicated in the inscription over the door of his house at Knumacht, which, translated, reads "God will be present whether called or not."

Jung's studies of religion revealed to him that the psychological concepts he and others had painstakingly discovered were even more clearly perceived much earlier by Eastern religious teachers. He notes: "Psychoanalysis itself and the lines of thought to which it gives rise—surely a distinctly Western development—are only a beginner's attempt compared to what is an immemorial art in the East. It should be mentioned that the parallels between psychoanalysis and yoga have already been traced by Oskar A. H. Schmitz."[5]

Further along this theme Jung comments on the teachings of the ancient Taoists:

My experience in my practice has been such as to reveal to me a quite new and unexpected approach to Eastern wisdom. But it must be well understood that I did not have a starting point, a more or less adequate knowledge of Chinese philosophy. . . . It is only later that my professional experiences have shown me that in my technique I had been unconsciously led along the secret way which for centuries has been the preoccupation of the best minds of the East.[6]

Another eminent psychologist who has recognized the value of Taoist teachings is Abraham Maslow,* who comments as follows on the value of Taoist concepts in counseling:

> Counseling is not concerned with training or with moulding or with teaching in the ordinary sense of telling people what to do and how to do it. It is not concerned with propaganda. It is a Taoistic uncovering and then helping. Taoistic means the noninterfering, the "letting be." Taoism is not a laissez-faire philosophy or a philosophy of neglect or of refusal to help or care. . . .
> What the good clinical therapist does is to help his particular client to unfold, to break through the defenses against his own self knowledge, to recover himself, and to get to know himself.[7]

Maslow further comments, "We as scientists, not to mention physicians, teachers, or even parents, must shift our image over to a more Taoistic one."[8]

In commenting on the importance of religion to mankind, Erich Fromm first defines his understanding of religion as "any system of thought and action shared by a group which gives the individual a frame of orientation and an object of devotion."[9]

He then goes on to state:

> The thesis that the need for a frame of orientation and an object of devotion is rooted in the conditions of man's existence seems to be amply verified by the fact of the universal occurrence of religion in history. This point has been made and elaborated by theologians, psychologists, and anthropologists.[10]

From the viewpoint of the psychoanalyst, Fromm offers as additional proof of this thesis his interpretation of "neurosis as a regression to primitive forms of religion,"[11] which an individual may develop, lacking the more conventional fulfillment of this need.

We see here a correspondence with the comment by Jung, quoted earlier, that problems with his patients over thirty-five years of age can universally be traced to the need for finding a religious outlook on life.

Fromm adds that "if a person has not succeeded in integrating his energies in the direction of his higher self, he canalizes them in the direction of lower goals; if he has no picture of the world and his position in it which approximates the truth he will create a picture which is illusory and cling to it. . . . Indeed, 'man does not live by bread alone.' "[12]

---

*Abraham H. Maslow was a pioneering psychological investigator, thinker, and author of many books and articles. He taught at Brooklyn College and the Western Behavioral Science Institute and was chairman of the Department of Psychology at Brandeis University. His books include *The Farther Reaches of Human Nature, Toward a Psychology of Being, Psychology of Science and Religions,* and *Values and Peak Experiences.*

We find concurrence in the theme that mankind shows an inherent tendency toward the pursuit of "religion" in the words of Roberto Assagioli, one of the pioneers of psychoanalysis in Italy and a colleague of Freud, Jung, and Maslow. Concerning different aspects of love, Assagioli writes:

> Finally, there is love of God, or whatever designation may be preferred to represent Universal Being or Beingness: The Supreme Value, Cosmic Mind, Supreme Reality, both transcendent and immanent. A sense of awe, wonder, admiration, and worship, accompanied by the urge to unite with that Reality, is innate in man. Present in every age and every country, it has given birth to the many varieties of religious and spiritual traditions and forms of worship, according to prevailing cultural and psychological conditions. It reaches its flowering in the mystics who attain the lived experience of union through love.[13]

Psychologist and author Robert Ornstein* has focused a great deal of attention on how the esoteric traditions of the Middle East and Far East; those of the Sufis, the Yogis, and Buddhist monks can be applied to further modern psychology. It is his opinion that:

> A new synthesis is in process within modern psychology. This synthesis combines the concerns of the esoteric traditions with the research methods and technology of modern science.

Ornstein goes on to explain that:

> When we refer to these traditions, we refer largely to teachers, exercises, and techniques of the past. The Buddha formulated his techniques especially for those in India 2,600 years ago. Muhammad's school and teaching were formulated for the Middle East 1,300 years ago. But Muhammad, although primarily speaking to those of his own time and place, made many statements which apply to many teachers of these traditions, independent of their situation. One which is relevant to this discussion was "Speak to those in accordance with their understanding."[14]

Psychologist and author Carl R. Rogers also comments on the synthesis of the esoteric and the scientific in the practice of psychology: "Our experiences in therapy and in groups, it is clear, involves the transcendent, the indescribable, the spiritual. I am compelled to believe that I, like many others, have underestimated the importance of this mystical, spiritual dimension."[15]

An excellent comprehensive summary of the essence of religion and its relationship to psychology is given in the following by Erich Fromm:

---

*Professor Robert E. Ornstern is a research psychologist at the Langley Porter Neuropsychiatric Institute and teacher at the University of California Medical Center in San Francisco. He is a graduate of Queens College of the City University of New York and of Stanford University. He is the author of numerous books and articles.

In trying to give a picture of the human attitude underlying the thinking of Lao-tse, Buddha, the Prophets, Socrates, Jesus, Spinoza, and the philosophers of the Enlightenment, one is struck by the fact that in spite of significant differences there is a core of ideas and norms common to all of these teachings. Without attempting to arrive at a complete and precise formulation, the following is an approximate description of this common core: man must strive to recognize the truth and can be fully human only to the extent to which he succeeds in this task. He must be independent and free, an end in himself and not the means for any other person's purposes. He must relate himself to his fellow men lovingly. If he has no love he is an empty shell, even if his were all power, wealth, and intelligence. Man must know the difference between good and evil, he must learn to listen to the voice of his conscience and to be able to follow it. . . . the aim of the psychoanalytic cure of the soul is to help the patient attain the attitude which I just described as religious.[16]

THE NATURE OF MAN

The similarity of concepts relative to man's nature between psychology and religion are apparent to those familiar with both fields. The psychologist talks about the superconscious, while religion speaks of the soul and the spirit; psychology speaks of the collective unconscious and religion talks of the universal mind. We find that some psychologists have taken note of the common elements in the two fields and have begun to integrate the concepts.

Ornstein comments that "in general the esoteric traditions characterize consciousness in terms similar to those of modern psychology."[17]

Roberto Assagioli writes as follows on an aspect of consciousness in man:

There is another dimension in man. Though many are unaware of it and may even deny its existence, there is another kind of awareness, to the reality of which the direct experience of a number of individuals has testified throughout history. The dimension along which this awareness functions can be termed "vertical." In the past it was generally considered the domain of religious or spiritual experience, but it is now gaining increasing recognition as a valid field of scientific investigation.

This is the specific domain of transpersonal psychology, which deals with what Maslow, a pioneer in the field, has called the "higher needs."[18]

Assagioli goes on to point out that a growing interplay between the personal and transpersonal selves leads ultimately to their fusion and "in turn to their relationship with the ultimate reality, the Universal Self,"[19] a viewpoint concurred in by esotericists. He provides the diagrammatic concept of the psychological constitution of man shown in Figure 11, which illustrates his contention that the conscious self is a "reflection or projection" of the "Transpersonal, or higher, Self."[20]

These same concepts are expressed using slightly different terms by Carl Jung, who writes, "Spirit is the living body seen from within, and the body the outer manifestation of the living spirit—the two being really one."[21]

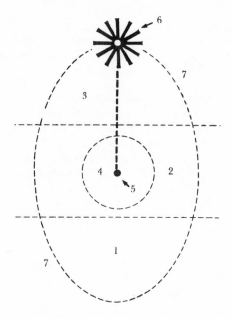

1. The Lower Unconscious
2. The Middle Unconscious
3. The Higher Unconscious, or Superconscious
4. The Field of Consciousness
5. The Conscious Self, or "I"
6. The Transpersonal Self
7. The Collective Unconscious

Fig. 11. The Psychological Constitution of Man

From Roberto Assagioli, M.D., *The Act of Will* (Baltimore: Penguin Books, 1973), p. 14. Used by permission of the publisher.

And in another writing he states, "I have called this center the *self*. It might equally well be called the 'God within us.' The beginnings of our whole psychic life seem to be inextricably rooted in this point, and all our highest and ultimate purposes seem to be striving toward it."[22]

Along the line of Assagioli's "Collective Unconscious," Jung states: "In some way or other we are part of an all-embracing psychic life, of a single 'greatest' man, to quote Swedenborg."[23]

Maslow concurs with the view that man's nature extends beyond that which is externally apparent. He phrases it as follows: "Man has a higher and transcendent nature, and this is part of his essence."[24] To this he adds: "Becoming divine or godlike is part of human nature, even though it is not often seen in fact. It is still a potentiality of human nature."[25]

Recognizing that there are deeper aspects to man's nature, Ornstein acknowledges that the techniques used by some religious communities and esotericists provide a means to expand consciousness into these dimensions. He writes:

> The traditional esoteric psychologies . . . constitute important new input for modern scientific psychology, about an area of inquiry and an area of the mind which has largely been ignored and forgotten in contemporary culture and psychology. . . . [They] proceed in another direction, to practical techniques such as meditation, for circumventing the "reducing valve" of normal consciousness, techniques for suspending the normal analytic, linear mode. More advanced techniques then tune the intuitive mode by working in its own tacit language.
>
> The further development of a modern psychology of consciousness may in large part rest on the integration of this new input, the extended perspective and practical exercises of the traditional psychologies, with the technology of the modern, making contemporary psychology more complete once again.[26]

Continuing along this line, Ornstein points out new directions in scientific inquiry concerning the nature of man.

> Our personal and scientific attention is being shifted inward, to the importance of consciousness itself as an object of inquiry, and to the self-control of internal states. Physiological feedback research thus involves a fundamental redirection of technology toward the internal rather than the external environment.
>
> Man is not so closed a system as the Western scientific community once thought. We are sensitive and permeable to subtle sources of energy from geophysical and human forces which often lie unnoticed in the brilliance of the day.[27]

Dr. Assagioli, concurring with Ornstein's view that man is not a closed system, expresses the following view of man's true nature, which agrees with that of the world's great religious teachers:

> Man can have the intuitive realization of his essential identity with the supreme Reality. In the East it has been expressed as the identity between the Atman and the Brahman. In the West some mystics have boldly proclaimed the identity between man and God. Others have emphasized that life is One, that there is only One Life. But this does not mean that man's mind can grasp the wonder and mysteries of the cosmic manifestation. Only through a series of expansions of consciousness, only by reaching ever higher states of awareness, may he gradually experience some of those wondrous mysteries.
>
> Of such transpersonal possibilities the most enlightened men and women of all ages have given testimony, expressing them in basically the same way, above the differences and colorings due to individual and cultural conditionings.[28]

The importance of exploring and developing man's inner nature expressed earlier by Ornstein is pointed out even more forcefully by Assagioli:

Only the development of his inner powers can offset the dangers inherent in man's losing control of the tremendous natural forces at his disposal and becoming the victim of his own achievements. A vivid realization that this is indispensable for maintaining the sanity and indeed the very survival of humanity, that only thus can man fulfill his true nature, should spur him on to tackle this task with an intensity of desire and determination equal to that which he has previously devoted to his external attainments.[29]

Jung concurs in this view: "We moderns are faced with the necessity of rediscovering the life of the spirit; we must experience it anew for ourselves. It is the only way in which we can break the spell that binds us to the cycle of biological events."[30]

THE MYSTICAL EXPERIENCE

We shall see from what follows that rather than being scoffed at, dismissed, ignored, or taken lightly by the modern science of psychology, the mystical experience—the experience of expanded consciousness—is recognized as being of great significance to the past and future progress of the race.

That there are modes of consciousness beyond those we are accustomed to in our everyday working lives is widely recognized by psychologists as exemplified by the following four quotations.

> Our normal waking consciousness, rational consciousness as we call it, is but one special type of consciousness, whilst all about it, parted from it by the filmiest of screens, there lie potential forms of consciousness entirely different.[31]
>
> —William James

> Two major modes of consciousness exist in man, and function in a complementary manner. Since the dominant mode in our culture is the verbal and rational, recognition of their existence involves us in a cultivation of the second mode, the intuitive and holistic.[32]
>
> —Robert Ornstein

> I have come to the conclusion that man always lives in two spheres of experience: the sphere in which subject and object are experienced as separate and only secondarily related, and another one in which he experiences oneness with the world.[33]
>
> —Kurt Goldstein

> Hard-headed research seems to be confirming the mystics' experience of union with the universal.[34]
>
> —Carl Rogers, referring to researches by Grof and Grof [1979] and Lilly [1973]

This state of consciousness, in which oneness with the world is experienced, is mentioned also by Erich Fromm in the following observations concerning religious experiences:

It seems that there is a factor common to certain kinds of religious experience which goes beyond the purely ethical. But it is exceedingly difficult if not impossible to formulate this factor of religious experience. Only those who experience it will understand the formulation, and they do not need any formulation.[35]

Fromm then adds in a footnote:

The kind of religious experience which I have in mind in these remarks is the one characteristic of Indian religious experience, Christian and Jewish mysticism, and Spinoza's pantheism. I should like to note that, quite in contrast to a popular sentiment that mysticism is an irrational type of religious experience, it represents—like Hindu and Buddhistic thought and Spinozism—the highest development of rationality in religious thinking.

Fromm attempts to describe this experience in spite of the difficulty, dividing it into three categories. After discussing the first two, he goes on to say:

Beyond the attitude of wonder and of concern there is a third element in religious experience, the one which is most clearly exhibited and described by the mystics. It is an attitude of oneness not only in oneself, not only with one's fellow men, but with all life and, beyond that, with the universe.[36]

Along a similar line, Abraham Maslow expresses the desirability of fostering the kind of viewpoint that results from the mystical experiences: "We need to teach our children unitive perception, the Zen experience of being able to see the temporal and the eternal simultaneously, the sacred and the profane in the same object."[37]

Roberto Assagioli notes Maslow's recognition of the powerful influence of higher states of consciousness in the following:

There is another and higher condition in which the personal will is effortless; it occurs when the willer is so identified with the Transpersonal Will, or, at a still higher and more inclusive level, with the Universal Will, that his activities are accomplished with free spontaneity, a state in which he feels himself to be a willing channel into and through which powerful energies flow and operate. This is wu-wei, or the "taoistic state," mentioned by Maslow in The Further Reaches of Human Nature.[38]

Dr. Assagioli also acknowledges that higher states of consciousness are not confined to great religious leaders and those universally recognized as mystics of a high order:

Experiences of spontaneous illumination have been reported by many, and many of these experiences are detailed in R. M. Bucke's *Cosmic Consciousness,* and William James' *The Varieties of Religious Experience. . . .* A collection of firsthand reports of spontaneous illumination occurring to "ordinary" people is contained in Winslow Hall's *Observed Illuminates.*[39]

The book *Cosmic Consciousness,* mentioned by Assagioli, has long been considered a classic in this area. Bucke was a physician and thus brings some scientific background to the subject. His book discusses thirty-six cases which appear to indicate expanded consciousness, by individuals ranging from the great religious leaders, such as Jesus Christ, Buddha, Lao-tzu, and Muhammad, to individuals unknown to the general public. Bucke also reports on a number of well-known poets, authors, philosophers, and a scientist—Blaise Pascal. Among the poets, which include Yeats, Blake, Carpenter, and others, he focuses especially on Walt Whitman, whom he knew personally. Bucke also reveals that he had himself experienced states of higher consciousness.

Robert Ornstein also makes note of the widespread occurrence of mystical experience and mentions Whitman in this context:

The "mystic" consciousness is described by many, in almost every esoteric tradition, from the ancient Hindu to the contemporary European. It is described in the Bible, in the Koran, in Whitman, in James's *The Varieties of Religious Experience.* It is the "mysterious darkness" of Augustine Poulain, a mode in which ordinary consciousness of a "multiplicity" of people and objects disappears, to be replaced by the awareness of "unity."

A second characteristic of these experiences, as described both by William James and by Arthur Deikman, is their sense of "realness"; they involve reliance on a type of verification that is more intuitive than our usual linear and inferential one. . . . [and] linear time, as we know it, has no meaning.

The contents of this experience are often said to be "ineffable," incapable of being fully communicated by words or by reference to similar experiences in ordinary life.[40]

The concept of unity described by the mystics is further explained by Ornstein:

This statement does not mean that "We are all the same thing and exactly alike," as it is often interpreted. Rather, it means that people are all individual components in an emergent level of organization, and that this level, this organization, may become perceptible in the same way that the sum of cells in a body are individual, yet make up one person.[41]

And with respect to time, he explains that "in this mode, all action occurs in an infinite present. There is no attribution of causality or construction of a sequence. All events occur simultaneously.[42]

Ornstein summarizes the mystical consciousness and the well-known way of achieving it in this way:

The "mystic" experience—brought about by concentrative meditation, deautomatization exercises, and other techniques intended to alter ordinary, linear consciousness—is, then, a shift from that normal, analytic world containing separate, discrete objects and persons to a second mode, an experience of "unity," a mode of intuition. This experience is outside the province of language and rationality, being a mode of simultaneity, a dimension of consciousness complementary to the ordered sequence of normal thought.[43]

He then goes on to state one of the reasons why this mode of consciousness is important:

A growing body of evidence demonstrates that each person has two major modes of consciousness available, one linear and rational, one arational and intuitive.

Our highest creative achievements are the products of the complementary functioning of the two modes. Our intuitive knowledge is never explicit, never precise in the scientific sense. It is only when the intellect can begin to process the intuitive leaps, to explain and "translate" the intuition into operational and functional knowledge that scientific understanding becomes complete.[44]

It should be noted that with regard to intuitive perception, especially with one not accomplished in sustaining an altered mode of consciousness, such terms as "flashing forth of the intuition" are used to connote a brief sudden and often fleeting intuitive insight, and it is in recognizing, grasping, and cultivating these that capability in this direction grows. It is said that Whitman, for example, always carried a stub of a pencil and a bit of paper to jot down whatever came to him.

CONCLUDING COMMENTS

It is clear from the preceding that some of the most advanced thinkers in the field of psychology are not at variance in their viewpoint either with those who founded the world's great religions or with the great saints and mystics who carried on their traditions Maslow also sees an encouraging sign in the issues that modern theologians are beginning to focus on. He comments:

The questions that theologians consider of prime importance nowadays are questions such as the meaning of the universe, and whether or not the universe has a direction. The search for perfection, the discovery of adherence to values, is the essence of the religious tradition, and many religious groups are beginning to declare openly that the external trappings of religion, such as not eating meat on Friday, are unimportant.[45]

Speculating on the just-mentioned subject of the direction of the universe from his viewpoint as a psychologist, Assagioli finds his perceptions in agreement with those of a man of religion who was also a scientist and a mystic. Assagioli writes:

Universal life appears to us as a struggle between multiplicity and unity—a labor and an aspiration towards union. We seem to sense that—whether we conceive it as a divine being or as cosmic energy—the Spirit working upon and within all creation is shaping it into order, harmony, and beauty, uniting all beings (some willing but the majority as yet blind and rebellious) with each other through links of love, achieving—slowly and silently, but powerfully and irresistibly—the Supreme Synthesis.[46]

Assagioli notes that this conclusion which he reached in a 1934 paper, he later found to be in agreement with the writings of Teilhard de Chardin concerning the logical goal of the evolutionary process.

Carl Rogers indicates that his views are along similar lines as follows:

I hypothesize that there is a formative directional tendency in the universe, which can be traced and observed in stellar space, in crystals, in micro-organisms, in more complex organic life, and in human beings. This is an evolutionary tendency toward greater order, greater complexity, greater interrelatedness.[47]

A most appropriate conclusion to this review of psychology and religion is given by Erich Fromm. In a discussion of the question "Is psychoanalysis a threat to religion?" Fromm makes the following observations:

The attitude common to the teachings of the founders of all great Eastern and Western religions is one in which the supreme aim of living is a concern with man's soul and the unfolding of his powers of love and reason. Psychoanalysis, far from being a threat to this aim, can on the contrary contribute a great deal to its realization. Nor can this aspect be threatened by any other science. It is not conceivable that any discovery made by the natural sciences could become a threat to religious feeling. On the contrary, an increased awareness of the nature of the universe in which we live can only help man to become more self-reliant and more humble. As for the social sciences, their growing understanding of man's nature and of the laws governing his existence contributes to the development of a religious attitude rather than threatens it.[48]

14. Healing

Healing is an area where some significant interaction between science and what was once considered a strictly religious or miraculous phenomenon is taking place. Certainly the ability to heal without the use of medicines or other visible means of assistance is something that has been attributed to many great religious leaders throughout history. The New Testament of the Bible is full of such stories with respect to Jesus and his disciples. Many great saints are reported to have had such powers.

There have also been over the years—and still are today—many less-well-known individuals and groups who are quite successful in healing in this way. Books such as *We Are All Healers*, by Sally Hammond; *Psychic Healers*, by David St. Claire; and *Healers and the Healing Process*, edited by George M. Meek, report in detail on many individuals who successfully practice psychic or religious healing.

An interesting set of developments has now coupled psychic healing techniques to physical measurements and thus opened up a possible avenue for extended scientific investigation. Some of the experiments performed along this line were mentioned earlier in that portion of the chapter on the esotericists devoted to describing the etheric body. As discussed there, Kirlian photography has been successfully used to show changes in the energy field of patients and healers as a result of the healing process.

Another impressive series of experiments, which detected energy directed by a healer at a great distance, are those conducted by Robert N. Miller,[*] a research scientist who headed a team including Dr. Philip B. Reinhart, chairman of the physics department at Agnes Scott College in Atlanta. For a detector they used a modern cloud chamber ordinarily used to observe the paths of subatomic particles by means of saturated air and alcohol vapor.

The cloud chamber experiments were conducted with the help of psychic healer Olga Worrall. First, Mrs. Worrall placed her hands near the

---

[*]Dr. Miller is a former professor of chemical engineering at Georgia Institute of Technology and is now a research scientist for the Lockheed Aircraft Company in Georgia.

215

cloud chamber and visualized healing energy flowing from her hands, as she does when conducting a healing. After about a half-minute, a wave pattern developed in the chamber and was aligned between her two hands held one on each side of the chamber. After several minutes she shifted the position of her hands 90°, and the waves began to change direction and line up 90° from the original path. Other members of the research team then placed their hands around the cloud chamber, yielding no visible effect.

Several weeks later the experiment was repeated, with Mrs. Worrall about 600 miles from the cloud chamber. At a predetermined time, Mrs. Worrall mentally visualized holding her hands at the sides of the chamber and caused the same sort of oriented wave motion as in the earlier experiment.[1]

In other experiments Dr. Miller determined, through brain-wave measurements on effective healers, that they operate in the alpha state of consciousness, or a combination of alpha and beta states, when performing psychic healing. The alpha state is a deep relaxation or meditative state that is characterized by brain-wave frequencies of between 8 and 13 cycles per second. The healers were able to move quickly from the beta (normal waking consciousness) state, with brain waves between 14 and 25 cycles per second, into the alpha state. One healer operated in both the alpha and theta states. Theta is a light-sleep state with frequencies of 3 to 7 cycles per second.

In another series of experiments conducted by Dr. Miller in an attempt to determine a method of measuring healing energy, it was determined that water treated by healers showed a decrease in surface tension compared with untreated water. A healer placed the forefingers of each hand in a specimen of water for three minutes. The energized water exhibited a surface tension of 62.9 dynes and the control sample 70.1 dynes. Both samples were Atlanta city water. Other healers obtained comparable results, while samples "treated" by non-healers showed some decrease in surface tension but not nearly as pronounced as those treated by the healers. These tests were also successfully repeated with distilled water.

Dr. Miller also determined by the use of spectrophotometer tests that water treated by healers showed changes in the hydrogen bonding of the H_2O molecules.

Another investigator in the area of healing energies is Dr. Thelma Moss, assistant professor of psychology at the University of California Neuropsychiatric Institute, Los Angeles. She has used the earlier-mentioned Kirlian photography technique to show that with a number of healers there is a marked change in the auric fingertip emanations from these healers during healing. Plate I shows an orange-yellow color appearing during healing, but changes can be different with different healers. Dr. Moss has also

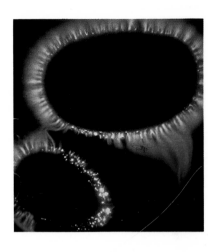

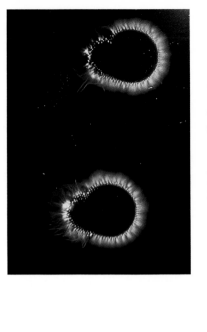

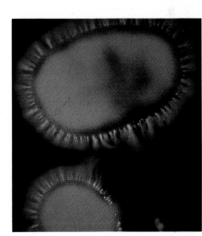

BEFORE HEALING

DURING HEALING

PLATE I. KIRLIAN PHOTOGRAPHS OF FINGER PADS OF TWO PSYCHIC HEALERS
BEFORE AND DURING HEALING (see ch. 14, p. 216)

demonstrated that with patients who are ill, the auric discharge pattern is small and often shows gaps. After healing, these patients often show a larger pattern with the gaps filled in.

In addition, Dr. Moss conducted controlled experiments to authenticate psychic healings. She described two "last chance" cases, where doctors had given up on curing a condition, and she used healer Jack Gray to successfully effect a cure under controlled laboratory conditions. Medical doctors could provide no explanation for the healing.

Dr. Moss also performed another type of photographic experiment with the help of healer Olga Worrall. After establishing with the Kirlian technique that Mrs. Worrall showed a modification in fingertip "corona" discharge during healing (see Plate I, top), another experiment was run with ordinary black-and-white film without any high voltage applied. Mrs. Worrall simply held the film between her fingertips without exposing it to light. When the film was developed, the resulting picture showed a cloud-like wave pattern described by one observer as "surrealistic hands." This phenomenon was again duplicated on five stacked layers of film, which all showed the same pattern. A control film developed with the same chemicals showed no effect.

Very significant accomplishments in the investigation of psychic healing have been made by psychologist Lawrence LeShan. Dr. LeShan brought to the study of psychic healing a background of fifteen years' full-time work on a project in psychosomatic medicine. He therefore approached the subject initially by questioning whether the phenomena actually existed, recognizing the possibility of "hysterical symptoms and hysterical suppression of symptoms." He concluded after a survey of the literature in the field that the phenomenon of psychic healing did exist, finding that "there was enough careful evaluation of reported claims to make this clear."[2]

After studying the methods used by a group of what he terms "serious psychic healers," who worked consistently at healing and had a record of accomplishment, he determined that a pattern of two basic techniques of healing emerged.

In the first method, which he terms *Type 1* and considers the more important, "the healer goes into an altered state of consciousness in which he views himself and the healee as one entity."[3] LeShan quotes healer Ambrose Worrall in describing this method: "I followed a technique I have of 'tuning in' to become, in a metaphysical sense, one with the patient." Healer Harry Edwards similarly writes that in psychic healing the healer "then draws 'close' to the patient so that his being is merged, as it were, into that of the patient, so that 'both' are 'one.'"[4] LeShan stresses that the other factor involved in this type of healing is the need for the healer to be focused by love and caring for the one to be healed. He quotes healer

Agnes Sanford: "Only love can generate the healing fire"[5] and Ambrose and Olga Worrall: "We must care. We must care for others deeply and urgently, wholly and immediately; our minds, our spirits must reach out to them."[6]

LeShan reports that the healers used a wide variety of techniques to reach this altered state of consciousness, including prayer or attempting to look at the one to be healed from God's viewpoint or as he would look from the spirit world. Again quoting Ambrose and Olga Worrall: "In true prayer our thinking is an awareness that we are part of the Divine Universe."[7]

In thinking through the process that might be taking place in a *Type 1* healing, LeShan takes note of a comment made by George Bernard Shaw concerning the lack of discarded artificial limbs or glass eyes at the shrine at Lourdes while there were mountains of crutches, wheelchairs, and braces. LeShan also found in his study of psychic healing that there was never a case of the regrowth of an amputated limb. Turning then to the observation, under a lens, made by Alexis Carrel of the cure of an open visible cancer during a "miraculous healing," LeShan notes the reported course of this cure. Carrel, author of *Man, the Unknown* and whom LeShan characterizes as a "very highly trained and reliable observer, reported that the cancer followed the usual, well-known course a cancer follows when it regresses . . . but many times faster than he had ever seen or heard of it happening before."[8]

LeShan concludes from this that in a *Type 1* healing the healee's self-healing abilities are brought to a much-higher-than-usual state of effectiveness, somewhere close to their ultimate potential:

> Type 1 psychic healing was not a "doing something" to the healee, but a meeting and uniting with him on a profound level, a uniting that permitted something new to happen. The reason, then, behind Shaw's comment on the lack of wooden legs at Lourdes is that the regrowth of a severed limb is beyond the ability of the body's self-repair systems. The rapid remission of a cancer is not.[9]

In a *Type 2* healing "the healer perceives a pattern of activity between the palms of his hands," which are placed on either side of the healee's pathological area so that the flow of energy is perceived to pass through the area. "Some healers perceive this as a flow of energy, some as a sphere of activity."[10] LeShan notes that about 50 percent of the healees treated in this way report feeling heat in the area. In a *Type 2* healing the healer tries to heal through the healing flow, and in both types the healer must care completely at the time of the healing. The fundamental difference is that in *Type 1* the healer unites with the one to be healed.

In *Type 2* healing some healers see themselves as originators of the healing power and some as transmitters. LeShan notes that Frank Loer has called them the "God Withiners" and the "God Beyonders" respectively.

What is most interesting concerning LeShan's work with healing is that after he carefully studied the methods used by healers he was able to teach himself the methods and successfully perform healings. It took LeShan about a year and a half of experimentation with meditation techniques to be able to achieve the state of consciousness that he believed to be associated with successful psychic healing. He reports his surprise (and his surprise at his surprise) when positive biological changes occurred in healees when he was able to go into his special altered state of consciousness.

After some experience he set up a basic rule of always proceeding with a *Type 1* healing first and only going into a *Type 2* healing if it felt like the right thing to do during the process of his *Type 1* healing. In general he found that *Type 2* results when done alone were transient, whereas *Type 1* healings tended to be permanent.

LeShan found that a factor preventing successful psychic healing exists where the patient does not want the healing. LeShan comments that "it is impossible to 'unite' with someone who does not want to unite with you."

In addition to teaching himself to heal, LeShan set up and conducted seminars in which he taught others who he believed (after screening) might have the capability to become effective healers. In his first five seminars he generally ruled out people who had a number of psychic experiences or who had ever been involved in psychic healing, in order to determine if those without background in this area could be effectively trained. LeShan concludes from his experience with healing seminars that these techniques can be effectively taught. He also determined the effectiveness of healing circles (where a number of trained individuals work as a group), describing a case in which a boy with a broken back was healed at a distance by a group of his seminar graduates.

In summing up, LeShan describes a second state of consciousness or point of view that applies to *Type 1* healing in addition to the state where the healer and healee are perceived to be one. This is an approach where "the healer attempts to send messages to the greater One of which he is a part, and tries to influence the One to move to the aid of another small part. To put it differently, the healer prays to the All for the best for another part of it! The word 'prays' is indeed appropriate here, since there may be a deep feeling of awe and reverence connected with the full attainment of the state of consciousness."[11]

LeShan adds that "the 'All' is the 'One' is 'God' and at these moments this becomes clear. Very strong feelings of humility and reverence may come to consciousness with the full realization of what one is a part of and of its awesome and overwhelming nature."

Another concept LeShan used to describe this process is in terms of energy: "Knowing yourself a part of an all-encompassing energy system, you will the total system to divert additional energies to the repair and harmonization of a part that needs it." LeShan also commends a viewpoint described to him by Dr. Robert Laidlaw: "If I can perfectly align myself with the harmonies of the universe, then their energies can flow through me toward the healee, whom I hold in my consciousness."

LeShan makes an important point in connection with activities of this sort:

> One can only really pray for the best for another part of the whole, for its increased harmony. Prayer that is specific beyond this . . . implies greater knowledge of what is "best" for one part of the All by another part, and then leads to a division and separation of the parts from the whole that . . . returns one to the Sensory Reality [i.e. the altered state of consciousness gives way to normal consciousness].[12]

"In addition," states LeShan, "prayers must be 'pure,' that is, without reference to one's own best interest."

LeShan finishes with an observation that we have commented on earlier (ch. 7):

> The recurring theme "God is Love" appears to mean exactly what it says, that there is a force, an energy, that binds the cosmos together and moves always in the direction of its harmonious action and the fruition of the separate connected parts. In man, this force emerges and expresses itself as love, and this is the "spark of the divine" in each of us.[13]

Psychologist Carl Rogers gives the following description of experiences that are similar to those of LeShan.

> When I am at my best, as a group facilitator or as a therapist, I discover another characteristic. I find that when I am closest to my inner, intuitive self, when I am somehow in touch with the unknown in me, when perhaps I am in a slightly altered state of consciousness, then whatever I do seems to be full of healing. Then, simply my presence is releasing and helpful to the other. There is nothing I can do to force this experience, but when I can relax and be close to the transcendental core of me, then I may behave in strange and impulsive ways in the relationship, ways which I cannot justify rationally, which have nothing to do with my thought processes. But these strange behaviors turn out to be right, in some odd way: it seems that my inner spirit has reached out and touched the inner spirit of the other. Our relationship transcends itself and becomes a part of something larger. Profound growth and healing and energy are present.[14]

Another individual who has pursued extensive investigations in psychic healing is Jose Silva, the founder of the Silva Mind Control training courses that are taught in many major cities. The courses teach techniques for entering a relaxed state of consciousness (alpha level), which appears to be a useful first step for successful healing. This background, coupled with methods similar to those used by other healers, has been reported to be successfully used by graduates of the training in effecting successful healings.

Spiritual-healing abilities have generally been associated with mystics and esotericists throughout history. Mike Samuels, M.D., and his wife, Nancy, comment as follows on this in their book *Seeing with the Mind's Eye*, which has a chapter covering "Medicine and Healing" and, specifically, the use of visualization in this regard:

> This mystical tradition (relative to healing) permeated the thoughts of Hermetic philosophers in Egypt, Platonic Philosophers in Greece, Sufis in Persia, and Buddhists and Hindus in India and the Orient. In the Middle Ages in Europe it expressed itself in the mysticism of Christian Gnostics, Jewish Kabbalists, and secret occult societies like the Rosicrucians. . . . These philosophies believed in the primacy of spirit over matter, of mind over body; they believed that matter is a manifestation of spirit. They believed that visualizations manifest themselves as health or disease in the physical body.

The Samuelses comment also on Paracelsus, the "Renaissance physician whose medicine embodied the link between occult mysticism and science":

> He worked in the early 1500's in Switzerland. He is considered to be the father of modern drug theory and scientific medicine. Nevertheless, Paracelsus opposed the idea of separating the spirit from the healing process.
>
> Paracelsus also said that "The power of the imagination is a great factor in medicine. It may produce disease in man and in animals, and it may cure them. . . . Ills of the body may be cured by physical remedies or by the power of the spirit acting through the soul." . . . He believed that a physician could heal by tapping the power of God. . . .
>
> Since Paracelsus' time "religious" and practical scientific methods of healing have split into distinct systems.[15]

Probably the most comprehensive and advanced writing available concerning spiritual healing from the viewpoint of the esotericist is the book *Esoteric Healing* by Alice Bailey. It is not practical to attempt to review the vast amount of material (771 pages) covered there, but a few observations are appropriate. Her book covers the basic causes of disease, the basic requirements for healing, and the laws and modes of healing, and it relates diseases to the subtle vehicles in man with which they are most closely associated (mental, emotional, or etheric). The significance and importance of the seven major force centers in man's subtle bodies relative to disease and healing are reviewed. Death and dying are discussed and Laws and Rules for healing are stated and discussed in some detail.

It might be of interest to repeat and briefly discuss one of these rules because it corresponds closely to the conclusions reached by Lawrence LeShan concerning the fundamental methods of healing. Rule Five from *Esoteric Healing* reads as follows:

The healer must seek to link his soul, his heart, his brain and his hands. Thus can he pour the vital healing force upon the patient. *This is magnetic work.* It cures disease or increases the evil state, according to the knowledge of the healer.

The healer must seek to link his soul, his brain, his heart and auric emanation. Thus can his presence feed the soul life of the patient. *This is the work of radiation.* The hands are needed not. The soul displays its power. The patient's soul responds through the response of his aura to the radiation of the healer's aura, flooded with soul energy.[16]

The correspondence between the two methods of healing mentioned in this rule and the *Type 2* and *Type 1* healings described by LeShan is clear. In commenting on Rule Five, Mrs. Bailey makes the following observation:

From just casually reading this Rule it will be obvious that its significance is vital to all successful healing work. It sums up the two modes of healing, based on two capacities of the healer, founded on two groups of related aspects in the healer's personality, and indicating two different points in evolution on the part of the healer. . . . In one case the patient's physical body is the objective of the healing art, whilst in the other it is the patient's soul which feels the effect of the healing energy. In the first case the healer works with the prana or vital planetary fluid, and in the other with soul energy. . . . The two types of energy are of a widely different quality, for one is purely of the personality and is sometimes called *animal magnetism*, and the other is of the soul, involving a type of work called radiation.

Mrs. Bailey goes on to comment that there are three types of healers: those who work purely through magnetism, those who work only at higher levels with the energy of the soul, and those who work in both of these ways. She also states that "at present [1953] in the modern world, there is no true system of spiritual healing taught to would-be healers."[17] This, of course, is not meant to imply that there are no successful healers at work. The book concludes with the prediction that there will be significant future advances in spiritual healing based on increased knowledge of the true energy nature of the matter that makes up man's physical body as brought out by advances in atomic physics and by greater understanding of the etheric body.

With the introduction of acupuncture to the West, its acceptance and use by many doctors, and its unquestioned success in many cases, the idea of the existence of subtle energy fields is given a significant scientific boost. The theory of acupuncture is based on the existence of an invisible energy flow pattern associated with the human being. This energy is called *Chi* by the Taoists and *prana* by the Hindus. The framework of its flow, as earlier mentioned, is called the *etheric body* by the esotericists, and it has been seen and reported by Dr. Kilner through his special screens and apparently photographed in both humans and plants by means of Kirlian photography. Figure 12 shows Kirlian thumb pad photographs, supplied by

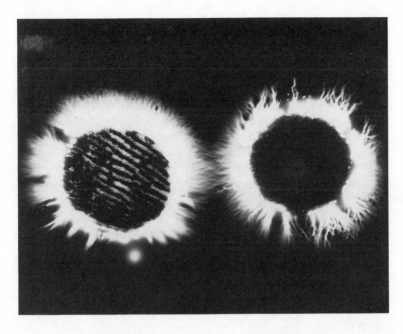

NORMAL   SPRAINED

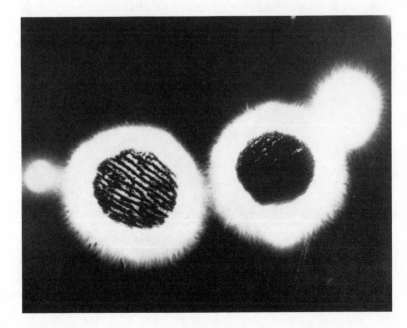

Fig. 12. Kirlian Photographs of the Thumb Pads of a Person with a
Sprained Thumb Before and After Acupuncture

Dr. Thelma Moss, of a person with a sprained thumb before and after acupuncture treatment. Dr. Moss's Kirlian photographs have also shown up the acupuncture points in the body. These points have been detected by an electrical-resistance measurement technique as well.

Eight different measurement methods for detecting and mapping the energy fields associated with living things are tabulated on pages 55 and 56 of the *Handbook of Psychic Discoveries* by Sheila Ostrander and Lynn Shroeder. One of these methods, the Burr voltmeter (which was designed to draw no current from life forms to be studied) was used by Yale University medical doctor and anatomist Harold Saxton Burr in collaboration with philosopher F. S. C. Northrop to measure electrical fields around humans, plants, trees, and even seeds. Burr measured what he termed the "lifefields" of trees on the Yale campus over a period of almost twenty years and found correlation with phases of the moon and sunspots and other cyclic variations with three- and six-month periods.[18]

Energy fields and healing are clearly areas where science and religion have the potential for converging. Religion and esotericism have already provided certain hypotheses concerning approaches to healing; force centers and flows and the Chinese acupuncture charts provide additional information. With this background and the new investigative techniques mentioned, perhaps a more complete theory with scientific substantiation can be developed for beneficial use by future practitioners.

15. Psychic Phenomena

Psychic phenomena such as precognition and the reading of thoughts have been associated with many great religious figures. The gospel accounts depict Christ as predicting his crucifixion and the events surrounding it as well as reading the thoughts of various individuals. Many of the writings of the Old Testament prophets are said to have been psychically received, and many of their prophecies were later demonstrated to be correct. The Koran is said to consist of the statements made by Muhammad as a result of instructions received by psychic means from a high authority, and the events of the Bhagavad Gita are stated in the introduction to be psychically observed by the one who described them.

The Yoga Sutras of the ancient Indian sage Patanjali discuss the sequential steps to be taken by the mentally focused members of the human race in order to progress spiritually. The process is called Raja Yoga, the yoga of the mind (lit. "kingly yoga"), and Patanjali mentions that certain psychic capabilities may emerge as this development proceeds. He also provides a warning, echoed by many other spiritual teachers, that excessive fascination with psychism can be an obstacle to further development.

More than simply being associated with or related to religion, psychic phenomena, scientifically verified, tend to prove the existence of an unseen world that can interact with the physical world. This, then, supports and validates one of the major claims of religion, that such a world (or worlds) exists. Further, certain types of psychic phenomena provide evidence of contact with entities whose physical life on earth has ended, thus supporting another claim of religion, that life in some form continues after physical death.

Thus the scientific investigation of psychic phenomena represents an area with potential for the melding of science and religion or perhaps for the partial validation of religion by science.

It also appears to be an area where there has been a significant level of activity in recent years. A *Los Angeles Times* article[1] estimates that there are 100 colleges and universities offering courses in parapsychology and

200 U.S. scientists involved in studies of this subject. Early milestones in the scientific investigation of psychic phenomena were the founding of the British Society for Psychical Research in 1882 and its American counterpart three years later. In more recent years the work done by Dr. J. B. Rhine and his wife, Louisa, at Duke University is widely recognized as a most significant pioneering effort in the field. The Rhines came to Duke University in September 1927 to do post-doctoral study under William McDougall, who had just taken over the Duke psychology department. McDougall had earlier been a professor of psychology at Oxford and then taken over the chair in psychology vacated by William James at Harvard in 1920. At the same time, McDougall became president of the American Society for Psychical Research, which had earlier been under the intellectual leadership of William James.

It is interesting to note that it was the investigation of the problem of postmortem survival that brought the Rhines to Duke and that interested Dr. McDougall when the work in parapsychology commenced there. The focus of attention in Rhine's experiments at Duke changed after a short while to telepathy, clairvoyance, and precognition. Convincing statistical evidence was produced under carefully controlled test conditions. This resulted in a great deal of publicity and no small amount of controversy. Today there are a number of colleges and universities throughout the world conducting experiments in parapsychology.

Psychic research has attracted the interest and support of two prominent individuals involved in the U.S. space program. The late rocket expert Dr. Wernher von Braun was a strong supporter of psychic research, calling it "one of the most promising fields of modern science." Former astronaut Dr. Edgar D. Mitchell, who became the sixth man on the moon during the Apollo program, has become deeply involved in the field of psychic research, founding the Institute of Noetic Sciences in Palo Alto, California. Dr. Mitchell recently compiled a book that provides an excellent review of some of the serious scientific work being done in the field of psychic phenomena. The book, entitled *Psychic Exploration: A Challenge for Science*, has chapters by thirty investigators (the majority being PhDs or MDs) covering a number of areas of psychic phenomena. It demonstrates a growing interest on the part of the scientific community in this field.

Another significant publication, which gained a great deal of attention, surveys psychic research in Russia, Bulgaria, and Czechoslovakia. This is the book entitled *Psychic Discoveries behind the Iron Curtain*, by Sheila Ostrander and Lynn Schroeder, which shows that there is a great deal of serious work occurring in these countries and that much has been achieved.

The information presented in both of these books strongly reinforces evidence presented by earlier investigators that psychic phenomena are real in spite of the many instances of deception uncovered among paid psychics and fortunetellers in the past.

Examples of investigation performed by scientists in the area of psychic phenomena include the demonstration of psychokinesis, or the influencing of physical events by the power of the mind. Tests conducted using two different types of random sources—a radioactively-based source constructed by theoretical physicist Dr. Helmut Schmidt, and a thermal noise random source used by researcher Charles Honorton at Maimonides Medical Center in Brooklyn, New York—both demonstrated that certain subjects appeared to be able to control these otherwise random processes wtih their thought.

Researchers at Stanford Research Institute have shown that many subjects are able to accurately describe in detail randomly selected distant sites they have never physically seen, including buildings, roads, and gardens.

These experiments are described in a book entitled *Mind Reach*[2] by researchers Russell Targ and Dr. Harold Puthoff of Stanford Research Institute and also in the international journal of science *Nature* and the *Proceedings of the Institute of Electrical and Electronics Engineers.*

16. The Vegetable Kingdom

In the attempt by man to understand the forces and mechanisms at work in the vegetable kingdom we have a field where experimental evidence shows a blending of the seen and the unseen, an interplay between dense physical matter and subtle energies that control this matter. It is a field where the areas usually addressed by religion and those traditionally explored by science are intermingled by the most successful investigators of the plant world.

In recent years a new surge of interest in the investigation of the effect human beings can have on plants through thought, emotion, or sound has been initiated as a result of experiments performed by lie-detector expert Cleve Backster. In 1966, on an impulse, Backster hooked the electrodes of one of his polygraph (lie detector) machines to the leaf of a large, palm-like plant in his office. He then watered the plant to see if this would have an effect on the polygraph, which measures electrical resistance. He did not notice any particular effect from the watering but did observe that the polygraph trace in general was similar to what he would expect from a human subject. Knowing that humans show strong polygraph reactions to physical danger, Backster decided to experiment along this line with the plant and dunked the end of a leaf into hot coffee. There was no significant reaction. Pondering this, he conceived the idea of burning the leaf of the plant that the electrodes were attached to. The instant he pictured this idea in his mind there was a dramatic reaction in the polygraph trace. This initial reaction led to a great many experiments by Backster and others, showing that plants respond to human thought about their well-being; that they can faint or swoon if threatened with overwhelming danger; that they can develop an affinity for those who care for them and respond to the thoughts or emotions of these persons over great distance; that they can respond to the death or danger of other living things (e.g. brine shrimp and spiders); and that they may have memory. These experiments have led Backster to conclude that, "Staggering as it may be to contemplate, a life signal may connect all creation."[1] Experiments similar to Backster's have been successfully conducted and reported on by Dr. Marcel Vogel of California.[2]

PIONEERS OF PLANT RESEARCH

More about Backster's experiments, along with a great deal of additional revealing information about the plant world, is found in the fascinating book by Peter Tompkins and Christopher Bird, *The Secret Life of Plants*.[3] The book reviews the findings of a number of individuals who have made contributions to our understanding of plants, and in reading about these people a common factor is noted. Those who had the most significant influence in pioneering plant research were men of deep spiritual perception. They can indeed be classified as "practical mystics." A few comments on each of these individuals will illustrate the point.

It should be noted initially that the ancient Zoroastrians attributed the initial breeding of the plants that we currently cultivate for food to the teaching of the religious leader Zarathustra, who founded their religion.

GEORGE WASHINGTON CARVER

The black scientist George Washington Carver is probably best known for bringing the peanut (which was previously judged useful only for hog food) and the unknown sweet potato to public attention as valuable foods, and for creating from them hundreds of products, "ranging from cosmetics and axle grease to printer's ink and coffee."[4]

From the time he was very young, Carver exhibited an ability to heal sick animals with certain varieties of plants and to bring ailing house plants back to health. They were brought to him by local farmers' wives in his Ozark foothill community of Diamond Grove, Missouri. Asked how he accomplished this, the young Carver replied: "All flowers talk to me and so do hundreds of little living things in the woods. I learn what I know by watching and loving everything."

Carver received a master's degree from Iowa State College of Agriculture, and turning down an offer to join the faculty there, he accepted instead a lower-paying post offered to him by Booker T. Washington at the Normal and Industrial Institute in Tuskegee, Alabama. He set out there to solve the main problem he saw facing farmers in the South: soil depletion through repeated planting of a single crop, cotton. He set up an experimental station with a laboratory he called "God's Little Worshop" and experimented with different natural fertilization techniques and with the peanut plant, which could grow well in poor soil. In one sleepless week Carver broke the peanut down into its chemical constituents, discovered that the peanut contained seven different varieties of oil, and, working with the different chemical parts of the peanut, created two dozen brand-new products.

He then set upon the difficult but ultimately successful task of convincing the farmers to plow under their cotton and plant the more valuable peanut. One of his bulletins to the farmers at the time pointed out that a good-tasting, nutritious butter could be made from the peanut. Anyone with young children will recognize the extent to which this idea of Carver's has become a staple in the American diet.

Carver made it a practice to rise each day at four o'clock and walk in the woods before the start of his working day, often bringing back plants to illustrate his lectures. Commenting on this habit he said, "Nature is the greatest teacher and I learn from her best when others are asleep. In the still dark hours before sunrise God tells me of the plans I am to fulfill." When questioned about where his ideas came from, he said they came to him in flashes of inspiration while walking in the woods. When there was a shortage of dyestuffs in World War I, "Carver rambled at daybreak through the mist and dew, inquiring from plant friends which of them could alleviate the deficit. From the leaves, roots, stems, and fruits of twenty-eight volunteers he coaxed 536 separate dyes."[5]

Carver received offers of employment at very substantial salaries from both Thomas Edison and Henry Ford, who called him "the greatest living scientist." He turned down both offers.

Clearly, Carver demonstrated great spiritual insight in his life and accomplishments. In responding to an inquirer who questioned why so few had his power and who besides Carver could do what he could, he replied: "Everyone can if only they believe it." Tapping a Bible on a table he added, "The secrets are all here in God's promises. These promises are real—as real as, and more infinitely solid and substantial than, this table which the materialist so thoroughly believes in."

On another occasion, touching a little flower on his workbench, Carver said, "When I touch that flower, I am touching infinity. . . . Through the flowers I talk to the Infinite, which is only a silent force."[6]

LUTHER BURBANK

In 1892, Luther Burbank, a New England transplant to Santa Rosa, California, published a 52-page nurseryman's catalogue called *New Creations in Fruits and Flowers* that created a sensation.

The catalogue did not contain a single plant previously known to man. As a result of his work with plants, he became known as "The Wizard of Horticulture," and his accomplishments led to the inclusion in Webster's dictionary of the verb *burbank*, which means "to modify and improve (plants or animals) by selective breeding. Also to cross or graft (a plant). Hence, . . . to improve anything . . . by a selecting of good features and rejecting of bad.''

Burbank's comments before a 1901 floral congress gives some indication of how he viewed his work:

> The chief work of botanists of yesterday was the study and classification of dried, shriveled plant mummies whose souls had fled. They thought their classified species were more fixed and unchangeable than anything in heaven or earth. . . . We have learned that they are as plastic in our hands as clay in the hands of the potter or color on the artist's canvas and can readily be moulded into more beautiful forms and colors than any painter or sculptor can ever hope to bring forth.[7]

Burbank is responsible for developing the potato that today ''dominates the U.S. potato market'' and varieties of prunes and plums that still account for half of California's crop. Peaches, nectarines, and quinces developed by Burbank are also widely used today. All in all, Burbank introduced over a thousand new plants.

When the 1906 earthquake that caused the near-destruction of San Francisco reduced Santa Rosa to a mass of rubble, citizens of the town were amazed that there was not even a pane of glass broken in Burbank's greenhouse. Tompkins and Bird note that, ''Burbank was less amazed than his fellow townsmen, though careful not to broach the subject directly in public, surmising that his communing with the forces of nature and the cosmos and his success with plants might well have protected his greenhouse.'' They also state that Burbank revealed to Manly P. Hall, founder of the Philosophical Research Society of Los Angeles, ''that when he wanted his plants to develop in some particular and peculiar way not common to their kind he would get down on his knees and talk to them.''[8]

Helen Keller wrote after a visit to Burbank, ''He has the rarest of gifts, the receptive spirit of a child. When plants talk to him he listens. Only a wise child can understand the language of flowers and trees.''[9]

Along the same line, Burbank used the following words in a lecture before the American Pomological Society entitled ''How to Produce New Fruits and Flowers.'':

> Some conditions are necessary before we can become one of nature's interpreters or the creator of any valuable work for the world. Preconceived notions, dogmas and all personal prejudice and bias must be laid aside. Listen patiently, quietly and reverently to the lessons, one by one, which Mother Nature has to teach, shedding light on that which was before a mystery, so that all who will, may see and know. She conveys her truths only to those who are passive and receptive. Accepting these truths as suggested, wherever they may lead, then we have the whole universe in harmony with us.

JAGADIS CHANDRA BOSE

More than fifty years ago a scientist from India devised and used instruments that measure the growth and behavior of plants in the greatest of detail by magnifying movements and changes up to 100 million times. The inventor and user of these instruments was Sir Jagadis Chandra Bose, a genius whose scientific work embraced the fields of physics, physiology and psychology. No attempt will be made to catalog his accomplishments here, but the extent of his work is indicated by the following statement made by the authors of *The Secret Life of Plants*: "[He] found out more about plants than anyone before and perhaps after him." The *Encyclopaedia Britannica* commented on his work in plant physiology almost a half-century after his death: "It was so much in advance of his time it could not be precisely evaluated."[10]

Among Bose's most fascinating achievements was his demonstration through carefully conducted measurements that similar response curves were obtained with metals or animal muscles after exposure to the effects of fatigue or stimulating, depressing, or poisoning drugs. Reflecting on these results, Bose turned to the vegetable kingdom. He showed that response to "blows" was essentially the same as with metals and muscles. He showed that when he chloroformed plants, they were anesthesized, just as in the case of animals, and when he blew away the vapors they revived. After a great deal of detailed work Bose concluded that "plants have a sensitive nervous system and a varied emotional life."[11] It was his contention that they responded to stimuli with the equivalent of love, hate, joy, fear, and other appropriate responses, as in the case of animals.

Describing his findings in experiments with metals and with what we normally refer to as living things before the evening session of the Royal Institution on May 10, 1901, Bose concluded:

> I have shown you this evening autographed records of the history of stress and strain in the living and the non-living. How similar are the writings! So similar indeed that you cannot tell one apart from the other. Among such phenomena, how can we draw a line of demarcation and say, here the physical ends, and there the physiological begins? Such absolute barriers do not exist.
>
> It was when I came upon the mute witness of these self-made records, and perceived in them one phase of a pervading unity that bears within it all things . . . it was then that I understood for the first time a little of that message proclaimed by my ancestors on the banks of the Ganges thirty centuries ago: "They who see but one, in all the changing manifoldness of this universe, unto them belongs Eternal Truth."

One of the world's authorities on metals at the time, Sir Robert Austen, praised Bose's lecture and commented: "I have all my life studied the properties of metals and am happy to think they have life." He acknowledged he had formed a similar view but had been rebuffed when he hinted at it before the Royal Institution.

Bose's perception of the unity of all things arrived at from the perspective of the scientist agrees, of course, with the declaration of many mystics throughout the ages; and his conclusion, that even objects as apparently unchanging as metals have life, agrees with the view consistently expressed by esotericists.

GOETHE

Long before Bose did his remarkable work, a genius of plants lived in Europe who, although well known to the public, is rarely recognized for his accomplishments in this field. Johann Wolfgang von Goethe was considered Germany's greatest poet when he died on March 22, 1832, but was relatively unknown as a scientist. Yet the famous biologist Ernst Haeckel viewed Goethe along with Lamarck as standing "at the head of all the great philosophers of nature who first established a theory of organic development, and who are the illustrious fellow workers of Darwin."

Through a deep study of the structure and growth of plants, Goethe perceived an inner identity in the various structures formed in different parts of a plant and concluded that nature could bring out many variations of form through modifications of a single organ. He clearly recognized and stated the principle that Luther Burbank used so successfully at a much later time: "The variations of plant forms whose unique course I had long been following, now awakened in me more and more the idea that the plant forms round about us are not predetermined, but are happily mobile and flexible, enabling them to adapt to the many conditions throughout the world, which influences them, and to be formed and re-formed with them."

What Goethe called his doctrine of the metamorphosis of plants was in effect a theory of evolution that preceded Darwin by more than thirty years. But unlike Darwin, who attributed evolutionary changes to purely external material and mechanical causes, Goethe believed that an inner essence was involved in the process, creating the outer modifications that made the plant more adaptable to its environment. It is interesting that Luther Burbank was very impressed and inspired by Darwin's extensive writings on plants but was more aligned with Goethe relative to the hidden forces behind the outer forms in the vegetable kingdom.

Rudolf Steiner, the esotericist who introduced a very successful cultivation method called *biodynamic farming*, was in his early years a deep student of Goethe's life and work. He writes as follows concerning the different viewpoints of Darwin and Goethe:

> It was from observations similar to those of Goethe that Darwin proceeded when he asserted his doubt as to the constancy of the external forms of genera

and species. But the conclusions which the two thinkers reached were entirely unlike. Whereas Darwin considered that the whole nature of the organism was, in fact, comprised in these characteristics, and came to the conclusion, therefrom, that there is nothing constant in the life of the plant, Goethe went deeper and drew the inference that, since those characteristics are not constant, what is constant must be sought in something else which lies beneath changeable externalities.

In his early years, in an attempt to better understand the hidden forces of nature, Goethe studied the works of esotericists, mystics, and philosophers such as Paracelsus, Jacob Boehme, Giordano Bruno, and Spinoza. Perhaps as a result of this background, his approach to the study of plants had a mystical element to it. In the words of Tompkins and Bird:

> Above all, Goethe learned that the treasures of nature are not discovered by one who is not in sympathy with nature. He realized that the normal techniques of botany could not get near to the living being of a plant as an organism in a cycle of growth. Some other form of looking was needed which could unite itself with the life of the plant. To obtain a clearer picture of a plant, Goethe would tranquilize himself at night before going to sleep by visualizing the entire cycle of a plant's development through its various stages from seed to seed.[12]

GUSTAV THEODOR FECHNER

Goethe's contention that there was some spiritual essence behind the outer appearance of plants was concurred in by a later investigator who published in 1848 a book called *Nanna, or the Soul Life of Plants*. The writer of this book was Gustav Theodor Fechner, a medical doctor and professor of physics at the University of Leipzig with over forty technical papers to his credit.

Fechner gained his deep insight into plants following a long period during which he lived in seclusion in a darkened room with a mask over his face, praying for recovery from near blindness caused by staring at the sun in an attempt to understand the nature of the afterimages that persist after looking at a bright object.

Three years after the incident, realizing that his sight had been restored, he emerged into the light of a spring morning and recognized that the trees and flowers he saw were "be-souled."

> As I stood by the water and watched a flower, it was as though I saw its soul lift itself from the bloom and, drifting through the mist, become clearer until the spiritual form hung clearly above it.[13]

Fechner also expressed the view that all life is one, and in a book on atomic theory published two years after *Nanna* he "argued that atoms were centers of pure energy and the lowest elements in a spiritual hierarchy."[14]

THE FINDHORN COMMUNITY

In modern times an agricultural marvel has emerged from some barren sandy soil in a remote area of northern Scotland. This community, called Findhorn, has produced vegetables and flowers unheard of in size and quality any place on earth, much less in the forbidding climate and soil of northern Scotland, bordering the Arctic Circle.

This community used organic farming methods in producing their results, and while it has been shown elsewhere that these techniques are beneficial in producing larger crops and healthier food, the accomplishments at Findhorn were not logically explainable as resulting from these methods alone. Such things as 42-pound cabbages simply do not grow in northern Scotland. Agricultural experts were amazed at what had been achieved at Findhorn and uniformly concluded that the plant growth and quality was far beyond what could be expected from the external methods used, the soil, the weather conditions in the area, and the fertilizer applied.

One of these experts, Sir George Trevelyan (who also pioneered adult education in England), after seeing the garden and tasting the vegetables, realized that something very unusual was happening and was determined to understand it.

The founders of the community, Peter and Eileen Caddy, had up until that time been reluctant to discuss any factors behind their success other than organic farming. But Sir George refused to accept that, and his questioning was so intense and persistent that Peter (who had formerly been an R.A.F. squadron leader and a hotel-keeper, and who had some Rosicrucian training) finally revealed the remarkable sequence of events behind Findhorn.

Fortunately Sir George was somewhat prepared to accept what they were to tell him, having been a student of Rudolf Steiner and his biodynamic methods of agriculture based on Steiner's investigation of "etheric formative forces."

Sir George wrote a memo following his visit to Findhorn in 1968, and after describing the remarkable growth he saw in the poor and sandy soil, he went on to write: "There must be, I thought, a Factor 'X' to be taken into consideration."[15]

The memo went on to outline the remarkable story Peter Caddy revealed to him. He described Caddy's group as living a "God-centered life," with Caddy's wife making daily contact through meditation at a high spiritual level and thereby bringing direction for the activities. He was told that another member of the group, a sensitive named Dorothy, obtained practical advice for the group of amateurs in working this difficult land. Knowing that "Devas"* were described as the architects of the plant world, she

*See Angels, chapter 5.

asked for and received advice from certain of the Devas in meditation. Another key participant was an older man named Roger Ogilvie Crombie, who was called Roc. Caddy explained that Roc's consciousness was opened up to the elemental world, a part of the Deva evolution, and he was able at times to communicate with these beings. All three provided the inputs for Caddy, who did and directed the practical work.

The Findhorn community were not the only ones who had testified as to the existence of the Deva kingdom and that nature spirits of that kingdom were involved with plants. In *The Secret Life of Plants*, we read:

> Carver's insistence that nature spirits abound in the woods and take part in the growth of plants may have to be reviewed in the light of the discoveries of the Theosophists and especially of such extraordinary seers of nature spirits as Geoffrey Hodson. The ancient wisdom, as detailed by seers like Mesdames Helena P. Blavatsky and Alice A. Bailey, throws quite another light on the energy of bodies, both of humans and of plants, as well as the relations of individual cells to the entire cosmos.[16]

Esotericists have insisted that the stories of fairies, elves, and nymphs from earlier cultures had their foundation with individuals whose clairvoyant vision could detect the etheric or astral images of these beings who do not possess dense physical bodies. As noted in chapter 5, "The Esotericists," Geoffrey Hodson in his book *Kingdom of the Gods* has provided illustrations of his clairvoyant observations of these colorful beings.

As Findhorn's reputation began to spread, the community grew to almost two hundred people and a new role emerged, that of teaching. Both through example and more formal methods (a "college" was formed by the community), "New Age" spiritual principles were taught. The interrelationship between man and the other kingdoms of nature and the significance of the proper handling of the energies that flow through man, and especially through groups such as that at Findhorn, were emphasized. A key individual in helping to lead this phase of the work was David Spangler, who came to Findhorn in June of 1970 and stayed during the following three years of the community's greatest growth. Spangler began having psychic experiences when he was still a baby and has had since he was very young a sense of being in two dimensions simultaneously. His lectures to the community were the base on which the teaching activities grew. His creative output is prolific and exhibits deep spiritual insight. His lectures at Findhorn have been termed "lectures that changed lives." Spangler saw the significance of Findhorn as "a demonstration that people can take the fate of the world into their hands."[17]

17. Astrology: A Dilemma for Religion and Science

I never behold the stars that I do not feel that I am looking in the face of God. I can see how it might be possible for a man to look down upon the earth and be an atheist but I cannot conceive how he could look up into the heavens and say there is no God.

—Abraham Lincoln

Astrology is a subject that is not universally held in high regard by either science or religion, but there are some who believe it has a significant relationship to both. We will explore this later in the chapter, following a brief review of the history of astrology.

HISTORICAL BACKGROUND

The beginnings of astrology are lost in antiquity, but records indicate that the Sumerians, Babylonians, Chaldeans, Assyrians, and Egyptians practiced astrology, and in the western hemisphere the Mayans and Aztecs had developed a complete system of astrological delineation. It was also well developed in the pre-Christian era in China.

Astrology was practiced in ancient Greece and Rome, and Pythagoras, Plato, and Aristotle believed in the influence of the stars in human activities. Hippocrates used astrology as an aid in practicing medicine. In A.D. 140, the Greek astonomer Claudius Ptolemeus (Ptolemy), who is viewed as the creator of mathematical astronomy, wrote the most famous and detailed work on Greek astrology, called *Tetrabiblos* or *Quadripartitum* (The Four Books). The names given to the planets by the Greeks correspond to their principal deities, and the corresponding names given by the Romans (Mars, Mercury, etc.) are still used today. Julius Caesar and Pompey were firm believers in astrology, which was in high regard in the early Roman era.

Astrology flourished in early Islam and was spread by the Saracen conquest. The sources of Arab astrology are neo-Platonic in origin, with the fundamental teachings said to be related back to Hermes. Astrology blossomed in Baghdad at the height of its glory and included the construction of an observatory that was a working place for astrologers. The most famous astrologer of this era was Albumasar, who died in A.D. 886. His book *The Flowers of Astrology*, translated into Latin, was one of the first books published in Germany by Gutenberg.

In Europe through the Middle Ages and the Renaissance we find many well-known individuals closely associated with astrology. Paracelsus, the famous physician and alchemist, was convinced of the influence of the sun, the planets, and the stars on man, and Roger Bacon was similarly both an alchemist and astrologer.

In France and England in the 14th, 15th, and 16th centuries, many prominent individuals were believers in astrology. Kings Charles V, Charles VI, and Charles VII of France, as well as Francis I and the Duke of Berry, all used astrologers. Catherine de Medici, the Florentine wife of Henry II, was a protector of a number of astrologers, including Luc Gauric, Cosme Ruggieri, and the famous doctor Michel de Nostredame, better known as Nostradamus. In addition to being one of the most famous doctors of his time, he was an astrologer and prophet whose work *Centuries* saw continuous reprints and contained some amazingly accurate predictions. He died at the exact time and under the conditions he had himself predicted.

Among the scientists of that era who set the stage for modern astronomy, we find that the most important were either astrologers themselves or men who expressed conviction in the principles. Copernicus "did not deny his belief in planetary influences."[1] Tycho Brahe, the great Danish astronomer, and Johann Kepler, his student who formulated the three great laws of planetary motion, both spent some of their time preparing horoscopes. Galileo, who assembled one of the first telescopes and discovered the moons around Jupiter, Saturn's rings, hills and valleys on the moon, and spots on the sun, was also an astrologer.

Francis Bacon wrote *Astrologia-Sana* and expressed the opinion that astrology had validity; and Giordano Bruno was likewise convinced of its merits.

William Lilly was a well-known astrologer in the 1600s who issued an early prophetic almanac and was summoned to appear before a committee of the House of Commons to be questioned about his accurate prediction of the Great Fire of London. (He was cleared of having any part in causing the fire.) John Flamsteed, the first Astronomer Royal of England, used astrology to determine the best time for laying the cornerstone for the Greenwich Observatory.

Astrology played an important part in Rosicrucianism, which saw an upsurge of interest in the early 17th century. One of the well-known figures associated with the fraternity "which had as its aim the reintegration and regeneration of humanity,"[2] was Robert Fludd, an English alchemist and well-known doctor. Fludd stated in his writings, as Paracelsus had also done, that each part of the human body has a planetary influence corresponding to it. This correspondence is well known to modern astrologers.

Mystic Jacob Boehme commented on astrology in the introduction to his three principles: "Good reader, I compare all philosophy, astrology and theology, as joined at the source from where they are derived, to a beautiful tree which grows in a garden of beauty."[3] Goethe was also an enthusiastic defender of astrology.

One of the most important individuals in reintroducing astrology in modern times was William Frederick Allan (1860–1917), who used the pen name Alan Leo. He wrote thirty books that constitute a modern restatement of astrology. A visit to a library or bookstore today will reveal that there are a whole host of modern writers on the subject of astrology.

There is a medieval adage concerning astrology which it is important to keep in mind when considering this subject: *Astra inclinant, non necessetant*—"The stars influence, they do not compel." This adage is also subscribed to by competent modern astologers. Astrology, they claim, indicates influences which one can work with but that should not lead to a fatalistic outlook.

PHYSICAL SCIENCE AND ASTROLOGY

The skepticism concerning astrology among today's scientists is forcefully illustrated by science writer Lawrence E. Jerome's success in obtaining the signatures of 192 scientists (including a number of Nobel Prize winners) on a statement he wrote in collaboration with a professor of astonomy and a professor of philosophy. The statement is entitled "Objections to Astrology" and cautions "the public against the unquestioning acceptance of the predictions and advice given privately and publicly by astrologers"—a caution that cerainly seems appropriate. The statement goes on to say, among other things, that there is no verified scientific basis for the belief in astrology.

Jerome includes the statement, with the list of signers, in his book *Astrology Disproved*. In spite of the title, the book does not contain statistical information to disprove astrology in a scientific sense but does offer some theories on how astrology might appear to be valid even if it is not. Jerome contends that the power of suggestion and the use of the conscious and unconscious mind by the astrologer in gathering clues from the subject's involuntarily responses figures in the success of astrologers. This, of course, does not explain how astrologers can give credible indications of a person's strengths, weaknesses, and other characteristics by working only from date and time of birth and without ever meeting the individual involved. However, Jerome does pose a line of argument that if the astrologer can keep his statements sufficiently vague and general, he can come up with a fair number of right-sounding comments with most individuals just through the laws of probability.

On the other hand, Jerome notes the "alarmingly accurate" predictions of astrologer Karl Ernst Kraft, who correctly indicated the time and place of the 1939 assassination attempt on Adolf Hitler. He acknowledges that Kraft was gifted with "mathematical brilliance and psychological talents" and adds that "there have always been a few successful astrologers who seemed to be able to achieve well-above-chance results." Jerome suggests that this may be related to his earlier-mentioned theories as well as to some sort of statistical phenomena by adding, "Since there have no doubt been millions of astrologers in the history of the world, it is to be expected that a few should achieve high scores."[4] Carl Jung, also noting that certain astrologers were capable of remarkably accurate predictions, suggested that their success might involve psychic ability, which Dr. Rhine's experiments had shown could improve predictions.

It is perfectly logical for scientists to seriously doubt that astrology has validity. Astrology does not fit any of the well-known principles in physical science today, and so there is no easily made connection between science and astrology. There is nothing that science can presently measure to indicate that the location of the planets, sun, and moon relative to the fixed stars as viewed from earth at a given time should make any significant difference to life on earth. Further, those who read the astrological columns in newspapers will not find a particularly high degree of correlation between what is predicted and what occurs.

Concerns similar to these undoubtedly motivated the astronomer Halley, the discoverer of the comet named after him, to express his doubts about astrology to Sir Isaac Newton. Newton's famous reply in defense of astrology was "Sir, I have studied it, you have not." As we have seen in the historical survey, a number of other early scientists were also astrologers.

A comment might be appropriate here concerning the astrological forecasts given in newspapers. These should not be used to evaluate the validity of astrology because even astrologers do not consider them to be very accurate. The problem is that there is a great deal of detail, considered important by astrologers, that is omitted by the newspaper columns that attempt to cover all individuals born under a given sun sign (in effect for about one month of the year) independent of the year, date, or time of birth of the individual. This, astrologers state, is so superficial as to be of extremely limited significance. Thus, even if astrology were completely valid, the information given in newspapers could not be expected to have a very high degree of accuracy and could even provide misleading information, as compared with a more detailed analysis for a given individual.

A STATISTICAL LOOK AT ASTROLOGY

An impressive statistical survey of the influence of the stars on people's destiny has been performed by the French statistician Michel Gauquelin. He feels that his statistical investigations do not support a number of contentions about stellar influences made by astrologers, but he does find a clear correlation between the planetary configuration at the time of birth and the talents and tendencies later exhibited by the individual. Initially, Gauquelin did a chart analysis of 576 members of the French Academy of Medicine and discovered a high incidence of the planets Mars and Saturn in prominent position* in the horoscopes of these individuals, while similar studies made on individuals at random did not show this result. An additional review of the horoscopes of 508 famous physicians showed results similar to the first physicians' group. These data motivated Gauquelin to compile data on the birth dates of 25,000 people in many occupational groups and in different countries. Gauquelin wrote concerning some of his conclusions:

> A great many individuals born when Mars was appearing over the horizon or passing at the highest point of its course later became famous doctors, great athletes, or military leaders, while future artists, painters or musicians were seldom born at the times propitious for doctors or athletes. Actors and politicians were born more frequently when Jupiter rose or culminated but scientists were rarely born at that time. Thus, as far as vocational success was concerned, the moon, Mars, Jupiter, and Saturn were found to act as planetary clocks.[5]

In another study, Gauquelin compared the charts of 15,000 couples and their children and showed, as would be predicted by astrologers, that a high degree of correlation between such charts was validated, with odds of 500,000-to-1 against chance correlation.

In spite of this, Gauquelin himself does not believe in astrology but believes that there are undiscovered scientific laws that cause inherent hereditary tendencies in an individual to bring about birth under certain planetary configurations.

John Anthony West and Jan Gerhard Toonder, who have made an extensive study of astrology, disagree with this conclusion. In a book entitled *The Case for Astrology*,[6] they state that "Gauquelin's work proves once and for all that there is *something* to astrology." They acknowledge that "it does not prove that astrologers know what they are doing . . . . But it does prove beyond any possible shadow of doubt, that there is a direct correlation between the position of planets at birth and the profession a man subsequently practices." They believe that Gauquelin is so blinded by modern science and so opposed to astrology (which he set out to disprove) that he talks in terms of a new science rather than working at applying his results to the tradition of astrology.

West and Toonder also cite the results of three well-controlled sets of experiments conducted by psychologist Vernon Clark, each of which tested

---

*Aspecting the ascendant or mid-heaven.

the ability of a group of twenty or more astrologers to make judgments about people based only on horoscopes provided to them. The first experiment was to show whether astrologers could determine character from birth data. The second tested their ability to match key events in a person's life with a horoscope, and the third asked astrologers to pick people who were victims of cerebral palsy from others with similar charts who were above average in intelligence and exceptionally gifted in some way. Elaborate steps were taken in the last two tests to minimize the possibility of the astrologer's obtaining data through extrasensory perception.

In all of these tests, the astrologers scored very well; statistically, in each of the tests the odds against their results being attributable to chance was 100-to-1 or greater.

PSYCHOLOGY AND ASTROLOGY

In addition to early astronomer-astrologers, an area where there has been a certain amount of cooperative work between science and astrology is the field of psychology and psychiatry. Carl Jung had experts in astrology on his staff and used astrological information in some difficult cases under his care. In *Modern Man in Search of a Soul*, Jung writes: "We are born at a given moment in a given place, and we have (like the best wines) the qualities of the year and the season which witnessed our birth. Astrology claims no more than this." Commenting on the increased serious interest in astrology, he further notes: "The Philistines believed until recently that astrology had been disposed of long since, and was something that could be safely laughed at. But today, rising out of the social deeps, it knocks at the doors of universities from which it was banned some three hundred years ago."[7] There have also been recent newspaper reports of psychiatrists using astrologers to aid in character analysis and especially to predict periods of stress in suicidal and other seriously afflicted patients so that preventative measures could be taken.

HOW THE STARS MIGHT AFFECT US

Let us consider very briefly the sort of concepts described by the advocates of astrology to explain how stellar influence might affect us. Because of the rotation of the earth about the sun once a year, the sun when viewed from the earth appears to move relative to the fixed stars. The plane of this relative motion is called *the ecliptic*. The planets and the moon also move in this approximate plane. The Zodiac is a circular band of sky intersected by the ecliptic and extending 8 degrees on either side of it as viewed from earth (see Fig. 13). The Zodiac is divided into twelve equal sections, and each section is given the name and sign of the constellation within it. These names—Aries, Taurus, Gemini, etc.—are well known to those familiar with astrology. The information used by astrologers in making their analyses is the position of the sun, moon, and planets within the

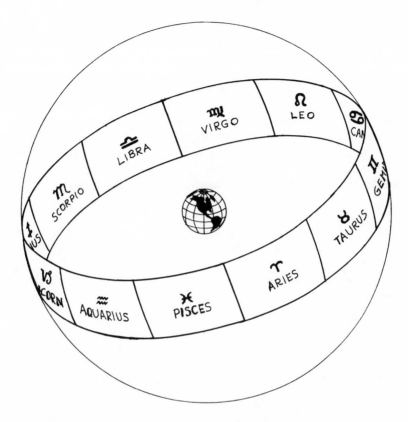

Fig. 13. The Zodiac

Zodiac as viewed from earth at the time in question. The imparting of astrological influences can be conceptualized in terms of energy from a given section of the Zodiac, which has its own peculiar characteristics, being focused and conditioned by a planet, the sun, or the moon aligned between this section of the Zodiac and the earth. The planet in this case is believed to bestow its own distinctive influence on energy from that area of the Zodiac. The types of influences claimed to be imparted by the different zodiacal signs and the sun, moon, and planets have been catalogued over the years by astrologers and refined with experience. Astrologers also attach significance to certain angular relationships between the various bodies of the solar system as viewed from earth.

How and why the stars and solar-system bodies might have an influence here on earth is easier to comprehend today than in Newton's time. Today the public is familiar with such concepts as invisible forms of energy. Invisible electromagnetic waves are transmitted and transformed by television and radio to sights and sounds that the physical senses can detect.

Coupling this understanding with the concepts, discussed earlier, of invisible levels of existence interpenetrating and influencing our physical world makes at least some level of comprehension of astrological influences a possibility. We can conceive of the possibility of energy from a constellation being focused and qualified by the invisible aura of an aligned planet before impinging on earth, where it somehow influences the subtle mechanism of a human being or animal. The ability to explain these influences accurately in terms of our present scientific knowledge is virtually nonextistent, but when the methods of astrological analysis that have been accumulated through the ages are applied by a skilled practitioner, they sometimes seem to provide remarkably accurate results.

ASTROLOGY AND RELIGION

Astrology is far more widely accepted among religious people in the East than in the West. Among Hindus an astrological chart is often drawn up at the birth of a new child.

Dr. W. Y. Evans-Wentz comments on astrology in Buddhism and Hinduism:

> Astrology . . . is known to have been in the lives of many . . . if not all, of the Sages of the Mahayana [branch of Buddhism] and as it still is in the life of every Oriental who has remained true to his or her wisdom-born ancestral heritge.

> Learned Indian astrologers maintain that astrology *per se* is of all sciences the most important, because there can be no true art of living apart from it. In so viewing astrology, they exclude, as being unworthy of the name astrology, almost all of that which poses for astrology in the Occident and the greater part of that which is popularly called astrology in the Orient.

He comments further:

> Astrology does not, however, imply fatalism; for the master of yoga is also the master of astrological influences and by knowing them, is enabled scientifically to chart the course of his Vessel of Salvation across the Sea of Existence in such a manner as to avoid the hidden reefs and shallows; and be prepared for tempests and contrary currents and at last, attain the safety of the Other Shore.[8]

Astrology plays virtually no part in organized Western religion, but as we shall see, the Bible contains quite a bit of astrological symbolism.

As to church attitudes on astrology, Serge Hutin concludes in his study, *History of Astrology*: "In fact there was never to be in the Church any express condemnation of astrology; and many clerics would cultivate the discipline, right up to modern times." He adds in a footnote: "The condemnations would only be aimed at charlatanism, or really deliberate belief in total planetary fatalism."[9]

The new English translation of the Bible that is presently used in the

Roman Catholic church has substituted the name "astrologers" for "wise men" in the story of the birth of Jesus, thus lending some measure of biblical credibility to the practice of astrology.[10]

In the New Testament story we find Jesus often associated with fish—having selected fishermen for some of his disciples, causing them to draw in a miraculous catch of fish, speaking of his disciples as fishers of men, and performing the miracle of the loaves and the fishes. The symbology persists in churches to this day. Those familiar with astrology will recognize that Christ's appearance coincided with the start of the Piscean age, a period of approximately 2000 years, during which the vernal equinox has occurred in the constellation Pisces, and during which Christianity has spread and flourished. The astrological symbol for Pisces is, of course, a pair of fishes.

It is also claimed that Christ symbolically referred to the Aquarian age, and the task he would return to perform when that age began, in the New Testament story of the Last Supper. In Luke 22 we read that he sent Peter and John to prepare the Passover, telling them, "Behold, when ye are entered into the city, there shall a man meet you, bearing a pitcher of water; follow him into the house where he entereth in" (Luke 22:10). The disciples were instructed to prepare for what was to become the communion meal in a large upper room that the man of the house would show them.

The symbol for the astrological sign Aquarius, the age we are in the process of transitioning into, is a man carrying a jar of water. Alice Bailey writes, in connection with this Bible symbology, that "the great spiritual achievement and evolutionary event of that age will be the communion and human relationships established among all peoples, enabling men everywhere to sit down together in the Presence of the Christ, and share the bread and wine (symbols of nourishment.)"[11]

Another piece of astrological symbolism which appears in the New Testament is that of the fixed cross of the Zodiac. This is the cross made by the fixed* signs Taurus, Leo, Scorpio, and Aquarius (see Fig. 14). In the fourth chapter of Revelation, John writes: "I was in the spirit: and behold, a throne was set in heaven, and one sat upon the throne." John goes on to describe the four and twenty elders and seven spirits before the throne and then describes four beasts "in the midst of the throne, and round about the throne. . . . And the first beast was like a lion, and the second beast like a calf, and the third beast had a face as a man, and the fourth beast was like a flying eagle" (Rev. 4:2,6,7). If we take into account that the constellation Aquila the Eagle rises at the same time as the zodiacal sign Scorpio the Scorpion, and if we recognize that in early astrology the eagle symbol was often used for this section of the Zodiac, we realize that these

---

*The signs of the Zodiac are characterized by astrologers as fixed, mutable, or cardinal signs, and the four signs in each category are positioned so that they form three crosses.

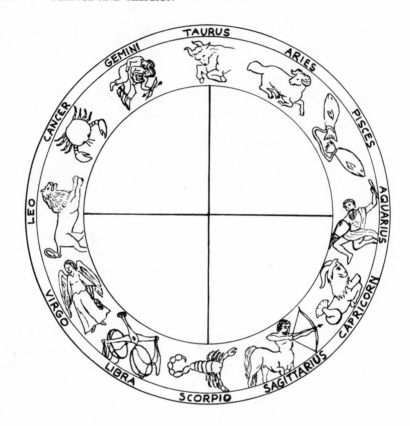

Fig. 14. The Fixed Cross of the Zodiac

beasts correspond to the four fixed signs of the Zodiac. Esoteric writings refer to these four signs, or the Fixed Cross of the Zodiac, as the cross of the second Person of the Trinity.[12]

In the Old Testament we find Ezekiel experiencing a vision with similar symbology. He describes seeing four living creatures with faces of a man, a lion, an ox, and an eagle (see Ezek. 1:10).

We also find on some Catholic church pulpits the writers of the four gospels symbolized by these four fixed signs. Matthew is symbolized by the face of a man, Mark by the face of a lion, Luke by the face of a bull or ox, and John by the face of an eagle.

Many have asserted that the twelve tribes of Israel mentioned in several places in the Bible are associated with the twelve signs of the Zodiac. Table 4 shows the connections made between the characteristics of the twelve signs of the Zodiac and the twelve tribes described in the words of the dying Jacob to his sons as he projects the future of the tribes (Gen. 49).

TABLE 4. SIGNS OF THE ZODIAC AND THE 12 TRIBES OF ISRAEL.

SIGN	TRIBE	CHARACTERISTIC
Aquarius	Reuben	"Unstable as water."
Gemini	Simeon and Levi	"Simeon and Levi are brethren."
Leo	Judah	"A lion's whelp."
Pisces	Zebulon	"Shall dwell at the haven of the sea."
Taurus	Issachar	"A strong ass crouching down between burdens." (The association with the stables is cited here.)
Scorpio and Virgo	Dan	"A serpent by the way, an adder in the path that biteth."
Virgo independent of Scorpio	Dina	(The only daughter of Jacob)
Aries	Gad	"He shall overcome at the last."
Libra	Asher	"His bread shall be fat."
Capricorn	Naphtali	"A hind let loose."
Sagittarius	Joseph	"His bow abideth in strength."
Cancer	Benjamin	"Shall devour the prey."

The twelve tribes of Israel are mentioned also in connection with the symbol of the New Jerusalem in the twenty-first chapter of Revelation. The city is described as having twelve gates with "names written thereon, which are the names of the twelve tribes of the children of Israel" (Rev. 21:12). The term *gates* is sometimes used in symbolic esoteric writings in connection with the signs of the Zodiac to illustrate that they can be thought of as different entryways to life, since a person comes into life under a given sign. Gates may also relate to viewing the signs as different places from which energies enter. The New Jerusalem, "the holy city" (Rev. 21:2), the city that "lieth four square," is considered to be a symbol for man.

In the twenty-second chapter of Revelation the number twelve is found again. The tree of life mentioned there is described as having "twelve manner of fruits, and yielding her fruit every month." One could speculate that this refers to the fruits of the tree of life as being those born into incarnation, and that the twelve different types refer to the fact that individuals are born under twelve different signs of the Zodiac corresponding approximately to the twelve months of the year.

The zodiacal references associated with the opening of the seven seals in chapter 6 of Revelation were discussed earlier in chapter 9, "Symbolic Writing and Allegory."

ESOTERICISTS AND ASTROLOGY

Esotericists have made some very clear statements about both the significance and the limitations of astrology as understood today. The formation of the Theosophical Society at the end of the last century brought with it a growth of interest in the serious study of astrology among many learned individuals. Madame Blavatsky's writings did not concern themselves with any of the details of astrology, but she did acknowledge the influence of the stars, stating that "Astrology is built on the mystic and intimate connection between the heavenly bodies and mankind."[13]

On the subject of astrological fatalism, however, she notes: "All the great astrologers have admitted that man could react against the stars."[14] Alice Bailey's writings reflect the following similar view: "An advanced individual can offset the influence of the planets and thus so dominate his personality life that prediction and certainty, as to activity and circumstance, are no longer possible."[15]

In connection with the validity of astrology, Mrs. Bailey observes:

> That astrology is a science, and a coming science, is true. That astrology in its highest aspect and its true interpretation will enable man eventually to focus his understanding, and to function rightly, is equally true. That in the revelations that astrology will make in time to come will be found the secret of the true coordination between soul and form, is also correct. But *that* astrology is not yet to be found. Too much is overlooked and too little known, to make astrology the exact science that many claim it is. The claim will be fulfilled at some future date, but the time is not yet.[16]

She gives some idea of the limitations of the present astrology:

> Orthodox astrology sets up a chart (the horoscope) which gives the fate and destiny of the personality, and when that personality is little evolved or is only of an average development, it can be, and often is, amazingly cor-

rect. . . . However, in the case of highly developed people, . . . who are beginning to control their stars and consequently their actions, the events and the happenings in their lives become unpredictable. The new and future astrology endeavors to give the key to the Horoscope of the soul.[17]

Esotericists claim that the energy transmissions associated with astrology take place on etheric levels and influence man through the etheric body. They also show a link between astrology, religion, and mythology. Blavatsky indicates that there "are the primeval seven Rays. . . . Hence there are seven chief planets, the spheres of the indwelling seven Spirits" [mentioned in the Book of Revelation].[18] She also claims that "the seven planetary Spirits or Angels . . . are identical with the Dhyan Chohans of the esoteric doctrine and have been transformed into the archangels and the Spirits of the Presence by the Christian Church."[19] As noted earlier, gods of Greek and Roman mythology were also related to the planets.

In connection with mythology, the legend of the twelve labors of Hercules has been linked by many to the twelve signs of the Zodiac. Mrs. Bailey affirms this relationship, indicating that the legend is representative of lessons to be learned in each of the signs by each person as he grows spiritually. She connects each of the labors with its zodiacal sign, and her detailed discussion of the symbology and significance of each element of the legend has been published in a book entitled *The Labours of Hercules*.[20]

THE PROBLEM OF TWINS

A question that is brought up often in connection with astrology is that twins or others born at almost the same time and place do not necessarily lead identical lives or have the same personality. However, there are many recorded cases of people born at approximately the same time who did lead remarkably similar lives, with identical timing of key, similar events and close personality correspondences. A number of these are detailed in *The Case for Astrology*, by West and Toonder.

The more sophisticated practitioners of astrology point out that there are many more influences than those from the stars. Esotericists, as we have noted, indicate that a person's state of development significantly affects how he or she will react to a given influence. People bring different fundamental equipment to their lives. Esotericists maintain that each of the different vehicles they claim make up a person (physical, astral, mental, etc.) is under the basic influence of one of the Seven Rays. The ray influence for each vehicle varies from individual to individual, and therefore each person may respond differently for that reason as well as because of the state of development of the different vehicles that reflects in the responsiveness of the various force centers associated with the vehicles. There are many forms of energy impacting on an individual other than stellar. The factor of free will also comes into play, and thus the subject is far too complex for the average astrologer to do more than estimate the effect of certain major influences and provide guidance on timing. Certainly with all the variables involved, one would not expect identical lives for two persons born at the same time and place, but if astrology has any validity, there should be correspondences in the timing of some key events even if the exact event and the way it plays out differ somewhat. Also, a character analysis by an astrologer would be expected to apply reasonably closely to both individuals.

CONCLUDING COMMENTS

In summary, astrology is an attempt to characterize the effects of a system of energies believed by some to exist and to have a significant influence on the life of our planet. Astrology, as practiced today, is not totally accepted by science, religion, or even the esotericists, but there have been members of the religious and scientific communities who have indicated their belief that these energies are real and do have a somewhat predictable influence. Most experienced astrologers do not take a fatalistic approach toward the influence of astrology but believe that there is advantage in learning to work in harmony with this influence.

PART III

SUMMING UP

18. The Message of the Teachings and Daily Life

On hearing of the Way, the best of men
Will earnestly explore its length.
The mediocre person learns of it
And takes it up and sets it down.
But vulgar people, when they hear the news,
Will laugh out loud, and if they did not laugh,
It would not be the Way.[1]

—Lao-tzu

This chapter is a commentary on the guidance contained in the writings of the great teachers summarized in chapters 1–4 and elsewhere in this book as well as on the direction they provide for mankind in facing the task of living useful and meaningful lives in the world. Referring to chapter 1 and specifically to the listing of topics covered in the scripture comparisons on pages 5 and 6, we can see the outlines of a message from these great religions on the way people should conduct themselves and the direction in which they should be progressing.

In our daily activities we are urged to love and serve humanity, to work diligently at performing the duties we find it our place to perform, and to control our lower nature in order to become effective in carrying all this out.

The scriptures tell us that there is a higher authority transcending the physical world we see around us and that our existence is controlled by a body of laws. One of these is the law of cause and effect.

They further declare that man has a spiritual nature and that cultivation of greater rapport with this aspect is the path of progress.

We are told that right outward and inward effort will lead to the development of a number of desirable qualities that will be signs of spiritual growth.

Clearly, if a significantly larger proportion of mankind followed these precepts and consistently applied them to everyday life, most of the problems with which humanity is faced would quickly be solved.

253

LOVE, SERVICE, AND DUTY

The comparison in chapter 1 begins with love, which St. Paul in I Corinthians 13 calls "the way which surpasses all others."[2] He counts extraordinary powers of no value without love and characterizes love as patient and kind, and not jealous, snobbish, rude, self-seeking, or prone to anger. He states that love rejoices in the truth and that there is no limit to its forbearance, trust, hope, and power to endure.

Much of the world confuses love with desire, an aspect of the lower nature, to which it has a correspondence. Love, however, is a spiritual quality and has no element of selfishness associated with it.

In speaking of this love, Nobel Prize–winner Mother Teresa of Calcutta, who has demonstrated its expression in the world, says:

> Love is a fruit in season at all times, and within the reach of every hand. Anyone may gather it and no limit is set. Everyone can reach this love through meditation, the spirit of prayer and sacrifice and an intense inner life.[3]

Concerning the relationship of love and service, Alice Bailey writes: "A man . . . in service learns the power of love in its occult significance. He spends and consequently receives; he lives the life of renunciation and the wealth of the heavens pour in on him; . . . he asks nothing for himself and is the richest man on earth."[4] And further along this same line:

> True service is the spontaneous outflow of a loving heart and an intelligent mind; it is the result of being in the right place and staying there; it is produced by the inevitable inflow of spiritual force and not by strenuous physical plane activity; it is the effect of a man's being what he truly is, a divine Son of God, and not by the studied effect of his words or deeds. A true server gathers around him those whom it is his duty to serve and aid by the force of his life and his spiritualized personality, and not by his claims or loud speaking. . . . He lives, serves, works and influences, asking nothing for the separated self.[5]

Christ taught the importance of love as well as service. He gave us a new commandment, that we love one another, and added: "Whoever wants to rank first among you must serve the needs of all. Such is the case with the Son of Man who has come not to be served by others, but to serve" (Matt. 20:27–28).[6] He emphasized this by washing the feet of his disciples shortly before he was crucified.

Christ dramatically conveyed the need for compassion and charity by his words in the twenty-fifth chapter of Matthew:

> Then the just will ask him: "Lord, when did we see you hungry and feed you or see you thirsty and give you drink? When did we welcome you away from home or clothe you in your nakedness? When did we visit you when you were ill or in prison?" . . . "I assure you, as often as you did it for one of my least brothers, you did it for me."[7]

As a result of this emphasis in the teachings of Christ and his apostles, we find hospitals, educational facilities, and charitable organizations founded by Christian church-related groups all over the world.

It should be recognized that service to humanity is not accomplished only by acts of charity or compasion but by using the talents we have or can develop for the advancement or well-being of the world. Thus scientists, artists, writers, performers, educators, physicians, psychologists, economists, politicians, businessmen, and people in all walks of life serve humanity along with those associated with religious or charitable activities.

Leaders in government and business are in a position to influence the well-being of many individuals. Government's role, along with its other functions, is to provide a suitable atmosphere for growth and to work for right relations among all nations and groups. Those who lead well-run businesses where opportunity for learning, development, and advancement to greater responsibility are provided, along with a means to fulfill material needs, perform a valuable service.

Creative technical people have given us our present modern civilization, which has removed man's need for constant toil and provided the opportunity (not always taken) for greater mental and cultural development.

Artists and musicians can exert a very significant positive influence on mankind. Norman Rockwell's posters of the four freedoms conveyed that spiritual message to almost every classroom in the United States far more effectively than most history lessons could have. The widespread appeal of music and the ability of its message to reach and inspire many is apparent. Writers and performers have the opportunity today, with efficient distribution and publicity means, and with electronic communications media, to bring their messages to larger audiences than ever before. Television, radio, motion pictures, and paperback books can reach most of the civilized population.

Although all religions urge that we strive for peace in the world and make it clear that the ultimate goal should be the elimination of arms, it is nevertheless necessary at mankind's present stage of development to provide the means for defense. Since this is the case, those in the military who are of right motive also provide a necessary service; and the experiences and opportunities afforded, especially with today's technically complex systems, can provide learning and growth for those involved. Krishna conveys the need to fight, when conditions dictate, in his words to Ajurna, who is wavering over taking the lives of those he knows. Krishna says, "If you refuse to fight this righteous war, you will be turning aside from your duty."

The question of right action in the face of perceived evil is indeed a difficult one. Christ told us to turn the other cheek, but he also drove the moneychangers from the temple. He thus illustrates, as stated elsewhere in the Bible, that we should be slow to anger, especially when it is ourselves who may be wronged, but points out the need to take action when the spiritual welfare and growth of the people is being threatened. World War II was, in retrospect, a just war for the Allies, and one that ultimately could not be avoided; but for many it was not easy in the early stages to read Hitler's true motives and character. Some more recent world events have been even less clear, but the best-informed decisions possible nevertheless had to be made by those responsible at the time.

As a long-term goal, we need to continue to work at the task of bringing humanity and human relations to the point where mankind can, in the well-known words of the prophet Isaiah, "beat their swords into plowshares and their spears into pruning hooks" (Isa. 2:4).

We see that service to our fellow-men is possible in all walks of life through love and right motive and by living the principles taught by the great religions. We need not go out searching for a place and set of conditions where we can provide some service. The place we are in is the place to start, the duties we are faced with there should be carried out conscientiously, and opportunity for greater responsibility will come our way.

Many of the significant advances of benefit to mankind in today's complex world are made not by individuals but by groups or teams of individuals. By bringing together diverse talents, accomplishments beyond the scope of any one person are possible. The potency of a highly cooperative group is far beyond that of the sum of the individuals involved. One of the most important things to learn in group work is to avoid criticism. Differences sometimes need to be resolved for the work to proceed, but the constructive approach is far more conducive to team unity than the critical approach. The quotations under "Faultfinding and Harmlessness" in chapter 1 set the theme.

Service is not without its advantage to the server. We find that those who forget themselves in helping others or in some creative work are far happier than the dissatisfied people who are always seeking pleasure for themselves. There is great joy in creative accomplishment that brings enlightenment to the world, benefits mankind, or produces a thing of beauty. The esotericists also tell us that service is one of the most powerful and vitally necessary means of spiritual development.

Closely related to love and the Golden Rule are brotherhood and goodwill. We find these principles in the teachings of all great religious leaders. Christ's story of the Good Samaritan is an illustration that is easily understood and remembered by children as well as adults, and in I John 4:21 we read: "He who loves God loves his brother also." Speaking of one on the path to union with God, the Bhagavad Gita says, "By this sign he is known, being of equal grace to friends, strangers, lovers, enemies, aliens and kinsmen; loving all alike, evil or good." Muhammad's words on this theme, recorded in the *Hadith*, read: "No man can be considered a True Believer who does not seek for his brother what he seeks for himself."

If mankind is to progress beyond its present condition, which is characterized by constant strife and preparations for conflict, into an era where the emphasis is on growth and advancement, the principles of brotherhood, goodwill, and sharing need to be applied on a broader scale. We must go beyond helping our families and communities to greater national and international cooperation. We need to bridge the gaps between different religious, ethnic, and racial groups which make for severe problems in some countries. Teilhard de Chardin wrote: "No evolutionary future awaits man except in association with other men."[8] The following definition also warrants careful consideration: "Virtue is the manifestation in man of the spirit of cooperation with his brothers, necessitating unselfishness, understanding, and complete self-forgetfulness. Vice is the negation of this attitude."[9]

Albert Einstein wrote:

> Man can find meaning in life . . . only through devoting himself to Society.
>
> The education of the individual in addition to promoting his own innate abilities, should attempt to develop in him a sense of responsibility for his fellow men in place of the glorification of power and success in our present society.[10]

St. Paul states that: "There is one God and Father of all, who is above all, and through all, and in you all" (Eph. 4:6). He also declares that in a mystical sense we are all part of one body in Christ, and these passages provide a revealing way of viewing mankind.

Consider the working of the integrated human body. When one part of the body is in difficulty, there is a response from other parts of the body. If a thorn penetrates our foot, our hand will move quickly under control of the brain and nervous system to remove it. If infection penetrates our body as a result of injury, antibodies are sent to combat the infection.

Contrast this with the body of humanity. Do we, when one part of the body is in need, move to aid it? To some extent we do, but at mankind's present state of development, this cooperation is less than universal. In fact, we have the situation in human interaction where disputes arise, resulting in war in which various parts destroy each other.

The analogy can be carried still further. If one part of a man or woman's body becomes infected, there is the danger that the infection will spread to other parts. This is also true of humanity as a whole in ways that go beyond the spread of disease. Moral breakdown and poverty can lead to crime, for example, and antisocial attitudes tend to spread. Being our "brother's keeper" benefits all of us in the long run.

SELF-CONTROL

Looking next at the categories listed under the heading *Self-Control* in chapter 1, we see that we are enjoined to establish mastery over our physical, emotional, and mental aspects, this being necessary if we are to serve effectively, set a proper example for our fellow men, and attain further spiritual advancement.

It is clear that if we are to be effective and consistent in any worthwhile activities, it is necessary to have a high degree of control over our emotions. A person who is subject to uncontrolled anger, fear, possessiveness, or other passions will be greatly limited in working with others and in maintaining the consistent dedication to purpose necessary for success in any complex endeavor. The term *dispassion* is used to describe the quality to be cultivated, which does not imply the elimination of all emotion, but rather maintaining control.

The categories titled *Freedom from Worldly Desires* and *Renunciation* in chapter 2 relate to a quality called *detachment*, reference to which is found in the writings of sages and mystics. We shall see that detachment implies something more than control of desire for things; it also includes a spiritual focus.

Christ calls for this attitude of detachment in the Sermon on the Mount: "Lay not up for yourselves treasures upon earth, where moth and rust doth corrupt, and where thieves break through and steal: but lay up for yourselves treasures in heaven: . . . for where your treasure is, there will your heart be also" (Matt. 6:19–21).

The Hindu scriptures clearly teach the concept of detachment. In the Bhagavad Gita we read, "Perform every action with your heart fixed on the Supreme Lord. Renounce attachment to the fruits."[11] We also read:

> When men have thrown off their ignorance, they are free from pride and delusion. They have conquered the evil of worldly attachment. They live in constant union with the Atman. All craving has left them. They are no longer at the mercy of opposing sense-reactions. Thus they reach that state which is beyond all change.[12]

From the Brihadaranyaka Upanishad: "How does such a knower of Brahman act and conduct himself? Whatever he may do and however he may conduct himself, he is free from craving, and is forever established in the knowledge of Brahman."[13]

In the appendix to the translation of the Bhagavad Gita by Swami Prabhavanada and Christopher Isherwood are found the following comments relating to detachment:

> Attached action binds us to the world of appearances; to the continual doing of more action. But there is another way of performing action, and this is without fear and without desire. The Christians call it "holy indifference"

and the Hindus "non-attachment." Both names are slightly misleading. They suggest coldness and lack of enthusiasm. But the doer of non-attached action is the most conscientious of men. Freed from fear and desire, he offers everything he does as a sacrament of devotion to his duty.

Lao-tzu states the concepts as follows:

> If you can create things
> Without feeling the need to own them;
> If you can aid mankind
> Without waiting for reward;
> If you can learn to act as a leader
> While men still look on you as a brother;
> Then you have learned to travel The Way.[14]

In the Buddhist scriptures the need for detachment is also clearly stated, as in the second and third of the Four Noble Truths of the Buddha, which state:

> II. Unhappiness is caused by selfish craving.
> III. Selfish craving can be destroyed.[15]

Also, in chapter 16 of the Dhammapada we read: "Let, therefore, no man be attached to anything; . . . Those who are attached to nothing, and hate nothing, have no fetters."[16]

The well-known writer on Buddhism, D. T. Suzuki, in discussing detachment quotes the following words of the great Dominican mystic Meister Eckhart:

> I have read many writings of both heathen philosophies and sages, of the Old and New Testaments, and I have earnestly, and with all diligence sought the best and the highest virtues whereby man may come most closely to God. . . . And having dived into the basis of things to the best of my ability, I find that it is no other than absolute detachment from everything that is created.[17]

The esotericists also stress the importance of detachment and relate it to the cultivation of what is termed "the attitude of the observer"—that is, mentally stepping back and silently taking note of the activities of your own concrete mind and emotions and their interaction with the outside world. This attitude is fostered by a practice, encouraged by a number of esotericists, of acting as the silent noncritical observer in a nightly review of the day's activities, beginning with the latest events and working through to the earliest. The intent is not only to gradually achieve a more mature functioning of the mental and emotional nature, but also to foster the possibility of working at a higher level as a soul.

The following, from Alice Bailey's writings, gives an idea of the esotericists' view of the functioning and value of detachment:

It is a mental detachment which enables the thinker to dwell ever in the high and secret place, and from that center of peace calmly and powerfully to carry out the work he has set before himself. He works in the world of men; he loves and comforts and serves; he pays no attention to his personality likes and dislikes, or to his prejudices and attachments; he stands as a rock of strength, and as a strong hand in the dark to all whom he contacts. The cultivation of a detached attitude personally, with the attached attitude spiritually, will cut at the very roots of a man's life; but it will render back a thousand-fold for all that it cuts away.[18]

A spiritually advanced individual operating with detachment is able to work effectively in spite of physical disabilities or adverse conditions and other problems that would incapacitate the average person emotionally. He can place himself mentally above these things and continue to concentrate on that which is to be accomplished, relatively undistracted by surrounding conditions.

St. Paul indicates this in several passages. In Philippians 4:11 he writes: "I have learned, in whatever state I am therewith to be content." Commenting on the likelihood that "bonds and afflictions" await him, Paul says: "None of these things move me, neither count I my life dear" (Acts 20:24).

CONTROL OF THOUGHTS

An area of self-control that is receiving a great deal of attention today is control of the thought process. Many books are being published and courses conducted along the general line of mind control, which includes the additional factor of control of the emotions by the mind.

Ralph Waldo Emerson, who is a major inspirational force in churches emphasizing the power of the mind, wrote: "Great men are they who see that mental force is stronger than material force, that thoughts rule the world."

The Buddha clearly expressed the importance of thought in our lives, stating: "All that we are is the result of what we have thought: It is founded on our thoughts and is made up of our thoughts."

A major element in living right is thinking right, and St. Paul gives an admonition that has great psychological merit: "Whatsoever things are true, whatsoever things are honest, whatsoever things are just, whatsoever things are pure, whatsoever things are lovely, whatsoever things are of good report; . . . think on these things." (Phil. 4:8).

In the Bhagavad Gita Krishna speaks similarly: "The best remedy for evil is not the suppression but the elimination of desire, and this can best be accomplished by keeping the mind constantly steeped in things divine."[19]

This technique is, in fact, cited as the most effective way to change one's character and outlook. If we find that we have faults that need correcting, it is not advisable to attempt to suppress our negative desires or thoughts but rather to substitute the opposite virtue in our thinking. "Resist not evil" (Matt. 5:34) is an important principle to observe. If we focus attention on a fault in an attempt to suppress it, we are actually reinforcing it in our subconscious. If, instead, we substitute love for hate, courage for fear, cheerfulness for depression, and so on, we emphasize the desired quality; and since two opposite thoughts and emotions cannot exist simultaneously, we tend to starve the undesired quality rather than feeding it. Thus it is gradually eliminated. In another way of looking at it, we are directing the energies of the unwanted passion into a higher channel. By this means we can follow the guidance of St. Paul: "Be ye therefore transformed by the renewing of your mind."

With emotions or thought patterns that are very difficult to control—for example, an overwhelming fear of flying—a technique used by a number of "self-hypnosis" and "mind control" courses can be very helpful. A state of deep relaxation is induced by progressively relaxing all parts of the body, usually beginning with the feet and working gradually up to the head, paying particular attention to relaxing the eyes and tongue, which can be sources of tension. (This relaxation process can be greatly speeded up as experience is gained.) When a deeply relaxed state is achieved, the desired condition is visualized as clearly and in as much detail as possible.

In the case of fear of flying, you picture yourself cheerfully boarding the plane, enjoying the airplane ride, feeling perfect peace and contentment, and stepping off the plane at the end with the thought and feeling: "That was a most enjoyable and pleasant trip!" Repetition of this process will build a new positive subconscious reaction to flying, in place of the fear. Extrapolation to other situations is fairly obvious. It is important to avoid bringing any element of the undesired negative condition into the process, and a technique used by some for avoiding this is to visualize only the desired end-result rather than the activity itself.

The achieving of deep relaxation brings the brain-wave activity as measured on an e.e.g. machine into what is termed an *alpha* state, exhibiting a lower frequency than the *beta*, or normal waking consciousness, state. In the alpha state the subconscious mind is much more easily influenced, and the ability to change unwanted patterns of behavior, thought, or emotion and to instill new habits by visualizing or reflecting on the opposite is greatly heightened. When using this procedure, even though we are physically and emotionally deeply relaxed, the mind is maintained positive and alert, and it is not allowed to wander from the task at hand.

Spiritual teachers urge that we habitually control our line of thinking and think deeply along the desired direction, eliminating stray or idle thoughts. This advice, if followed, will result in a marked improvement in mental ability.

Another psychologically powerful technique for attaining a desired attribute is to begin to act as if we possess it. The Brihadaranyaka Upanishad states: "As a man acts, so does he become." This acting "as if" requires the use of the imagination, and through the application of the imagination we can achieve profound changes.

The habit of continuing to worry about some event that may take place or has taken place after all positive corrective steps have been taken can reduce effectiveness, dissipate energy, and even lead to physical problems. Attention to detail is a useful attribute; worry, which involves the repetition of a thought pattern again and again along the same mental channel, is not. We must break up the patttern by channeling our thoughts in the opposite direction to something higher and more useful and put worry behind us. Once again, St. Paul has good advice for us: "This one thing I do, forgetting those things which are behind, and reaching forth unto those things which are before" (Phil. 3:13).

A mental quality whose cultivation is stressed by the Eastern religions is discrimination. This is the ability to separate out the illusory and transitory from what is real and permanent. It is especially applicable to dealing with the emotional nature and the glamours that can easily mislead a person driven by desire for worldly things. The Bhagavad Gita asks: "Where is your sword, discrimination? Draw it and slash delusion to pieces."[20] One of the best-known prayers in the Upanishads touches on the theme of discrimination:

> Lead me from the unreal to the real;
> Lead me from darkness to light;
> Lead me from death to immortality.

According to the Hindu scriptures, discrimination is developed by careful attention to that which is to be learned from experience. In the Bhagavad Gita we read: "Confuse your mind and you forget the lesson of experience; forget experience and you lose discrimination; lose discrimination and you miss life's only purpose."[21] The Chandogya Upanishad states: "When a man discriminates by analyzing his past experiences and considering on the basis of these what may come in the future, he rightly wills in the present."[22]

SPIRITUAL DEVELOPMENT

When we reflect on the implications of controlling our thoughts, we can logically postulate that there must be a controlling factor independent of, and superior to our thoughts, emotions, and physical body. Thus in a fundamental sense we are not our thoughts, and it would appear that some higher element exists. All the great religions,* along with mystics, esotericists, and many great philosophers, agree with this concept.

The objective in spiritual development is to expand the consciousness so that the higher spiritual nature increases its control over the lower nature and so that we function more and more with our focus of attention at higher levels. This is what the devotion, good works, and meditation practices of the saints and mystics lead toward. Swami Vivekananda summarizes the process as follows:

> Each soul is potentially divine. The goal is to manifest this divinity within, by controlling nature, external and internal. Do this either by work, or worship or psychic control, or philosophy—by one, or more, or all of these—and be free. This is the whole of religion. Doctrines or dogmas, or rituals, or books, or temples, or forms, are but secondary details.[23]

Probably the most complete outline for spiritual development ever set down comes to us from Patanjali, a sage of ancient India, in the form of a work called the Yoga Sutras. The word *yoga* means "union," and the Yoga Sutras outline the means by which an individual can achieve union with his or her higher nature. The word *sutra* means "thread" and is believed to relate to the fact that the Yoga Sutras consist of a series of brief statements that give the basic thread or outline of the subject without elaborate explanation. It is theorized that this form was used so the statements could be readily memorized, since the sutras were composed when there were no books. Teachers of yoga would provide elaboration on the outline for students. There are a number of English translations of the Yoga Sutras available, and various individuals have written commentaries on the Sutras.

The form of yoga described in the Yoga Sutras is called *Raja Yoga* (the Kingly Yoga)—a yoga of the mind. There are a number of other forms of yoga, the most significant fundamental categories in addition to Raja Yoga being *Hatha Yoga* (relating to the physical body), *Laya Yoga* (relating to the force centers in the etheric body), and *Bhakti Yoga* (the yoga of devotion, which relates to the emotional body). The other forms of yoga are subsets of these four. In the introduction to Alice Bailey's book on the Yoga Sutras of Patanjali[24] she states that Hatha Yoga goes back to the very earliest races of man when the physical body was being developed and that Laya Yoga was introduced later in man's racial history, when the development of the etheric body was taking place. Bhakti Yoga was added to Laya Yoga with the development of the emotional or astral body.

Mrs. Bailey points out that all of the yogas have served a useful purpose but that "any return to Hatha Yoga practices or those practices which deal specifically with the development of the centers, brought about through

*See chapter 1 under the heading "The Spiritual Nature of Humanity."

various types of meditation practices and breathing exercises, is from a certain aspect, a retrogression. It will be found through the practice of Raja Yoga, . . . the other forms of yoga are unnecessary, for the greater yoga automatically includes the less in its results, though not in its practices." As mentioned earlier, it is also pointed out by Bailey and others that breathing exercises and concentration on the centers without proper guidance can lead to serious mental disorders.

Much of humanity is still centered more emotionally than mentally, and today we have a situation where both Bhakti and Raja Yoga are practiced in both the East and the West but not necessarily under those names. Both Christ and Krishna taught devotion along with other practices that are consistent with the overall teachings of Raja Yoga. In the same introduction from which we have just quoted, Mrs. Bailey adds her opinion that "there are three books which should be in the hands of every student, the Bhagavad Gita, the New Testament, and the Yoga Sutras, for in these three is contained a complete picture of the soul and its unfoldment."

In the Bhagavad Gita a number of different means of yoga are mentioned, as indicated by some of the chapter headings listed below:

II.	The Yoga of Knowledge
III.	Karma Yoga
V.	The Yoga of Renunciation
VI.	The Yoga of Meditation
IX.	The Yoga of Mysticism
XII.	The Yoga of Devotion[25]

All of these yogas are touched on in the sutras given by Patanjali as well. The Yoga of Knowledge is also called *Jnana Yoga* by the Hindus, and Karma Yoga is defined by Krishna as the path of selfless action—the Yoga of Action. Mysticism and devotion are, of course, related to Bhakti Yoga, which is the yoga of the devotee and mystic as contrasted with that of the esotericist or occultist, who works more along the path of knowledge, science, and understanding in achieving union. Meditation, covered in chapter 6 of the Bhagavad Gita, is the basic technique of Raja Yoga.

A few excerpts from the Yoga Sutras will provide an indication of some of the practices to be followed in order to achieve union and will also show that the teachings of all of the great religions are consistent with these practices. The Yoga Sutras are divided into four sections or "books"; the roman numeral preceding each verse gives the book number, followed by an arabic number designating the verse.[26]

I.2 . . . Union (or yoga) is achieved through the subjugation of the psychic nature and the restraint of the chitta (or mind).

I.3 When this has been accomplished, the Yogi knows himself as he is in reality.

I.4 Up till now the inner man has identified himself with his forms and with their active modifications.

I.14 When the object to be gained is sufficiently valued, and the efforts towards its attainment are persistently followed without intermission, then the steadiness of the mind . . . is secured.

I.15 Non-attachment is freedom from longing for all objects of desire, either earthly or traditional, either here or hereafter.

I.16 The consummation of this non-attachment results in an exact knowledge of the spiritual man when liberated from the qualities or gunas.

I.30 The obstacles to soul cognition are bodily disability, mental inertia, wrong questioning, carelessness, laziness, lack of dispassion, erroneous perception, inability to achieve concentration, failure to hold the meditative attitude when achieved.

I.33 The peace of the chitta (or mind stuff) can be brought about through the practice of sympathy, tenderness, steadiness of purpose, and dispassion in regard to pleasure or pain, or towards all forms of good or evil.

I.37 The citta is stabilised and rendered free from illusion as the lower nature is purified and no longer indulged.

II.3 These are the difficulty-producing hindrances: avidya (ignorance) the sense of personality, desire, hate, and the sense of attachment.

II.4 Avidya (ignorance) is the cause of all the other obstructions. . . .

II.5 Avidya is the condition of confusing the permanent, pure, blissful and the Self with that which is impermanent, impure, painful and the not-self.

II.10 These five hindrances, when subtly known, can be overcome by an opposing mental attitude.

II.11 Their activities are to be done away with, through the meditation process.

II.12 Karma itself has its root in these five hindrances and must come to fruition in this life or in some later life.

II.17 The illusion that the Perceiver and that which is perceived are one and the same is the cause (of the pain-producing effects) which must be warded off.

II.25 When ignorance is brought to an end through non-association with the things perceived, this is the great liberation.

II.26 The state of bondage is overcome through perfectly maintained discrimination.

II.29 The eight means of yoga are: the Commandments or Yama, the Rules or Nijama, posture or Asana, right control of life-force or Pranayama, abstraction or Pratyahara, attention [concentration] or Dharana, Meditation or Dhyana, Contemplation or Samadhi.

II.30 Harmlessness, truth to all beings, abstention from theft, from incontinence and from avarice, constitute yama or the five commandments.

II.32 Internal and external purification, contentment, fiery aspiration, spiritual reading and devotion to Ishvara constitutes nijama (or the five rules).

A few words of explanation in connection with the preceding three sutras may be helpful before continuing. Commentaries indicate that *asana*, or posture, refers to more than simply the physical position during meditation (which, as recommended for the Westerner, is to sit with the spine erect in a comfortable chair, with the eyes closed, feet on the floor, ankles crossed naturally, hands folded in the lap, and chin slightly dropped). Posture also concerns the poise and attitude of the emotions and mind as well. The physical body should be relaxed; the objective is to forget about it. There should be a steadiness and control of the mind and emotions. Abstraction in the same sutra refers to withdrawal from sense contacts or disturbances.

In commenting on the meaning of incontinence mentioned in II.30, Mrs. Bailey writes:

Celibacy is not enjoined. Self-control is. In the relatively short cycle of lives, however, in which the aspirant fits himself to tread the path, he may have to pass a life or maybe several in a definite abstention from the act of procreation in order to learn complete control. . . . The right use of the sex principle along with entire conformity to the law of the land is characteristic of every true aspirant.[27]

Spiritual reading relates to more than the study of scriptures or spiritual writings; it concerns also developing the ability to recognize the meaning behind the words and, in general, to recognize the hidden causes and significance behind all that we observe, feel, and think—in a manner of speaking, the spiritual essence behind the outer symbol.

Devotion to Ishvara refers to devotion to the divine aspect within oneself, the God or Christ within, in Christian terms. In a broader sense, it refers also to that which is divine in all creatures and therefore to God in the final analysis.

Returning now to the sutras:

II.33 When thoughts which are contrary to yoga are present there should be the cultivation of their opposite.

II.34 Thoughts contrary to yoga are harmfulness, falsehood, theft, incontinence, and avarice, whether committed personally, caused to be committed or approved of. . . .

III.2 Sustained Concentration (dharana) is meditation (dhyana).

III.3 When the chitta becomes absorbed in that which is the reality (or idea embodied in the form), and is unaware of separateness or the personal self, this is contemplation or samadhi.

III.4 When concentration, meditation and contemplation form one sequential act, then is sanyama achieved.

III.5 As a result of sanyama comes the shining forth of the light.

III.6 This illumination is gradual; it is developed stage by stage.

III.7 These last three means of yoga have a more intimate subjective effect than the previous means.

IV.2 The transfer of the consciousness from a lower vehicle into a higher is part of the great creative and evolutionary process.

IV.25 The state of isolated unity (withdrawn into the true nature of the Self) is the reward of the man who can discriminate between the mind stuff and the Self, or spiritual man.

IV.29 The man who develops non-attachment even in his aspiration after illumination and isolated unity, becomes aware, eventually, through practiced discrimination, of the overshadowing cloud of spiritual knowledge.

The commandments and rules laid down by Patanjali correspond to the rules of right living placed before us by all the great religions, and it is stressed in commentaries that these must be a part of a person's daily life before the other means of yoga can be followed with complete safety.

Man's objective in practicing yoga is, in the words of the parable of the Prodigal Son, to return to the "father's house." This ultimately means raising the consciousness to the point where we are one with our spiritual nature and, through this means, finally with God. This, of course, is a slow and gradual process that is referred to in symbolic terms as treading the path of return.

CONCENTRATION AND MEDITATION

The process of spiritual development can be speeded up by following the means of yoga. The mental steps of concentration, meditation, and contemplation—referred to in the Yoga Sutras as the means that have the "more intimate subjective effect"—have been used and described by saints and mystics of all faiths.

The ability to concentrate, in addition to being a means of spiritual culture, is the key to success in almost anything we set out to do. It is a capability that can be improved by practice, and we will find that the habit of maintaining a focus of attention on that which we wish to accomplish, observe, or learn will bring great rewards in increased effectiveness.

There are a number of books that discuss the benefits of concentration and that provide exercises and techniques for improving it. However, situations present themselves every day in the course of our lives where we can be more attentive and more observant. By taking ourselves in hand, we can utilize these opportunities for practice while also improving our performance.

We will find as we work at concentration that it is more difficult than we might have imagined, and at first continual effort is required to maintain attention. Krishna comments on this in the Bhagavad Gita: "The mind is restless . . . and hard to subdue. But it can be brought under control by constant practice, and by the exercise of dispassion."[28] Krishna makes clear in this passage that the emotional nature can, if uncontrolled, be an important deterrent to the control of the mind. Thus, before we can concentrate effectively, we must learn dispassion—control of the emotions.

The difficulty and importance of controlling thought is also mentioned by the Buddha in the Dhammapada: "As the arrow-maker makes straight his arrow, so the wise man makes straight the trembling and unsteady thought which is difficult to control and difficult to hold back."[29] When control is obtained, we can direct our thoughts along the lines we wish and not be subject to an uncontrolled and emotionally colored stream of thoughts that can disrupt our attention, dissipate our energy, and keep us from accomplishing what we seek to achieve.

If we attempt to concentrate while sitting quietly relaxed as a first stage of meditation, we will be impressed in starting out by the many ways in which the mind can be distracted from the line of concentration we have chosen to pursue. Constant unemotional drawing back of the mind is required, and our ability should improve with experience. Intense interest in what one is concentrating on is a most important factor in successful concentration.

We can see from the sections entitled *Meditation* and *The Self* in chapter 1 that the idea of going inward to achieve illumination is contained in the scriptures of the great religions. We also find that the practice of meditation is found in connection with every major religion and is especially prevalent among those who are recognized as the most holy and the greatest spiritual contributors to each religion.

Patanjali defines meditation as sustained concentration and speaks of "meditation with seed," which means that some seed thought is selected as a subject for concentrated thought to begin the meditation process. In

Raja Yoga the mind is alert and is not dulled by continuous repetitions, nor is any attempt made to blank the mind, which could lead to a dangerous trance state. The mind concentrates on developing the seed thought to increase and expand the understanding of the object of meditation. If concentration is carried to the point where the stage of meditation is reached, a new clarity of thought will be achieved that transcends any emotional reactions.

The state of contemplation may be entered when, following the meditative state's having been carried to its highest level, the mind is held in a positive waiting attitude while the consciousness shifts to a higher level. Then the activity of the soul comes into play and may be registered by the waiting quiescent mind and brain. This is contemplation, and contemplation is an activity of the soul.

All these steps are easy to write about, but, as one might suspect, they are far more difficult to accomplish. We are assured that, independent of results achieved during meditation, no effort along this line is wasted, and a positive effect in the outer life—including greater efficiency and capability—will gradually be evidenced. We are also urged not to seek after dramatic or phenomenal effects but simply to persist in the effort daily, even if progress is not apparent. A time period of fifteen minutes per day is recommended when starting out on concentration or meditation exercises, and a maximum of forty minutes should not be exceeded, even when a great deal of experience has been gained. Morning is considered the best time for meditation, since we are more awake and alert then and our minds are not distracted by the events of the day.

The effects of meditation are described as follows:

> This process of ordered meditation, when carried forward over a period of years and supplemented by meditative living and one-pointed service, will successfully arouse the entire system, and bring the lower man under the influence and control of the spiritual man; it will awaken also the centers of force in the etheric body and stimulate into activity that mysterious stream of energy which sleeps at the base of the spinal column [kundalini]. When this process is carried forward with care and due safeguards, and under direction, and when the process is spread over a long period of time, there is little risk of danger, and the awakening will take place normally and under the law of being itself. If, however, the tuning up and awakening is forced, or is brought about by exercises of various kinds before the student is ready and before the bodies are coordinated and developed, then the aspirant is headed toward disaster.[30]

The stress laid on selfless service in connection with the overall work of spiritual development has importance beyond its contributions to humanity in that it provides a safe and beneficial channel for the release of energies that are induced as a result of the meditation process. This outlet permits a desirable and useful flow and prevents congestion and resulting difficulties.

We will not delve further here into the techniques of meditation; there are other books that cover the subject.[31]

Referring again to the excerpts from the Yoga Sutras given earlier, we note in III.5 and III.6 that a state termed *illumination* may be achieved beyond the state of contemplation. In III.5 "the shining forth of the light" is mentioned, and, indeed, the inner vision of light is an experience reported by mystics. It is commented on as follows by Dr. Carl Jung: ". . . the light vision is an experience common to many mystics and one that is undoubtedly of the greatest significance, because in all times and places it appears as the unconditional thing, which unites in itself the greatest power and the profoundest meaning."[32] Jung also speaks of knowing individuals who had personally experienced this inner light. Referring to the section on *The Light Within* in chapter 1, it is seen that this light is mentioned also in scripture. For example, in the Svetasvatara Upanishad we read: "The yogi experiences directly the truth of Brahman by realizing the light of the Self within."

More important than this phenomenal appearance of light, which is not always present, is the intuitive perception and intellectual illumination that come as results of this stage. The recognition of the source of intuition gives us an indication of the nature of true genius. The intuitive faculty is related to the spirit in man rather than to the soul, and by means of the intuition we do not have to come to a conclusion analytically—we simply *know*. Perhaps St. Paul is referring to this intuitive perception in the earlier-quoted passage when he writes that there is "a mysterious, a hidden wisdom . . . revealed to us through the Spirit. The Spirit scrutinizes all matters, even the deep things of God" (I Cor. 2:7–10).[33]

Because of the ascetic practices of some yogis involved with Hatha Yoga, people sometimes associate yoga with extremes of behavior. Extremes, however, are not recommended by the great teachers, as the following from the Bhagavad Gita indicates:

> Yoga is not for the man who overeats, or for him who fasts excessively. It is not for him who sleeps too much or for the keeper of exaggerated vigils. Let a man be moderate in his eating and his recreation, moderately active, moderate in sleep and in wakefulness.[34]

Daily practice of meditation for a brief period is considered far more valuable than occasional prolonged attempts. With daily repetition there is help from the automatic habitual response of the body and the mind. Some believe that St. Paul referred to the daily practice of meditation and raising the consciousness when he said, "I die daily" (I Cor. 15:3). Paul speaks in other passages with considerable authority about the spiritual nature of man, which may lend some credibility to this belief.

Another passage in the New Testament is cited as a symbolic hint linking the Christian scripture with the yoga of the East. In Matthew 11:20, Jesus says: "Take my yoke upon you and learn of me; . . . and ye shall find rest unto your souls." We are told that "The word yoga is the Sanskrit ancestor of the English word yoke."[35] Compare these words of Christ with the following spoken by Krishna: "Devote your whole mind to me and practice yoga. Take me for your only refuge" (Bhagavad Gita, ch. 6).

Meditation has not been stressed much in Christianity, even though it has been practiced by saints, mystics, and monastics—but it has not been totally overlooked by the clergy, either. We find, for example, Bishop Fulton Sheen writing: "Just try meditation for at least fifteen minutes a day, and in the end you will make great discoveries: What you really are, and what you are on the way to becoming."[36] Bishop Sheen also remarks that "Never has there been a sad saint! And if he is sad he is not a saint. The reason is very simple: 'The fruit of the spirit is joy!' "

Speaking of saints, if we consider the lives of those outstanding figures from all religions who have done much to shape and bolster the faith of men and women throughout the ages, we find two common elements that characterize them. They all spent much of their time in service to their fellow men, and they all practiced some form of meditation. They also experienced profound inner joy, without requiring the external material possessions that many crave.

We are advised that if we begin to practice meditation, we should follow the example of the saints and not withdraw from the world; nonattachment must not become detachment from life. The Upanishads sound a particularly strong warning along this line: "To darkness are they doomed who devote themselves only to life in the world, and to a greater darkness those who devote themselves only to meditation." In *Agni Yoga*[37] we read, "When you will be asked how you affirm the Teaching, answer, 'Only by application to life.' "

Lawrence LeShan comments as follows:

> The great mystics have . . . functioned strongly in both worlds. W. R. Inge, a scholar of the subject, has pointed out that "all the great [Western] mystics have been energetic and influential, and their business capacity is specially noted in a curiously large number of cases." The lives of St. John of the Cross, St. Teresa of Avila, Kabir, Vivekananda, and many others show the understanding, concern, and active involvement with the world of multiplicity.[38]

LeShan also cites Plotinus, Ramakrishna, and the anonymous author of the mystical manuscript *The Cloud of Unknowing* as stressing the need to be active in the two worlds.

Psychologist Abraham Maslow notes: "The great lesson from the true mystics, from the Zen monks, and now also from the Humanistic and Transpersonal psycholgists [is] that the sacred is in the ordinary, that it is to be found in one's daily life, in one's neighbors, friends and family, in one's back yard."[39] Maslow goes on to point out: "The 'spiritual disciplines,' both the classical ones and the new ones that keep on being discovered these days, all take time, work, discipline, study, commitment."[40]

The Yoga Sutras point out that meditation may lead to the unfolding of psychic powers but further explains that "these powers are obstacles to the highest spiritual realization, but serve as magical powers in the objective worlds."[41] One difficulty is that a person may become so fascinated and distracted by the psychic world that the more important activities may be given too little time. If psychic powers do develop, they may prove useful to some extent in serving mankind, but too great an attraction to them should be avoided. Mental and moral qualities are more important, and psychic development is not necessarily a sign of great progress.

Aldous Huxley writes as follows on the subject:

> The Sufis regard miracles as "veils" intervening between the soul and God. The masters of Hindu spirituality urge their disciples to pay no attention to the Siddhis, or psychic powers, which may come to them unsought, as a byproduct of one-pointed contemplation. The cultivation of these powers, they warn, distracts the soul from reality and sets up insurmountable obstacles in the way of enlightenment and deliverance. A similar attitude is taken by the best Buddhist teachers.[42]

Indicators of true spiritual progress are a growing sense of responsibility, a selfless point of view that is inclusive rather than exclusive, concern for the good of all humanity, and a tendency to be more intuitive.

In the Bhagavad Gita we find the following comment regarding a state of spiritual perception: "When you have reached enlightenment ignorance will delude you no longer. In the light of that knowledge you will see the entire creation within your own Atman and in me."[43]

In his *Autobiography of a Yogi*, Paramahansa Yogananda writes of an experience of samadhi, or higher consciousness, in which he is suddenly able to see in all directions simultaneously. His description is essentially the same as the following by Ralph Waldo Emerson:

> Standing on the bare ground—my head bathed by the blithe air, and uplifted into infinite space—all mean egotism vanishes. I become a transparent eyeball; I am nothing; I see all; the currents of the universal being circulate through me; I am part or parcel of God.

Although the aviator Charles A. Lindbergh was not noted as a mystic, he reported a remarkable experience that reveals an element of similarity to the above description by Emerson. The following, from *Reincarnation: the Phoenix Fire Mystery*, by S. L. Cranston and Joseph Head, describes how Lindbergh "during his historic 34-hour flight across the Atlantic, after not sleeping for the day and night before the flight . . . had to wage a superhuman battle to stay awake."

First a separation was observed to take place between mind and body—aspects of himself he usually regarded as inseparable. Overwhelmed with drowsiness, the senses and organs sought sleep . . . but the mind entity standing "apart" held firm. In turn, the mind became unable to preserve wakefulness only to give way to a transcendent power that Lindbergh hardly suspected was within him. Finally in midocean the conscious mind fell fast asleep and a third element, this new "extraordinary mind," which at first he feared to trust, now directed the flight. Then the fuselage behind became crowded with ghostly human presences. No surprise is experienced at their arrival; without turning his head he sees them all, for his skull has become "one great eye, seeing everywhere at once." What connection exists between these "spirits" and "himself"? . . . It is "as though I've known all of them before in some past incarnation."

OTHER FORMS OF MEDITATION

Considering the definition of meditation given by Patanjali—"sustained concentration"—the question arises, are there not other activities, unrelated to religion or self-culture, that can be classed as meditation? The answer is yes. If we consider the activities of the most creative scientists, artists, composers, writers, and philosophers, it will be apparent that in their work they engage in a form of meditation. The same is true of business people who organize, plan, review details, and concentrate deeply in arriving at the decisions that set the directions for their company in some area.

Psychologist Roberto Assagioli makes the following observation:

It is only when a dominating interest backed by a firm, a decided, will is able to hold the mind concentrated on an idea or task that it really "thinks" and we can say that it reflects, it meditates. Thus there are those who meditate without calling their mental activity that; for example, the scientist seeking the solution to a problem, the businessman working out a program for the conduct of his affairs.[44]

Abraham Maslow makes an interesting point along a similar line:

Because it will be so difficult for so many to believe, I must state explicitly that I have found approximately as many transcenders among businessmen, industrialists, managers, educators, political people, as I have among the professionally "religious," the poets, intellectuals, musicians, and others who are supposed to be transcenders. . . . Any minister will talk transcendence even if he hasn't got the slightest inkling of what it feels like. And most industrialists will carefully conceal their idealism . . . under a mask of "toughness," "realism," "selfishness" and all sorts of other words which would have to be marked off in quotes to indicate that they are only superficial and defensive.[45]

CREATIVITY

The way in which some of the most creative people get their ideas is useful to consider. As we know, Einstein used his imagination and visualization in working out his theory of relativity and created a relaxing mental atmosphere when doing this deep thinking. Thomas Edison would relax on his workshop couch after working intently on a difficult problem and come up with ideas for a solution. The pattern of intense study and conscious thought toward the solution of a very difficult problem, followed by the appearance of a solution when in a relaxed state, often while engaged in an activity unrelated to the problem, is many times reported. The 19th-century French mathematician Henri Poincaré reports making some of his more important discoveries in this way, and the same is true for Newton. Richard Wagner reported that once, when he needed a piece of music for an opera, the complete concept for one of his great works came to him as he stood outdoors on a porch reflecting.

Meditative thinking is clearly indicated by the actions of many creative people. Mathematician Norbert Wiener was reported to walk around so deep in thought that he hardly noticed his surroundings. While composing, César Frank is said to have walked around as in a dream, apparently unaware of his surroundings, and Brahms found that only in a state of deep reflection did his ideas come effortlessly. Brahms also indicated that he felt himself to be inspired by a power external to himself when composing and stipulated, in making this confession, that it not be published until fifty years after his death.[46]

While on the subject of music, we may digress for a moment and consider the effect of music on the listener. Abraham Maslow, reporting on what he terms *peak experiences*, observes:

> So far, I have found that these peak experiences are reported from what we might call "classical music." I have not found a peak experience from John Cage or from an Andy Warhol movie, from abstract expressionistic kind of painting, or the like. I just haven't. The peak experience that has reported the great joy, the ecstasy, the visions of another world, or another level of living, has come from classical music—the great classics.[47]

The esotericists agree with this observation, recommending great music as having a beneficial effect. A most interesting book by British composer Sir Cyril Scott called *Music: Its Secret Influence throughout the Ages*[48] discusses the psychological and spiritual effects the music of the great composers has had on mankind and also discusses the sources of inspiration for certain great musical works. Scott claims that composers with the required sensitivities and talent can be, and have been, inspired by higher powers associated with the Spiritual Hierarchy (mentioned in chapter 5) or by members of the Deva or Angel Evolution. This contention is supported by Arthur M. Abell's book *Talks with Great Composers*. Scott attributes the basic information on the effects of music in his book to one of the Masters of the Wisdom communicating through an acquaintance of Scott's named Nelsa Chaplin, who had displayed psychic ability from a very early age.

Scott discusses the process by which composers find their ideas for new works as follows:

> How does a composer fish for ideas? He improvises in his head or on the piano until he strikes something or something strikes him which he happens to like; when this occurs, he writes it down, and having done so resumes his fishing. The Germans have an expressive phrase for this "striking" process . . . which, literally translated, means "something falls into him." But it stands to reason that nothing could "fall into him" unless he held himself receptive or opened his mind to catch it; the "fishing process," therefore, is simply a process of opening the mind.[49]

It is clear that in addition to being able to find a desirable idea with the receptive mind, the great composer has the ability to recognize its value and to apply it properly in the context of the entire work. It is generally true that in any field one must have a good background in order to make effective use of inspiration and that thinking about the problem to be solved sets the stage for the appearance of the new idea.

Creativity requires openness to new ways of viewing things along with an ability to recognize and appreciate a new concept of value. The use of the imagination, the ability to visualize, and the ability to mentally exercise different combinations and alternatives are important.

John Dewey makes the following observation in connection with creative work:

> I do not think it can be denied that an element of reverie, of approach to a state of dream, enters into the creation of a work of art, nor that the experience of the work when it is intense often throws one into a similar state. Indeed, it is safe to say that creative conceptions . . . come only to persons who are relaxed to the point of reverie.

Annie Besant stresses the importance of reflection in training our minds. She writes:

> We should read less and think more, if we would have our minds grow, and our intelligence develop. If we are in earnest in the culture of our minds, we should daily spend an hour in the study of some serious and weighty book, and reading for five minutes, we should think for ten, and so on through the hour.[50]

Abraham Lincoln was reported by his law partner William Herndon to be "the most continuous and severest thinker in America. He read but little and that for an end." One of the writers he did read repeatedly was Shakespeare. Herndon also reported that Lincoln had a deep interest in metaphysics. As to Lincoln's writings and speeches, it is commented that "he became a master of our most difficult language, and the odd music to his sentences is unlike that of anyone else—with the possible exception of Walt Whitman."[51] Whitman would appear to provide an example of the inner sources of inspiration. As noted earlier, Whitman was said by his close acquaintance Dr. R. M. Bucke* to have experienced higher levels of consciousness, and lines such as the following in his writings suggest this: "Light rare, untellable, lighting the very light."[52]

ATTITUDES

The section under the scripture comparisons in chapter 1 entitled *Qualities to Be Gained* (section 9) provides an excellent guide to attitudes that make for peace of mind and that help equip us to be a positive force in our environment.

Faith is the first quality listed, and as we learn more of the spiritual side of life and begin to recognize it at work in the world, our faith is strengthened. Faith contributes to the development of another quality—*courage*; and as we become convinced of man's immortality, we are less influenced by one of the great causes of fear in the world: death. Another important source of fear that limits accomplishment is fear of failure. We need to realize that almost everyone who has made significant accomplishments in life has also had failures along the way and has learned from them. By analyzing the worst that can happen, we can put our fears in proper perspective; by preparing diligently for our task and visualizing success, we enhance the probability of a positive outcome. Having done all this, we then need to use mind and will to focus on what we are to do and then drive forward despite any remaining emotional reactions of fear. Starting out is usually the hardest part, and once we are under way, we generally become absorbed in the task at hand and leave no room for negative emotions.

We are told by the great religions to acquire a "selfless" attitude. For example, the Buddha tells us that unhappiness is caused by selfish craving. This advice sets the stage for the quality of *contentment*, which in turn allows us to be "serene in the face of pleasure or pain," as the scriptures enjoin.

Regarding the quality of *humility*, a good attitude to cultivate is not to take ourselves too seriously. A sense of humor about the minor humbling

*The author of *Cosmic Consciousness*.

occurrences that life sometimes sends our way will avoid useless anxiety. Humility should not, however, be carried to the point of false modesty. We need to be realistic with others about our capabilities if we are to be effective. The biblical saying "Pride goes before destruction and a haughty spirit before a fall" (Prov. 16:18) implies that life will eventually teach us the lessons we need to learn in the area of humility. We will find that it is difficult for people to sympathize with the overproud person who runs into problems.

Wisdom comes with experience and spiritual growth as we work toward the goal of *Perfection. Peace* does not imply a life devoid of the actions it is our duty and destiny to perform. On the contrary, failure to carry out our role in life will lead to uneasiness and discontent rather than peace. The great spiritual leaders of the world were able to be active and accomplish much, often in the midst of controversy and conflict, while maintaining inner peace.

All of the qualities mentioned are in a very real sense the outgrowth of spiritual development, but, as we saw earlier, the process of development is enhanced by "acting as if" we already possess the desired attributes.

MAN'S NATURE AND DIRECTION

If we consider the underlying direction for man which the scriptures of the world seek to impart through their teachings, we find that this direction is universally consistent with the premise stated earlier in the quotation from Vivekananda—that man in his fundamental nature is divine and that he should work toward bringing out that divinity.

Christ, quoting Psalm 82:6, says, "Is it not written in your law, I said, Ye are gods" (John 10:34). He also says, "The kingdom of God is within you" (Luke 17:21). St. Paul adds "You are the temple of God (I Cor. 3:16) and "Your body is a temple of the Holy Spirit who is within" (I Cor.19). In the Upanishads we read: "The Lord God, all-pervading and omnipresent, dwells in the heart of all beings" (Svetasvatara Upanishad); "The Self is one with Brahman" (Brihadaranyaka Upanishad); and "That Self . . . is the kingdom of Brahman" (Brihadaranyaka Upanishad). Muhammad tells us: "The one who knows his self knows God."

Recognizing this basic premise, we can see that the scriptures of the world, each in its own way, give guidance toward bringing out the divine potential of man. From time to time great teachers, saints, and leaders in various fields appear to inspire mankind on its way.

The various scriptures are focused for different people at different times, but all contain truths that are independent of time or place and that taken collectively, provide a broader and clearer picture of our nature and the steps to be taken to fulfill our destiny than is given in any one work.

It seems fitting to close this chapter with the following from the poem *Paracelsus* by Robert Browning:

> Truth is within ourselves; it takes no rise
> From outward things, whate'er you may believe.
> There is an inmost center in us all,
> Where truth abides in fullness and around,
> Wall upon wall, the gross flesh hems it in,
> This perfect, clear perception—which is truth.
> A baffling and perverting carnal mesh
> Binds it, and makes all error: and, to KNOW
> Rather consists in opening out a way
> Whence the imprisoned splendour may escape,
> Than in effecting entry for a light
> Supposed to be without.

19. Conclusion

What can we conclude from the comparison of the teachings of the great religions in this book? First, we note that on the variety of subjects that make up the basic rules of behavior and spiritual growth, all of the major religions are in agreement on what constitutes right action. Further, these rules of right action have found their way into the laws and customs of temporal society and thus influence those who are not outwardly religious.

These facts could lead to the conclusion that the founders and teachers of the great religions were all interpreting, in terms appropriate for the people and times they served, the teachings of certain universal laws. If we read the section in chapter 1 entitled "The Law," we find that this appears to be what is implied by the scriptures quoted there. This is also the view expressed by the esotericists, who indicate that when one works in harmony with these laws, progress is quickly made. Working in opposition produces conflict, suffering, and deterioration.

We can also conclude from this study that science and religion need not be at odds. In both science and religion there are those whose dogmatism prevents them from recognizing interpretations and possibilities beyond their particular view of things, and for them it can be difficult to bridge the gap. In the Christian religion, for example, there are some who insist on a strictly literal belief in some particular translation of the Bible. They recognize no possibility of allegorical interpretation or that teachings were perhaps simplified to suit the people and the times and therefore may not be the last word on a particular subject. Truth is ever unfolding.

In the field of science, there are those who are just as dogmatic as some in religion. They are open only to their own view of things and are totally closed to concepts that cannot be directly related to what science has proved at a given point in time. This attitude, of course, can lead to a rejection of religion, which speaks of events and happenings not explainable by today's science. The idea that what some religions call "miracles" may ultimately be explainable in terms of a science that is not yet recognized by most of humanity is not even admissible as a hypothesis subject to later proof or disproof in their thinking.

Dogmatists have, of course, always been present, and any new concept in science, religion, or any other field seems to have its detractors when first introduced. Caution and quesitoning is, of course, normal, proper, and useful when coupled with an open mind and not colored by a blind clinging to the status quo.

Religion has usually been one of the great forces for good in the world, but at times great wrongs have been committed in the name of religion, and it has been distorted into a means of fostering separateness between peoples. It has been used as the reason for so-called holy wars and has prevented understanding through the fostering of exclusiveness and by giving more emphasis to distinctive customs and rituals than to love and understanding.

If more religious leaders could comprehend, embrace, and live the concept of love for all mankind put forth by the founders of the great religions, the churches, temples, and mosques of the world could become a far more powerful force for true peace and brotherhood. Unfortunately, in some places of the world religious institutions are still used as forums to stir up conflict.

The deeper we study the subject, the more we realize that no one faith is the sole possessor of all truth. Great saints have come from all religious backgrounds, and men and women who did much for mankind have come from all races. Unfortunately, it seems to be in the nature of our background, training, and education that we tend to focus on differences. In the field of religion, this focus on small differences has tended to overshadow vast areas of agreement. The elaborate theology that has been added to the basic teachings of some religions tends to obscure and confuse these areas of fundamental agreement.

A wider recognition of the existence of common basic doctrines can do much toward eliminating religious intolerance and focusing attention on what is important in religion and away from those things that tend to divide. One writer who has made a comprehensive study of the world's great religions comments as follows: "The word 'heathen' should be deleted from our vocabularies. All faiths have their deep wells of inspiration, and every religion of man deserves our reverent study."[1]

Recognizing that many of the divisions that separate men today are related to religion, it is interesting to consider the effect of a widespread emphasis by the different religions on their fundamental unity. The world religions working together in a practical, cooperative way for peace and brotherhood might, because of the number of followers that could be united, present a formidable force for goodwill, against which the forces of division in the world would be hard pressed to succeed. Religions united in this way could inspire those youth of the world who now turn away because some of the practices of religion run counter to the fundamental principles taught by the founders and because claims of being the only true faith and other such dogmatic positions run counter to perceived reality.

Certainly there has been a growth of understanding and cooperation among many religious groups over the last thirty years. The changes in the Roman Catholic church have been noted earlier. The various ecumenical movements and the spread of interest in Eastern religions in the West have brought advances in understanding that are dramatic when compared with the preceding eras.

One might predict that, given the expanding knowledge and intellect of youth among the more advanced societies of the world, those religions that do not open themselves to growth in adjusting to the advances of science, civilization, and world understanding (while still holding to their truly fundamental principles) are facing diminishing influence and eventual extinction. All organizations that hope to be useful must progress and change if they are to remain responsive to the changing needs of the world.

Great leaders and teachers usually become involved in bringing about change, and the gospel story gives us a dramatic example of this. In the time of Jesus, the teachings given by Moses and the prophets had been formed into a dogmatic set of rules and practices dictated by the religious leaders of the time and imposed on the faithful. These practices lacked love, understanding, and compassion, and Christ preached against this dogmatic approach to God. It was time for a new dispensation, and, recognizing this, Christ declared, "A new commandment I give you, that you love one another," and proceeded to set in motion the events that brought into being a great new religion.

The periodic need to sweep away accumulated dogmatic interpretations and to modernize religious practice has brought forth many religious leaders in the East and the West, and this recurring need is not surprising when history and human nature are reviewed. There is a tendency in all fields of human thought—science, government, economics, religion, and others—for a period of consolidation to follow the introduction of new ideas.

When carried to an extreme, however, this can lead to stagnation, making it exceedingly difficult for any radically new lines of thought to be favorably considered. Human growth in understanding and intelligence, however, provides its own demand for new revelation as the limitations of old dogma begin to be recognized. Finally, a breakthrough is made when human advancement in ability to comprehend and the appearance of one or more individuals capable of bringing forth a new revelation coincide. A radically new teaching is usually strongly resisted by groups of individuals with vested interests or narrow dogmatic outlook, and violence may be the result, as it was with Christ and the other martyrs of both religion and science.

Certainly a spiritual revitalization is needed in the world today if we are to overcome the divisions that hold mankind poised on the brink of conflicts that could lead to the destruction of much of civilization. The principles of right action are contained in the great scriptures of the world; the difficulty is in conveying them with adequate conviction to those people who have not been exposed to them or who do not accept them. The great religions could contribute much by conveying a clearer message based on fundamental principles. Many of the difficulties in the world are aggravated by those things that make for separateness, and religion should strive to remove itself as a cause of conflict and become increasingly an instrument of understanding.

We should recognize that in today's inerdependent world we are citizens of the planet as a whole, along with our other allegiances, simply by virtue of being here. Our planetary civilization is at present not well organized and is experiencing great difficulty in some of its relationships. If we observe the world objectively, we will see that there are those whose motives are good in all nations, races, religions, and cultures, although they may at times be acting on limited knowledge. Similarly, those bent on destruction seem also to appear all over the world. Progress in solving the world's ills will be enhanced if the people of right motive pull in the same direction, and for this, knowledge of that direction is necessary. The works of the great teachers mentioned in this book provide the fundamental direction to follow. The task of applying this direction to some of the very complex challenges of our world is by no means simple and requires persistence and imagination, but it fosters the development of skill and wisdom. Through working in this demanding field of activity, we all have the opportunity of making our contribution and, in the process, growing toward our true potential.

Appendix

Messianic Prophecies and the Life of Jesus Christ

OLD TESTAMENT PROPHECY

Behold my servant, whom I uphold; mine elect, in whom my soul delighteth; I have put my spirit upon him: He shall bring forth judgment to the Gentiles. (Isa. 42:1)

I the Lord have called thee in righteousness, and will hold thine hand, and will keep thee, and give thee for a covenant of the people, for a light of the Gentiles. (Isa. 42:6)

The stone which the builders refused is become the headstone of the corner. This is the Lord's doing and it is marvelous in our eyes. (Ps. 118:22–23)

Therefore thus saith the Lord God, Behold, I lay in Zion for a foundation a stone, a tried stone, a sure foundation. (Isa. 28:16)

NEW TESTAMENT CORRESPONDENCE

And Jesus when he was baptized, went up straightway out of the water: and, lo, the heavens were opened unto him, and he saw the spirit of God descending like a dove, and lighting upon him: and lo a voice from heaven, saying, This is my beloved Son, in whom I am well pleased. (Matt. 3:16–17)

He came unto his own, and his own received him not. (John 1:11)

Jesus said unto them, Did ye never read in the scriptures, the stone which the builders rejected, the same is become the head of the corner: this is the Lord's doing and it is marvelous in our eyes? Therefore say I unto you, The Kingdom of God shall be taken from you and given to a nation bringing forth the fruits thereof. . . . And when the chief priests and Pharisees had heard his parables, they perceived that he spoke of them. (Matt. 21:42–45; see also Mark 12:10–11 and Luke 20:17)

The preceding passages foretell that the Messiah who was to come to the Jews would have a profound influence on the Gentiles. History leaves no doubt that Jesus Christ can be cited as fulfilling this prophecy. The comparisons which follow also show that the life and death of Jesus correlate with pronouncements of the Old Testament prophets. They begin with the predictions concerning his ancestry, that he would be of the line of Abraham and David, and that he would be born in Bethleham of Judea, and carry on through to predictions of the way he would die. In the interest of brevity, not all of the passages which could be cited as foretelling the life of Jesus Christ have been included.

OLD TESTAMENT PROPHECY

NEW TESTAMENT CORRESPONDENCE

And in thy seed [Abraham] shall all the nations of the earth be blessed. (Gen. 22:18)

The book of the generation of Jesus Christ, the son of David, the son of Abraham. (Matt. 1:1)

The Lord hath sworn in truth unto David; he will not turn from it; of the fruit of thy body will I set upon thy throne. (Ps. 132:11)

And the angel said unto her, Fear not, Mary, for thou hast found favor with God. . . . thou shalt . . . bring forth a son and shalt call his name Jesus. . . . and the Lord God shall give unto him the throne of his father David. (Luke 1:30–32)

For unto us a child is born, unto us a son is given: and the government shall be on his shoulder: and his name shall be called Wonderful, Counselor, The mighty God, The everlasting Father, The Prince of Peace.

Of the increase of his government and peace there shall be no end, upon the throne of David, and upon his kingdom, to order it, and to establish it with judgment and with justice from henceforth even for ever. (Isa. 9:6–7)

And the angel said unto her, Fear not, Mary: for thou hast found favor with God. And, behold, thou shalt conceive in thy womb, and bring forth a son, and shalt call his name Jesus. He shall be great, and shall be called the Son of the Highest: and the Lord God shall give unto him the throne of his father David: And he shall reign over the house of Jacob for ever; and of his kingdom there shall be no end. (Luke 1:30–33)

OLD TESTAMENT PROPHECY

The voice of him that crieth in the wilderness, Prepare ye the way of the Lord, make straight in the desert a highway for our God. (Isa. 40:3)

Behold, I will send my messenger, and he shall prepare the way before me: and the Lord, whom ye seek, shall suddenly come to his temple, even the messenger of the covenant, whom ye delight in: behold, he shall come, saith the Lord of hosts. (Mal. 3:1)

Rejoice greatly, O daughter of Zion, shout, O daughter of Jerusalem: Behold, thy King cometh unto thee: he is just and having salvation; lowly, and riding on an ass, and upon a colt the foal of an ass. (Zech. 9:9)

The Lord said unto my Lord, Sit thou at my right hand, until I make thine enemies thy footstool. (Ps. 110:1)

NEW TESTAMENT CORRESPONDENCE

He [John the Baptist] said, I am the voice of one crying in the wilderness, Make straight the way of the Lord, as said the prophet Esaias. (John 1:23)

And the disciples went and did as Jesus commanded them and brought the ass, and the colt, and put on them their clothes, and they set him thereon. And a very great multitude spread their garments in the way; others cut down branches from the trees and strewed them in the way. And the multitude that went before, and that followed, cried, saying, Hosanna to the son of David: Blessed is he that cometh in the name of the Lord; Hosanna in the highest. (Matt. 21:6–9)

While the Pharisees were gathered together, Jesus asked of them, saying, What think ye of Christ? whose son is he? They say unto him, The son of David. He saith unto them, How then doth David in spirit call him Lord, saying, The Lord said unto my Lord, Sit thou on my right hand, till I make thine enemies thy footstool? If David then call him Lord, how is he his son? (Matt. 22:41–45)

OLD TESTAMENT PROPHECY	NEW TESTAMENT CORRESPONDENCE

The Lord hath sworn, and will not repent, Thou art a priest forever after the order of Melchizedek. (Ps. 110:4)

Jesus [was made] an high priest for ever after the order of Melchisedec. . . . this Melchisedec, King of Salem, priest of the most high God, who met Abraham . . . and blessed him; to whom also Abraham gave a tenth part of all; first being by interpretation King of righteousness, and after that also King of Salem, which is, King of peace. (Heb. 6:20, 7:1-2)

And Melchizedek, king of Salem, brought forth bread and wine: and he was the priest of the most high God. And he blessed him, and said, Blessed be Abram of the most high God. (Gen. 14:18-19)

Jesus took bread, and blessed, and brake it, and gave to them, and said, Take, eat: this is my body. And he took the cup, and when he had given thanks, he gave it to them: and they all drank of it. And he said unto them, This is my blood of the new testament, which is shed for many. (Mark 14:22-24)

Awake, O sword, against my shepherd, and against the man that is my fellow, saith the Lord of hosts: smite the shepherd, and the sheep shall be scattered. (Zech. 13:7)

Then saith Jesus unto them, All ye shall be offended because of me this night: for it is written, I will smite the shepherd, and the sheep of the flock shall be scattered abroad. (Matt. 26:31)

Yea, mine own familiar friend, in whom I trusted, which did eat of my bread, hath lifted up his heel against me. (Ps. 41:9)

. . . that the scripture may be fulfilled, He that eateth bread with me hath lifted up his heal against me. . . . Verily, verily, I say, unto you, that one of you shall betray me. (John 13:18-21)

They weighed for me my price thirty pieces of silver. And the Lord said unto me, Cast it unto the potter . . . and I took the thirty pieces of silver and cast them to the potter in the house of the Lord. (Zech. 11:12-13)

Then one of the twelve, called Judas Iscariot, went unto the chief priests and said unto them, What will ye give me and I will deliver him unto you? And they covenanted with him for thirty pieces of silver. (Matt. 26:14-15)

OLD TESTAMENT PROPHECY	NEW TESTAMENT CORRESPONDENCE
	Then Judas, which had betrayed him . . . repented. . . . and he cast down the pieces of silver in the temple. . . . and the chief priests took the silver pieces. . . . and bought with them the potter's field, to bury strangers in. (Matt. 27:3–7)
He is despised and rejected of men; a man of sorrows. . . . he was wounded for our transgressions, he was bruised for our iniquities. . . . He was oppressed and he was afflicted, yet he opened not his mouth: he is brought as a lamb to the slaughter, and as a sheep before her shearers is dumb, so he openeth not his mouth. He was taken from prison and from judgment . . . he was cut off out of the land of the living: for the transgressions of my people was he stricken. (Isa. 53:3–8)	And the high priest arose, and said unto him, Answerest thou nothing? what is it which these witness against thee? But Jesus held his peace. . . . Then the high priest [said] What think ye? They answered and said, He is guilty of death. Then did they spit in his face, and buffeted him; and others smote him with the palms of their hands. . . . And Jesus stood before . . . the governor: . . . and when he was accused of the chief priests and elders, he answered nothing. (Matt. 26:62–67; 27:11–12)
My God, my God, why hast thou forsaken me? . . . All they that see me laugh me to scorn: they shoot out the lip, they shake the head saying, He trusted on the Lord that he would deliver him: let him deliver him, seeing he delighted in him. . . . I am poured out like water, and my bones are out of joint. . . . my tongue cleaveth to my jaws; and thou has brought me into the dust of death. . . . the assembly of the wicked have inclosed me: they pierced my hands and my feet. . . . They part my garments among them, and cast lots upon my vesture. (Ps. 22:1–18)	And they crucified him. . . . Then were there two thieves crucified with him, one on the right hand, and another on the left. And they that passed by reviled him, wagging their heads, . . . likewise also the chief priests mocking him, with the scribes and elders, said, "He saved others; himself he cannot save . . . . He trusted in God: let him deliver him now. . . . And about the ninth hour Jesus cried with a loud voice, saying . . . My God, my God, why has thou forsaken me? (Matt. 27:35–46)

OLD TESTAMENT PROPHECY	NEW TESTAMENT CORRESPONDENCE

And I will pour upon the house of David and upon the inhabitants of Jerusalem, the spirit of grace and of supplications; and they shall look upon me whom they have pierced. (Zech. 12:10)

And one shall say unto him, What are these wounds in thine hands? Then he shall answer, Those with which I was wounded in the house of my friends. (Zech. 13:6)

Many are the afflictions of the righteous: but the Lord delivereth him out of them all. He keepeth all his bones: not one of them is broken. (Ps. 34:19–20)

Then the soldiers, when they had crucified Jesus, took his garments, and made four parts, to every soldier a part; and also his coat; now the coat was without seam, woven from the top throughout. They said therefore among themselves, Let us not rend it, but cast lots for it, whose it shall be: . . . Then came the soldiers and brake the legs of the first, and of the other which was crucified with him. But when they came to Jesus, and saw that he was dead already, they brake not his legs: But one of the soldiers with a spear pierced his side, and forthwith came there out blood and water. And he that saw it bare record, and his record is true . . . . For these things were done that the scripture should be fulfilled, A bone of him shall not be broken. And again another scripture saith, They shall look on him whom they pierced. (John 19:23–37)

And he made his grave with the wicked, and with the rich in his death; because he had done no violence, neither was any deceit in his mouth. . . . He shall see the travail of his soul, and shall be satisfied: by his knowledge shall my righteous servant justify many; for he shall bear their iniquities. (Isa. 53:9–11)

Then were there two thieves crucified with him. (Matt. 27:38)

When the even was come, there came a rich man of Arimathaea, named Joseph, who also himself was Jesus' disciple: he went to Pilate, and begged the body of Jesus. . . . he wrapped it in a clean linen cloth, and laid it in his own new tomb, which he had hewn out in the rock. (Matt. 27:57–60)

OLD TESTAMENT PROPHECY	NEW TESTAMENT CORRESPONDENCE

And I saw in the night visions, and behold, one like the Son of man came with the clouds of heaven, and came to the Ancient of days, and they brought him near before him. And there was given him dominion and glory, and a kingdom, that all people, nations, and languages, should serve him: his dominion is an everlasting dominion, which shall not pass away, and his kingdom that which shall not be destroyed. (Dan. 7:13–14)

Jesus saith unto him . . . Hereafter shall ye see the Son of man sitting on the right hand of power, and coming in the clouds of heaven. (Matt. 26:64)

References

INTRODUCTION

1. *Teachings of Sri Ramakrishna* (Calcutta: Advaita Ashrama), pp. 249–50.
2. *The Upanishads, Breath of the Eternal*, trans. Swami Prabhavanada and Frederick Manchester (New York: Mentor Books), pp. 125–26. Copyright © 1948, by the Vedanta Society of Southern California. Quoted with permission of the Vedanta Society of Southern California.
3. *The Meaning of the Glorious Koran*, trans. Mohammed Marmaduke Pickthall (New York: Mentor Books), p. 250. Quoted with permission of the original publishers, George Allen and Unwin, Ltd.
4. E. A. Burtt, ed., *The Teachings of the Compasionate Buddha*, (New York: Mentor Books), p. 37. Quoted with permission.
5. J. Krishnamurti, *The Flight of the Eagle* (New York: Harper & Row, 1972), p. 38.

CHAPTER 1. Hinduism, Christianity, Buddhism, & Taoism: A Comparison

1. Robert Kirsch, review of *The Asian Journal of Thomas Merton, The Los Angeles Times* (July 22, 1973), Calendar Section, p. 56.
2. Manu-Smrti, quoted from Bhagavan Das, *The Essential Unity of All Religions* (Wheaton, Ill. Theosophical Press).
3. Kwan Tze, 23.8, quoted from ibid., p. 180.

REFERENCE KEY FOR TABULATION IN CHAPTER 1

Unless otherwise noted, quotations are from the sources listed below as identified in the text by the keys shown.

Reference Key	Hinduism
	Quotes from the Bhagavad Gita are taken from the two following sources:
BG-S	*The Song of God, Bhagavad Gita*, trans. Swami Prabhavanada and Christopher Isherwood (New York: Mentor Books). Copyright 1944, 1951, by the Vedanta Society of Southern California. Quoted with permission of the Vedanta Society of Southern California.
BG-A	*The Song Celestial or Bhagavad Gita*, trans. Sir Edwin Arnold. Roman numerals in the references refer to the chapters from which the quotations are taken.

| U | Quotes from the Upanishads are from *The Upanishads, Breath of the Eternal*, trans. Swami Prabhavanada and Frederick Manchester (New York: Mentor Books) Copyright © 1948, by the Vedanta Society of Southern California. |

Reference to the various Upanishads is keyed as follows:

U-K	Katha
U-M	Mundaka
U-T	Taittiriya
U-C	Chandogya
U-B	Brihadaranyaka
U-KV	Kaivalya
U-S	Svetasvatara

| W | Refers to quotations from Joseph Gaer, *Wisdom of the Living Religions* (New York: Dodd, Mead & Co., 1958). Quoted with permission of the publisher. |

Reference Key

Christianity

Bible quotations are taken from the Holy Bible, King James Version, and from the *New American Bible* (Catholic Press, Publishers).

Buddhism

Sources used for quotations from Buddhist scripture are:

| T | *Teachings of the Compassionate Buddha*, ed. E. A. Burtt (New York: Mentor Books). Quoted with permission. |
| W | *Wisdom of the Living Religions*, Joseph Gaer (New York: Dodd, Mead & Co., 1958). Quoted with permission of the publisher. |

| D | Quotes from the Dhammapada are followed by the verse number and are from *Sacred Books of the East*, vol. 10, trans. Max Müller (Oxford: Clarendon Press, 1881). |

Reference Key

Taoism

Reference sources used for quotations from the *Tao Te Ching* are:

B	*The Way of Life, Lao Tzu*, trans. R. B. Blakney. Copyright © 1955, 1983 by Raymond B. Blakney. Reprinted by arrangement with New American Library, New York, N. Y.
W	*Wisdom of the Living Religions*, Joseph Gaer (New York: Dodd, Mead & Co., 1958). Quoted with permission of the publisher.
S	*Lao-Tzu and the Tao Te Ching*, trans. Bennett B. Sims (New York: Franklin Watts, Inc.).

Numbers given are the number of the poem in the Tao Te Ching from which the quotation is taken.

CHAPTER 2. THE GOLDEN RULE & MORAL LAWS

1. *Tai-Shang, Kan-Ting-Pien.*
2. Yoga Sutras of Patanjali, Book II, no. 30, in Alice Bailey, *Light of the Soul* (New York: Lucis Publishing Co.). Copyright © Lucis Trust. Quoted with permission.

CHAPTER 3. RELIGIONS OF THE NEAR EAST: JUDAISM & ISLAM

1. Milton Steinberg, *Basic Judaism* (New York: Harcourt, Brace and Co.). Copyright © 1947 by Milton Steinberg; renewed 1975 by David Joel Steinberg and Jonathan Steinberg. Reprinted by permission of Harcourt Brace Jovanovich, Inc.
2. Quotations from the Koran in this chapter where the number of the Sura (chapter) is designated by a Roman numeral are from *The Meaning of the Glorious Koran*, trans. Mohammed Marmaduke Pickthall (New York: Mentor Books). Quoted with permission of George Allen and Unwin, Ltd.
3. Quotations from the Koran where the number of the Sura is Arabic are from Joseph Gaer, *Wisdom of the Living Religions* (New York: Dodd, Mead & Co., 1958). Quoted with permission of the publisher.
4. Quotations from the *Hadith* or Table Talk of Muhammad are from Joseph Gaer, *Wisdom of the Living Religions* (New York: Dodd, Mead & Co., 1958). These quotations were taken from Allama Sir Abdulla Al-Manum Al-Suhrowardy, *The Sayings of Muhammed*, and published in *The Wisdom of the East* series in London. The numbers correspond to the numbers in *The Sayings of Muhammed.*

CHAPTER 4. CONFUCIANSIM

1. Charles Francis Potter, *The Faiths Men Live By* (Englewood Cliffs, N.J.: Prentice-Hall, 1954). Copyright © 1954 by Charles Francis Potter. Reprinted with permission of the publisher, Prentice-Hall, Inc., Englewood Cliffs, NJ 07632, p. 80.
2. Ibid.
3. Ibid.
4. The quotations followed by roman numerals (designating the chapter of the Analects the quotation is from) are taken from *Wisdom of the Living Religions*, Joseph Gaer (New York: Dodd, Mead & Co., 1958). Quoted with permission of the publisher. Gaer used translations given in *Sacred Books of the East*, edited by Max Müller and translated by William Jennings with minor changes for clarity.

CHAPTER 5. THE ESOTERICISTS

1. H. P. Blavatsky, *Collected Writings*, vol. 8, p. 278.
2. Information on those familiar with Theosophy is taken from a compilation in Joseph Head and S. L. Cranston, *Reincarnation: the Phoenix Fire Mystery* (New York: Julian Press/Crown Publishers).
3. Quoted from *The New American Bible.*
4. II, 29.
5. From Alice Bailey, *Treatise on Cosmic Fire* (New York: Lucis Publishing Co.), p. 117. This and all subsequently referenced books by Alice Bailey are copyright © by Lucis Trust and quoted with permission of Lucis Trust.
6. From *The Theosophist* (December 1899).
7. From Max Heindel, *The Rosicrucian Cosmo-Conception* (Oceanside, Calif.: Rosicrucian Fellowship), p. 29.
8. H. P. Blavatsky, *The Secret Doctrine*, 3d rev. ed., pp. 85, 284.
9. *The Upanishads*, trans. Swami Prabhavananda and Frederick Manchester (New York: Mentor Books), p. 108.

10. These experiments were reported in the May 1907 issue of the *Journal of the American Society for Psychical Research*.

11. Dr. Kübler-Ross has authored a book entitled *On Death and Dying*.

12. Raymond A. Moody, Jr., *Life After Life* (Georgia: Mockingbird Books, 1975), Copyright © 1975 by Raymond A. Moody, Jr. Quoted with permission. Excerpts here and in chapter 6 are from pp. 21–22, 33–134, and 143 in the Bantam Books edition (1976).

13. C. W. Leadbeater, *A Textbook of Theosophy* (Wheaton, Ill: The Theosophical Press), p. 46.

14. Library of Devotion (London: Methuen & Co. Ltd.), 10th ed., 1919 (Lib. VII, xxii 2–3).

15. *Secret Science behind Miracles*, etc., published by DeVorss & Company, Marina del Rey, Calif.

16. Geoffrey Hodson, *The Kingdom of the Gods* (Wheaton, Ill.: Theosophical Publishing House).

17. Ibid.

18. Alice Bailey, *A Treatise on White Magic* (New York: Lucis Publishing Co.), p. 408.

19. Ibid., p. 490.

20. H. P. Blavatsky, *Isis Unveiled* (Pasadena, Calif.: Theosophical University Press), vol. 2, p. 349.

21. John Yarker, Jr., *Notes on the Scientific and Religious Mysteries of Antiquity: the Gnosis and Secret Schools of the Middle Ages; Modern Rosicrucianism and the Various Rites and Degrees of Free and Accepted Masonry* (London, 1872), p. 150. Quoted in H. P. Blavatsky, *Isis Unveiled*, p. 377.

22. Manly Palmer Hall, *Secret Teachings of All Ages* (Los Angeles: Philosophical Research Society, 1973).

23. Foster Bailey, *The Spirit of Masonry* (London: Lucis Publishing Co., 1957), p. 29. Copyright © by Lucis Trust. Quoted with permission of Lucis Trust.

24. Ibid., pp. 37–38.

CHAPTER 6. IMMORTALITY

1. See *William James on Psychical Research*, compiled and edited by Gardner Murphy and Robert O. Ballon (New York: Viking Press).

2. *The Song of God, Bhagavad Gita*, trans. Swami Prabhavananda and Christopher Isherwood (New York: Mentor Books), pp. 76–77.

3. Cunningham Press, Los Angeles.

4. From the *Books of Chuang-tzu*, quoted in Joseph Head and S. L. Cranston, *Reincarnation: The Phoenix Fire Mystery* (New York: Julian Press/Crown Publishers).

5. From *Contra Celsum*, quoted in Joseph Head and S. L. Cranston, *Reincarnation: An East-West Anthology* (Wheaton, Ill.: Theosophical Publishing House, 1968).

6. Hieronim, *Epistola ad Demetr.*

7. Head and Cranston, *Reincarnation: Phoenix Fire Mystery*. Copyright 1977 by Joseph Head and S. L. Cranston. Quoted with permission of the publisher.

8. Geddes MacGregor, *Reincarnation in Christianity* (Wheaton, Ill.: Theosophical Publishing House, 1978). Quoted by permission of the publisher.

9. Quoted in Head and Cranston, *Reincarnation: Phoenix Fire Mystery*, from *The Works of Flavius Josephus*, trans. William Wiston.

10. Quoted in E. D. Walker, *Reincarnation: A Study of Forgotten Truth*.

11. Quoted in *The Path* (New York), February, 1894, p. 359.

12. Letter to Joseph Head (Oct. 8, 1963) quoted in Head and Cranston, *Reincarnation: Phoenix Fire Mystery*.

13. Manly P. Hall, *Reincarnation: The Cycle of Necessity* (Los Angeles: Philosophical Research Society).

14. Alice Bailey, *The Reappearances of the Christ* (New York: Lucis Publishing Co.), p. 146.

15. From *Egyptian Hermetic Fragments*, quoted in Head and Cranston, *Reincarnation: Phoenix Fire Mystery*.

16. Ibid.

17. Published by the American Society for Psychic Research, 1966.

18. New edition (Garden City, N.Y.: Doubleday, 1965).

19. (Garden City, N.Y.: Doubleday, 1973).

20. (Harper & Row, 1978). See also *Life Before Life* (New York: Bantam Books, 1979), by the same author.

21. *There Is a River*, rev. ed. (Virginia Beach, Va.: A. R. E. Press, 1973), *Many Mansions* (New York: William Morrow & Co., 1968).

22. Jess Stern, *Yoga, Youth, and Reincarnation* (New York: Bantam Books).

23. *Reincarnation, Key to Immortality*, by Marcia Moore and Mark Douglas, discusses this and many other interesting cases.

CHAPTER 7. CREATION AND THE CREATOR

1. Alice Bailey, *The Rays and the Initiations* (New York: Lucis Publishing Co.), p. 556.

2. Marina del Rey, Calif.: DeVorss & Company.

3. Bailey, *Rays and Initiations*, pp. 51–55.

4. Ibid., p. 55.

5. From the description of the Sermon at Benares, *Teachings of the Compassionate Buddha*, E. A. Burtt, ed. (New York: Mentor Books), p. 31.

6. Ibid., from the Parable of the Burning House, p. 144.

7. James Churchward, *The Children of Mu* (New York: Paperback Library, 1931).

8. H. P. Blavatsky, *Two Books of the Stanzas of Dzyan*.

9. Leinani Melville, *Children of the Rainbow* (Wheaton, Ill.: Theosophical Publishing House, 1969). These illustrations are used with permission of the publisher.

10. Adolphe Franck, *The Kabbalah* (Secaucus, N.J.: University Books), pp. 96–97.

11. Ibid. Prov. 2:3–4 refers to understanding as being feminine.

12. *Philosphies of India* (Princeton University Press).

13. Nehru, who was a follower of Gandhi and succeeded him as India's national leader, made the remark in a speech delivered in 1949 at a celebration of the birthday of Sri Ramakrishna.

14. *Revelation: A Commentary on the Book* (Virginia Beach, Va.: A. R. E. Press, 1973). Copyright © 1969, 1952, 1945 by A. R. E. Press. Copyright assigned to The Edgar Cayce Foundation, June 25th, 1977. Quoted with permission, p. 91.

15. See, for example, Col. 1:16 and Gen. 3:24.

16. Daniel 7:22.

17. Alice Bailey, *A Treatise on Cosmic Fire*, (New York: Lucis Publishing Co.), p. 1136.

18. Alice Bailey, *Esoteric Psychology II* (New York: Lucis Publishing Co.), p. 229.

CHAPTER 8. CHRIST, KRISHNA, AND THE BUDDHA

1. Mentor Religious Classics, New American Library.

2. William Kingsland, *The Gnosis or Ancient Wisdom in the Christian Scriptures* (Wheaton, Ill.: Theosophical Publishing House, 1970). © George Allen & Unwin, Ltd., 1937, p. 156.

3. H. P. Blavatsky, *Studies in Occultism* (Pasadena, Calif.: Theosophical University Press), pp. 165–66.

4. Alice Bailey, *A Treatise on White Magic* (New York: Lucis Publishing Co.), p. 308.

5. H. P. Blavatsky, *Isis Unveiled*, vol. 2, p. 536.

6. E. A. Burtt, ed., *Teachings of the Compassionate Buddha* (New York: Mentor Books), p. 49.

7. Joseph Gaer, *Wisdom of the Living Religions* (New York: Dodd, Mead & Co., 1958), pp. 9–10.

8. Alice Bailey, *Problems of Humanity* (New York: Lucis Publishing Co.), pp. 150–51.

9. E.g. Max Heindel, *The Rosicrucian Cosmo-Conception*; Alice Bailey, *Initiation, Human and Solar*; C. W. Leadbeater, *The Masters and the Path*.

10. A Quest Book, Theosophical Publishing House.

11. *The Meaning of the Glorious Koran*, trans. Mohammed Marmaduke Pickthall (New York: Mentor Books), p. 66.

CHAPTER 9: SYMBOLIC WRITING AND ALLEGORY

1. Geoffrey Hodson, *Hidden Wisdom in the Holy Bible*, vol. 1 (Wheaton, Ill.: Theosophical Publishing House).

2. Bantam Books, 1973.

3. Alice Bailey, *A Treatise on White Magic* (New York: Lucis Publishing Co.), p. 303.

4. Alice Bailey, *Esoteric Psychology II* (New York: Lucis Publishing Co.), pp. 165–66.

5. Natalie N. Banks, *The Golden Thread* (New York: Lucis Publishing Co., 1963). Copyright © 1963 by Natalie N. Banks. Quoted with permission.

6. Geoffrey Hodson, *Hidden Wisdom in the Holy Bible*, vol. 1, p. 221.

7. Ibid., pp. 144, 108.

8. Bailey, *Treatise on White Magic*, pp. 94–96.

9. Manly P. Hall, *The Secret Teachings of All Ages* (Los Angeles: Philosophical Research Society, 1973). Copyright © by The Philosophical Research Society, p. 86.

10. Vol. 1, p. 549.

11. Charles Poncé, *The Kabbalah*.

12. Hall, *Secret Teachings of All Ages*, p. 185.

13. Published by Symbols and Signs, P.O. Box 4536, North Hollywood, CA 91507.

14. *Revelation: A Commentary on the Book* (Virginia Beach, Va.: A. R. E. Press, 1973), p. 47.

15. H. P. Blavatsky, *Isis Unveiled* (Pasadena, Calif.: Theosophical University Press), vol. 2, p. 351.

16. James M. Pryse, *The Apocalypse Unsealed* (Hollywood: Symbols and Signs), p. 35.

17. Hall, *Secret Teachings of All Ages*, p. 185.

18. Bailey, *Treatise on White Magic*, p. 285.

19. Alice Bailey, *The Rays and the Initiations* (New York: Lucis Publishing Co.), p. 336.

20. Alice Bailey, *A Treatise on Cosmic Fire* (New York: Lucis Publishing Co.), pp. 161–62.

21. Alice Bailey, *Letters on Occult Meditation* (New York: Lucis Publishing Co.), p.77.

22. Pryse, *Apocalypse Unsealed*, pp. 39–40.

23. C. W. Leadbeater, *The Chakras* (Wheaton, Ill.: Theosophical Publishing House), has paintings that show the configuration of the various chakras.

24. Bailey, *Treatise on White Magic*, pp. 199–200. See also Revelation 14:1, 5.

25. Bailey, *Treatise on White Magic*, p. 546, and *Discipleship in the New Age II* (New York: Lucis Publishing Co.), p. 130.

26. New York: G. P. Putnam's Sons, 1973.

27. Ibid., p. 225.

28. Ibid., p. 91.

29. Ibid., p. 289.

30. Chandogya Upanishad, from *Upanishads, Breath of the Eternal* (New York: Mentor Books), p. 75.

31. E. A. Burtt, ed., *Teachings of the Compassionate Buddha* (New York: Mentor Books), p. 138, from the *Bodhicharyavatara of Śantideva*.

32. Gershom Scholem, *Kabbalah* (New York Times Book Co.).

CHAPTER 10. DIFFERENCES & THEIR RESOLUTION

1. From Banesh Hoffmann and Helen Dukas, *Albert Einstein: The Human Side* (Princeton University Press).

2. H. P. Blavatsky, *The Secret Doctrine* (Theosophical University Press), vol. 2, p. 691.

3. H. P. Blavatsky, *Isis Unveiled* (Theosophical University Press), vol. 2, p. 422.

4. *The Theosophist*, vol. 3, p. 115, quoted in Alice Bailey, *A Treatise on Cosmic Fire* (New York: Lucis Publishing Co.), p. 39.

5. Published by W. W. Norton.

6. *New York Times Magazine* (June 1979).

7. From Fritjof Capra, *The Tao of Physics*. © 1975. This and all other excerpts from this book reprinted with permission of Shambhala Publications, Inc., Boulder, Colo.

8. Produced by Adrian Malone in association with KCET.

9. Max Planck, *Scientific Autobiography*, trans. F. Gaynor (New York: Philosophical Library, 1949), p. 113.

CHAPTER 11. MODERN PHYSICS

1. From Fritjof Capra, *The Tao of Physics*. © 1975. This and all other excerpts from this book reprinted with permission of Shambhala Publications, Inc., Boulder, Colo.

2. Lawrence LeShan, *The Medium, the Mystic and the Physicist* (New York: The Viking Press, 1974), p. 65. Copyright © 1966, 1973, 1974 by Lawrence LeShan. Reprinted by permission of Viking Penguin, Inc.

3. Capra, *Tao of Physics*, p. 131.

4. Alice Bailey, *A Treatise on Cosmic Fire* (New York: Lucis Publishing Co.).

5. Max Planck, *Where Is Science Going?* (London: G. Allen and Unwin, 1933), p. 24.

6. D. Bohm & B. Hiley, "On the Intuitive Understanding of Nonlocality As Implied by Quantum Theory," *Foundations of Physics*, vol. 5 (1974), pp. 96, 102.

7. Capra, *Tao of Physics*, p. 296.

8. *New York Post* (Nov. 28, 1972).

9. Quoted in Aldous Huxley, *The Perennial Philosophy* (New York: Meridian Books, 1970), p. 57.

10. Sri Aurobindo, *The Synthesis of Yoga*, pp. 989, 993.

11. D. T. Suzuki, *The Essence of Buddhism*, p. 52.

12. Capra, *Tao of Physics*, p. 139.

13. Ibid., p. 29.

14. *The Medium, the Mystic and the Physicist*, p. 36.

15. Capra, *Tao of Physics*, p. 164.

16. Louis de Broglie, in *Albert Einstein: Philosopher/Scientist*, ed. P. A. Schilpp, p. 144.

17. Mendel Sachs, "Space-Time and Elementary Interactions in Relativity," *Physics Today*, vol. 22 (Feb. 1969), p. 53.

18. J. Robert Oppenheimer, *Science and the Common Understanding* (New York: Simon and Schuster, 1964), p. 69.

19. Lincoln Barnett, *The Universe and Dr. Einstein* (New York: William Morrow).

20. J. A. Wheeler, *Superspace and Quantum Geometrodynamics*, pp. 252–53.

21. Quoted in Rudolf Otto, *Mysticism East and West*, p. 67.

22. Swami Vivekananda, *Jnana-Yoga* (New York: Ramakrishna-Vivekananda Center, 1949), p. 90 ff.

23. *On Indian Mahayana Buddhism*, pp. 148–49.

24. Quoted in Jiyu Kennett, *Selling Water by the River* (New York: Pantheon Books, 1972), p. 140.

25. Capra, *Tao of Physics*, p. 80.

26. Werner Heisenberg, *Physics and Beyond*, p.133.

27. Capra, *Tao of Physics*, p. 200.

28. Ibid., p. 75.
29. Adapted from *Foundations of Physics* (1973).
30. H. P. Blavatsky, *The Secret Doctrine*, vol. 1, p. 298.
31. G. F. Chew, "Impasse for the Elementary Particle Concept," *The Great Ideas Today* (Chicago: William Benton, 1974), p. 99.
32. Blavatsky, *Secret Doctrine*, vol. 2, p. 520.
33. Capra, *Tao of Physics*, p. 210.
34. Quoted in M. Capek, *The Philosophical Impact of Contemporary Physics*, p. 219.
35. Blavatsky, *Secret Doctrine*, vol. 1, p. 583.
36. Alice Bailey, *The Rays and the Initiations* (Lucis Publishing Co.), p. 437.
37. Capra, *Tao of Physics*, p. 211.
38. Chandogya Upanishad.
39. Capra, *Tao of Physics*, p. 212.
40. Blavatsky, *Secret Doctrine*, vol. 1, pp. 8-9.
41. Capra, *Tao of Physics*, p. 203.
42. Ibid.
43. Werner Heisenberg, *Physics and Philosophy*.
44. Werner Heisenberg, *Philosophic Problems of Nuclear Science* (Greenwich, Conn.: Fawcett, 1966), p. 64.
45. Sarvepalli Radhakrishnan, *Indian Philosophy*, p. 173.
46. Ibid., p. 369.
47. *Buddha and the Gospel of Buddhism* (Harper Torchbooks, 1964), p. 66.
48. Quoted in Capra, *Tao of Physics*, p. 204.
49. Blavatsky, *Secret Doctrine*, vol. 1, p. 633.
50. Max Born, *The Restless Universe* (New York: Dover Publications, 1951), p. 1.
51. Alice Bailey, *The Consciousness of the Atom* (Lucis Publishing Co.), p. 42.
52. Bailey, *Treatise on Cosmic Fire*.
53. Blavatsky, *Secret Doctrine*, vol. 1, p. 568.
54. Sir James Jeans, quoted in Paul Hawken, *The Magic of Findhorn* (New York: Bantam Books).
55. Arthur Eddington, *Nature of the Physical World* (New York: Macmillan, 1931), p. 414.
56. Quoted in R. Fisher, ed., *Interdisciplinary Perspectives on Time* (New York: New York Academy of Science, 1967), p. 16.
57. G. F. Chew, "Bootstrap: A Scientific Idea?" *Science*, vol. 161 (May 23, 1968), p. 763.
58. Quoted in Bailey, *Consciousness of the Atom*, pp. 38-39.
59. Quoted in Aldous Huxley, *The Perennial Philosophy* (New York: Meridian Books, 1962), p. 179.
60. Quoted in E. A. Burtt, *The Teachings of the Compassionate Buddha*, pp. 194-95.
61. Quoted in J. Needham, *Science and Civilization in China*, vol 2, p. 538.
62. Quoted in W. T. Stace, *The Teachings of the Mystics* (New York: Mentor Books, 1969), p. 58.
63. Blavatsky, *Secret Doctrine*, vol. 1, pp. 15-16.
64. From Laurence B. Chase, "The Black Hole of the Universe," *Intellectual Digest* (December 1972). Taken from an interview with John A. Wheeler in *University*, a Princeton Quarterly publication.
65. *The Song of God, Bhagavad-Gita*, trans. Swami Prabhavananda and Christopher Isherwood (New York: Mentor Books), p. 77.
66. Translation given in Blavatsky, *Secret Doctrine*, vol. 1.

CHAPTER 12. ESOTERICISM: COMMON GROUND

1. Alice Bailey, *The Rays and the Initiations* (New York: Lucis Publishing Co.), p. 666.
2. Alice Bailey, *Glamour, a World Problem* (New York: Lucis Publishing Co.), p. 187.

3. H. P. Blavatsky, *The Secret Doctrine*, vol. 1, p. 258. Blavatsky attributed this quotation to an ancient esoteric text called "The Book of Dzyan."

4. Alice Bailey, *A Treatise on White Magic* (New York: Lucis Publishing Co.), p. 28.

5. From a commentary on the *Tibetan Book of the Great Liberation*, ed. W. Y. Evans-Wentz (New York: Oxford University Press), pp. xxx–xxxi.

6. *The Song of God, Bhagavad-Gita*, trans. Swami Prabhavananda & Christopher Isherwood (New York: Mentor Books), p. 74.

7. From Joseph Head & S. L. Cranston, *Reincarnation: The Phoenix Fire Mystery* (New York: Julian Press/Crown Publishing), pp. 513–14.

8. Ibid., p. 513.

9. Quoted in Lincoln Barnett, *The Universe and Dr. Einstein* (New York: Mentor Books).

10. Robert Conot, *A Streak of Luck* (New York: Simon and Schuster), p. 17.

11. Manly Palmer Hall, *Secret Teachings of All Ages* (Los Angeles: Philosophical Research Society, 1973).

12. Blavatsky, *Secret Doctrine*, vol. 2.

13. *Fiery World*, I (New York: Agni Yoga Society), p. 659.

CHAPTER 13. PSYCHOLOGY

1. Erich Fromm, *Psychoanalysis and Religion* (New Haven: Yale University Press, 1950), p. 18. Copyright © 1950 by Erich Fromm. Quoted with permission.

2. From a commentary on the *Tibetan Book of the Great Liberation*, ed. W. Y. Evans-Wentz (New York: Oxford University Press), p. xxxi.

3. C. G. Jung, *Modern Man in Search of a Soul* (New York: Harcourt, Brace & World), p. 229.

4. Alfred Adler, *Beyond Good and Evil*.

5. Jung, *Modern Man in Search of a Soul*, p. 216.

6. From Jung's introduction to *The Secret of the Golden Flower* (Richard Wilhelm's German translation rendered into English by Carey P. Gazner), pp. 82–83.

7. Abraham H. Maslow, *The Farther Reaches of Human Nature* (New York: The Viking Press). Copyright © 1971 by Bertha G. Maslow. Quoted with permission of Viking Penguin, Inc., p. 52.

8. Ibid., p. 15.

9. Fromm, *Psychoanalysis and Religion*, p. 21.

10. Ibid., p. 26.

11. Ibid., p. 27.

12. Ibid., p. 28.

13. Roberto Assagioli, *The Act of Will* (Baltimore: Penguin Books, 1974), p. 95. Copyright © 1973 Psychosynthesis Research Foundation. Reprinted by permission of Viking Penguin, Inc.

14. Robert E. Ornstein, *The Psychology of Consciousness* (New York: Penguin Books, 1975), p. 244. Copyright © W. H. Freeman and Co., 1972. Quoted with permission of the author.

15. Carl R. Rogers, *A Way of Being* (Boston: Houghton Mifflin Co., 1981), p. 30. Copyright © 1981, Houghton Mifflin Company. Used with permission.

16. Fromm, *Psychoanalysis and Religion*, p. 76.

17. Ornstein, *Psychology of Consciousness*, p. 148.

18. Assagioli, *Act of Will*, p. 17.

19. Ibid., p. 18.

20. Ibid., p. 14.

21. Jung, *Modern Man in Search of A Soul*, p. 220.

22. C. G. Jung, *Two Essays on Analytical Psychology*.

23. Ibid., p. 210.

24. Maslow, *The Farther Reaches of Human Nature*, p. 349.

25. Ibid., 195.

26. Ornstein, *Psychology of Consciousness*, pp. 196–97.

27. Ibid., p. 205.

28. Assagioli, *Act of Will*, pp. 125–26.

29. Ibid., p. 6.

30. Jung, *Modern Man in Search of a Soul*, p. 122.

31. William James, *The Varieties of Religious Experience*, p. 388.

32. Ornstein, *Psychology of Consciousness*, p. 294.

33. Kurt Goldstein, "Concerning the Concept of Primitivity," in *Primitive Views of the World*, ed. S. Diamond (New York: Columbia University Press, 1964), p. 8.

34. Rogers, *Way of Being*, p. 128.

35. Fromm, *Psychoanalysis and Religion*, pp. 93–94.

36. Ibid., p. 95.

37. Maslow, *The Farther Reaches of Human Nature*, p. 191.

38. Assagioli, *Act of Will*, p. 21.

39. Ibid., p. 114.

40. Ornstein, *Psychology of Consciousness*, p. 154.

41. Ibid., p. 196.

42. Ibid., p. 107.

43. Ibid., p. 155.

44. Ibid., p. 28.

45. Maslow, *The Farther Reaches of Human Nature*, p. 195.

46. From a paper by Roberto Assagioli titled "Psychoanalysis and Psychosynthesis," *Hibbert Journal* (1934). Quoted in Assagioli, *Act of Will*, p. 34.

47. Rogers, *Way of Being*, p. 133.

48. Fromm, *Psychoanalysis and Religion*, pp. 99–100.

CHAPTER 14. HEALING

1. This experiment and others by Drs. Miller and Moss described here were presented at a symposium on "Thought as Energy," held at Founder's Church of Religious Science, Los Angeles, February 1975.

2. Lawrence LeShan, *The Medium, the Mystic, and the Physicist* (New York: Viking Press, 1974), p. 102.

3. Ibid., p. 106.

4. Harry Edwards, *Psychic Healing* (London: Spiritualist Press, 1946), p. 26.

5. Agnes Sanford, *The Healing Light*, 8th ed. (St. Paul: Manchester Park Publishing Co., 1949).

6. Worrall and Worrall, *Miracle Healers*, p. 165.

7. Ibid., p. 162.

8. LeShan, *Medium, Mystic, and Physicist*, p. 110.

9. Ibid., p. 111.

10. Ibid., p. 112.

11. Ibid., pp. 148–49.

12. Ibid., p. 161.

13. Ibid., pp. 166–67.

14. Carl R. Rogers, *A Way of Being* (Boston: Houghton Mifflin Co., 1981). Copyright © 1981, Houghton Mifflin Company. Used with permission, p. 129.

15. Mike Samuels, M.D., and Nancy Samuels, *Seeing with the Mind's Eye* (New York: Random House, Bookworks Books, 1975), pp. 215–18.

16. Alice Bailey, *Esoteric Healing* (Lucis Publishing Co.), pp. 642–43.

17. Ibid., p. 644.

18. See Peter Tompkins and Christopher Bird, *The Secret Life of Plants* (New York: Avon Books, 1974), p. 211.

CHAPTER 15. PSYCHIC PHENOMENA

1. *Los Angeles Times* (July 18, 1975).
2. Delacorte Press.

CHAPTER 16. THE VEGETABLE KINGDOM

1. Quoted in Sheila Ostrander and Lynn Schroeder, *Handbook of Psychic Discoveries* (New York: Berkeley Publishing, 1975), p. 15.
2. Edgar D. Mitchell, ed., *Psychic Exploration*.
3. Harper & Row; paperback: Avon Books.
4. Peter Tompkins and Christopher Bird, *The Secret Life of Plants* New York: Harper & Row, 1973). Copyright © 1973 by Peter Tompkins and Christopher Bird. Quoted with permission of Harper & Row, Publishers, Inc.; p. 150 in Avon Books edition (1974), hereafter cited.
5. Ibid., pp. 152–53.
6. Ibid., p. 156.
7. Ibid., p. 143.
8. Ibid., pp. 147–48.
9. "Outlook for the Blind."
10. Tompkins and Bird, *Secret Life of Plants*, p. 96.
11. Quoted in Ostrander and Schroeder, *Handbook of Psychic Discoveries*, p. 40.
12. Tompkins and Bird, *Secret Life of Plants*, p. 124.
13. Quoted in Tompkins and Bird, *Secret Life of Plants*, p. 135.
14. Ibid., p. 239.
15. Paul Hawken, *The Magic of Findhorn* (Harper & Row; paperback: Bantam Books), pp. 264–65. This memo is quoted from the "Findhorn Garden" book.
16. Tompkins and Bird, *Secret Life of Plants*, p. 382.
17. Hawken, *Magic of Findhorn*, pp. 294, 297.

CHAPTER 17. ASTROLOGY: A DILEMMA FOR RELIGION AND SCIENCE

1. Serge Hutin, *History of Astrology* (New York: Pyramid Communications), pp. 96–97.
2. Ibid., p. 110.
3. Quoted in Hutin, *History of Astrology*.
4. Lawrence E. Jerome, *Astrology Disproved* (Buffalo, N.Y.: Prometheus Books), p. 142.
5. Michel Gauquelin, *The Cosmic Clock* (Chicago: Henry Regnery, 1967), p. 191.
6. Baltimore: Penguin Books, 1970.
7. C. G. Jung, *Modern Man in Search of a Soul*, p. 216.
8. From introduction to the *Tibetan Book of the Great Liberation*, ed. W. Y. Evans-Wentz (New York: Oxford University Press), p. 63.
9. Hutin, *History of Astrology*, p. 65.
10. *New American Bible*, Matt. 2:1–12.
11. Alice Bailey, *Reappearance of the Christ* (New York: Lucis Publishing Co.), p. 80.
12. Alice Bailey, *Esoteric Astrology* (New York: Lucis Publishing Co.), p. 558.
13. H. P. Blavatsky, *The Secret Doctrine*, 3d ed., vol. 2, p. 525.
14. Blavatsky, *Secret Doctrine*, vol. 3, p. 482.
15. Bailey, *Esoteric Astrology*, p. 32.
16. Alice Bailey, *A Treatise on White Magic* (New York: Lucis Publishing Co.), p. 434.
17. Alice Bailey, *Discipleship in the New Age II* (New York: Lucis Publishing Co.), p. 780.
18. Blavatsky, *Secret Doctrine*, 3d ed., vol. 1, p. 626.
19. Blavatsky, *Secret Doctrine*, 3d ed., vol. 3, p. 160.
20. Published by Lucis Publishing Co., New York.

CHAPTER 18. THE MESSAGE OF THE TEACHINGS AND DAILY LIFE

1. *The Way of Life, Lao Tzu*, Translation of the Tao Te Ching by R. B. Blakney (New York: Mentor Books).
2. *New American Bible.*
3. Quoted in *Catholic Near East Magazine* (Winter 1976), p. 19.
4. Alice Bailey, *A Treatise on White Magic* (New York: Lucis Publishing Co.), p. 117.
5. Ibid., pp. 188–89.
6. *New American Bible.*
7. Matt. 25:37–40, *New American Bible.*
8. Teilhard de Chardin, *The Phenomenon of Man* (New York: Harper & Row), p. 246.
9. Alice Bailey, *Esoteric Psychology I* (New York: Lucis Publishing Co.), p. 284.
10. Albert Einstein, *Out of My Later Years*, (Secaucus, N.J.: Citadel Press, 1973), p. 130.
11. *The Song of God, Bhagavad-Gita*, trans. Swami Prabhavananda and Christopher Isherwood (New York: Mentor Books), p. 40.
12. Ibid., p. 111.
13. *The Upanishads*, trans. Swami Prabhavananda and Frederick Manchester (New York: Mentor Books), p. 94.
14. *The Tao Te Ching*, verse 10, trans. Bennett B. Sims.
15. E. A. Burtt, ed., *The Teachings of the Compassionate Buddha* (New York: Mentor Books), p. 28.
16. Ibid., p. 63.
17. D. T. Suzuki, *Mysticism, Christian and Buddhist* (New York: Harper & Row).
18. Bailey, *Treatise on White Magic*, p. 559.
19. Bhagavad Gita, Mohini translation, quoted in H. P. Blavatsky, *Practical Occultism* (Wheaton, Il: Theosophical Publishing House, 1972), p. 60.
20. Prabhavananda and Isherwood, *Song of God, Bhagavad-Gita*, p. 56.
21. Ibid., p. 42.
22. Prabhavananda and Manchester, *The Upanishads*, p. 72.
23. Swami Vivekananda, *Raja Yoga: Conquering the Internal Nature* (Hollywood: Vedanta Press).
24. Alice Bailey, *Light of the Soul* (New York: Lucis Publishing Co.).
25. Prabhavananda and Isherwood, *Song of God, Bhagavad-Gita.*
26. All excerpts are from the translation given in Bailey, *Light of the Soul.*
27. Bailey, *Light of the Soul*, p. 199.
28. Prabhavananda and Isherwood, *Song of God, Bhagavad-Gita*, p. 68.
29. Joseph Gaer, *Wisdom of the Living Religions.*
30. Alice Bailey, *The Externalisation of the Hierarchy*, (New York: Lucis Publishing Co.), p. 18.
31. See, for example, Alice Bailey, *From Intellect to Intuition* (New York: Lucis Publishing Co.).
32. Quoted in Bailey, *From Intellect to Intuition*, p. 170.
33. *New American Bible.*
34. Prabhavananda and Isherwood, *Song of God, Bhagavad-Gita*, p. 65.
35. *How to Know God: the Yoga Aphorisms of Patanjali*, trans. Swami Prabhavananda and Christopher Isherwood (New York: Mentor Books), p. 11.
36. *Los Angeles Herald-Examiner* (Feb. 8, 1975).
37. By Helena Roerich (New York: Agni Yoga Society), p. 176.
38. Lawrence LeShan, *The Medium, the Mystic, and the Physicist* (New York: The Viking Press), p. 52.
39. Abraham Maslow, *The Farther Reaches of Human Nature* (New York: The Viking Press, 1971), p. 345.
40. Ibid., p. 349.

41. Bailey, *Light of the Soul*, p. 325.

42. Aldous Huxley, *The Perennial Philosophy*, (New York: Meridian Books, 1970), p. 206.

43. Prabhavananda and Isherwood, *Song of God, Bhagavad-Gita*, pp. 54–55.

44. Roberto Assagioli, *The Act of Will* (Baltimore: Penguin Books, 1974), p. 220.

45. Maslow, *Farther Reaches of Human Nature*, p. 295.

46. Cyril Scott, *Music: Its Secret Influence throughout the Ages* (New York: Samuel Weiser, 1969), p. 28.

47. Maslow, *Farther Reaches of Human Nature*, p. 176.

48. First published by Rider and Co., 1933; revised 1958. Paperback edition published by Samuel Weiser, New York.

49. Scott, *Music: Its Secret Influence*, p. 25.

50. Annie Besant, *Thought Power* (Wheaton, Ill: Theosophical Publishing House, 1967), p. 28.

51. Gore Vidal, *Los Angeles Times* article on Lincoln (Feb. 28, 1981).

52. "The Prayer of Columbus," by Walt Whitman.

CHAPTER 19. CONCLUSION

1. Charles Francis Potter, *Faiths Men Live By* (Englewood Cliffs: N.J.: Prentice-Hall, 1954). Copyright © 1954 by Charles Francis Potter. Reprinted by permission of the publisher, Prentice-Hall, Inc., Englewood Cliffs, NJ 07632. Preface, pp. vi–vii.

ROLAND PETERSON is a long-time student of the physical, mental, spiritual, and esoteric sciences. In addition, he holds bachelor's (magna cum laude) and master's degrees in electrical engineering and is a Senior Corporate Vice President and Group Executive of a large U.S.-based high-technology corporation, with responsibility  for a number of divisions located in the U.S., Canada, Europe, and the Far East. Prior industrial experience includes a number of engineering management positions, Vice-President assignments in Engineering and Business Development, and a term as a Division President. Mr. Peterson was selected as a member of the Tau Beta Pi, Eta Kappa Nu, and Sigma Xi engineering and scientific honor societies and is the recipient of an award from the Institute of Navigation. He has served as Los Angeles Chairman of the American Electronics Association, as regional campaign chairman and regional board chairman of United Way, and as regional Vice President of the Institute of Navigation.